November 2006
To Pastor Lorna
Lozovsky from
Mike Shreve

Our GLORIOUS Inheritance

The Revelation of the Titles of the Children of God

Mike Shreve

VOLUME THREE

10-digit ISBN
ISBN: 0-942507-54-1
ISBN: 0-942507-71-1 (8-Volume Set)

13-digit ISBN
ISBN: 978-0-942507-54-6
ISBN: 978-0-942507-71-3 (8-Volume Set)

Library of Congress Control Number: 2006925817

All poetry is written by Mike Shreve unless otherwise noted.

Ministry website: www.shreveministries.org

Printed in the United States of America

All book orders and correspondence should be directed to:

Deeper Revelation Books
P.O. Box 4260
Cleveland, TN 37320-4260
Phone: 423-478-2843   Fax: 423-479-2980
Website: www.deeperrevelationbooks.org
Revealing "the deep things of God" (1 Cor. 2:10)

Daniel

God is My Judge

But God is the judge… Thou art the God
that doest wonders: thou hast declared
thy strength among the people.

Psalm 75 : 7, 77 : 14

DEDICATION

To Andrew and Winnie Shreve, who brought me into this world—"born of the water"—that I might then be "born of the Spirit" and enter the kingdom of God. I thank them for giving me 'roots' and 'wings'—and for providing a warm family 'hearth' to which we all gather.

COVER ART

This impressive scene depicts the Psalm 42 passage—"*Deep calleth unto deep at the noise of Thy waterspouts.*" (KJV) The individual believer is represented by the waterspout, while the dove speaks of the wooing Holy Spirit who hovers over our lives to draw us out from the ocean of humanity into the fullness of **Our Glorious Inheritance.** This Volume Three theme begins with the introductory chapter and reaches its peak with the revelation of "Waterspouts" in the last chapter of this book.

THE "OUR GLORIOUS INHERITANCE" CONCEPT

The **"OUR GLORIOUS INHERITANCE"** series (Volumes One through Eight) pursues one of the most relevant, inspiring and life-transforming subjects that believers can discover in the Word of God: **the revelation of over 1,000 names and titles God has given His offspring.** There are 195 revealed in this volume. Each one of these entitlements reveals a separate and unique portion of the full inheritance available to children of God. The comprehension of ALL of our God-given titles provides, quite possibly, the most comprehensive and compelling view of who we are and what we possess as sons and daughters of the Most High. Bestowing these names and titles on His people is *"the deep"* in God calling to *"the deep"* in every one of us. Seeking to walk in the fulfillment of these names and titles can be described as *"the deep"* in God's people calling out to *"the deep"* in God (the very reason for the subtitle of the volume). Understanding these names and titles makes us rich beyond description. Walking in their reality enables us to greatly enrich the lives of others and become a praise to God in the earth.

EXPLANATION OF THE TABLE OF CONTENTS

Each of the chapters listed in the table of contents contains one or more of the titles God has given us in His Word. Normally, only those names or titles which are related in meaning are grouped together into one chapter. Most are from either the King James Version or the New King James Version of the Bible. Some are from other versions. Usually, the main title of a chapter is listed first in the table of contents, with the subordinate, complementary titles following.

Only those titles which appear in larger print on the title-pages at the beginning of each chapter are listed in the table of contents. In a few chapters, there are a number of extra, less-important titles that are printed in small print on one of the beginning pages. When this takes place, a note will be placed in the table of contents.

There are hundreds of descriptive names and titles that God has given to us in His Word. Many are interwoven, lending richness of meaning to each other. The author has attempted to group all of those titles which convey a central theme in individual volumes, with many sub-groups in each book that also enhance this common theme. In Volume Three this underlying theme is best described by the Psalm 42 statement—*Deep Calls Unto Deep.*

TABLE OF CONTENTS

ഐ൪

THE HOST OF THE LORD
THE LORD'S HOST
THE SWORD OF A MIGHTY MAN
HIS BOW
HIS ARROW
A POLISHED SHAFT
WEAPONS OF GOOD
HIS ROYAL HORSE IN THE BATTLE
THE VIOLENT

Note: Twenty-six other associated titles are listed at the bottom of the third title-page at the beginning of this chapter.

TREES
TREES OF RIGHTEOUSNESS
THE PLANTING OF THE LORD
TREES PLANTED BY THE RIVERS OF WATERS
TREES PLANTED BY THE WATERS
THE TREES OF THE WOOD
THE TREES OF THE LORD
CEDARS OF LEBANON
BOUGHS
A MAJESTIC CEDAR
CEDARS
PALM TREES
THE OLIVE TREE
A CULTIVATED OLIVE TREE
A GOOD OLIVE TREE
A GREEN OLIVE TREE
OLIVE PLANTS
HIS FIG TREE
THE PINE TREES
THE FIR TREES

Note: Twenty-seven other associated titles are listed at the bottom of the third title-page at the beginning of this chapter.

Note: Three other associated titles are listed on the back of the first title-page at the beginning of this chapter.

ॐ

The third volume in
an eight-volume series on

The Revelation
of the
Titles of the Children
of God

DEEP CALLS UNTO DEEP

Down in the depths of my nature
Where the issues of life are born,
From that unknown mystical realm
Surviving through ages of storm.
A call is forever rising—
But its language I cannot speak.
It was born ere I had being.
'Tis the call of deep unto deep.

Our mother tongue here is awkward,
For no words can fully express
The needs in the depths of nature,
In bondage to sin and distress.
Our hearts in their depths sorely ache,
They hunger, they call, and they seek—
Then silently wait an answer
To the call of deep unto deep.

Down deep in the heart of our God,
In mystical regions sublime,
In the Godhead's holy council
Long before our world or our time,
An answer was fully prepared
Every pain, every ache to meet,
In Christ, God's only begotten,
In answer to deep unto deep.

The answer indeed was the Word,
The Word when expressed was the Son.
O, language of God how profound!
In answer what more could be done?
The heart of our God is hungry,
His portion, His people to seek.
"I thirst," was cried by the Answer—
'Tis the call of deep unto deep.

Rev. John Follette

DEEP CALLS UNTO DEEP

*Deep calleth unto deep at the noise of **THY WATERSPOUTS:** all Thy waves and Thy billows are gone over me.*

(Psalm 42:7 KJV)

❖ INTRODUCTORY CHAPTER ❖

Deep calleth unto deep
at the noise of
***THY WATERSPOUTS**:*
all Thy waves
and Thy billows
are gone over me.

(Psalm 42:7 KJV)

DEEP CALLS UNTO DEEP

*Deep calleth unto deep at the noise of **THY***
***WATERSPOUTS:** all Thy waves and Thy billows are*
gone over me.

(Psalm 42:7 KJV)

*I*t was God's ordained moment to reveal His sovereign power to a future apostle by means of a profound and unforgettable miracle. Simon Peter had unknowingly sown seed, on a small scale, that was about to return to him in a great way.

He had gladly loaned his ship to a poor, itinerant preacher from Nazareth. For a few choice hours he had seen that rough, weather-beaten fishing deck sanctified and transformed into a place of power, truth and deliverance.

It seemed a somewhat peculiar, though fitting pulpit for this holy, yet simple man who evidently had such a feeling for the common people.

Many were claiming that He was the Messiah, yet He did not come arrayed in noble garments or military garb. And He didn't seem the least bit interested in liberating the people from the iron-fisted rule of the Romans (which was, of course, what they all assumed the Messiah would come to do).

It was all somewhat confusing, but it really did not matter.

For when this man spoke, miracles always happened!

In fact, just to be there in His presence simply filled up the senses. It was almost too much to take in all at once—the former cripples walking surefooted for the first time, enthusiastically proclaiming to the crowd what God had done; the blind seeing and with the curiosity of newborn babes, joyously inspecting every detail of their surroundings; the deaf hearing, and with broad smiles stumbling over their newly-formed words, struggling to repeat whispered phrases from excited loved ones. And one of the most beautiful sights: hardened sinners weeping openly—so grateful to behold the power of God and so thankful to hear His precious and trustworthy words.

Yes, that was one of the most remarkable things about this prophet—His words—words He claimed were "spirit and life," flowing so gently, yet so firmly, from His impassioned heart.

Though He was near to being soft-spoken, still, His voice seemed to effortlessly reach every listener on the surrounding slopes. It was somewhat like the soft Galilee waves that seemed so small near the pulpit-ship, then suddenly swelled in size and volume as they reached the shoreline.

Yes, everything appeared to blend together so harmoniously that day—the warm, penetrating sun—the soothing wind—the timeless waves—the deepset, full-of-hope gaze in every person's eyes—and the *voice*—such a soothing, warm, penetrating *voice*—far deeper and far more full-of-hope than the gaze of the people and far more timeless than the waves.

For Simon Peter it was quite gratifying to have played even a small part in such a blessed happening. That in itself was sufficient return.

Besides, it had been a bad night anyway; they had not been able to catch one fish—even though Peter knew all the spots, and when the fish were there. (Why, he knew Galilee like the back of his skilled, calloused and leather-like hands. No one was any better at it. "Well, maybe tomorrow," he might have thought, "the wind will shift and the fish will be running more true to pattern.")

But then—quite possibly interrupting Peter's wandering thoughts—Jesus finished His sermon. Stepping out of the boat, He commanded:

> Launch out into **the deep** and let down your nets for a catch.

> (Luke 5:4)

Now this was an unexpected twist: a carpenter attempting to tell fishermen how to do their job. Of course, Peter knew it would not work. Out of respect for the Master, though, he obeyed—at least to a limited degree.

Rather than dropping all the nets, he half-heartedly dropped one, explaining:

> "...Master, we have toiled all night and caught nothing: nevertheless at Your word I will let down THE NET."

The next six verses in the Bible tell the rest of the story:

> And when they had done this, they caught a great number of fish, and their net was breaking.
> So they signaled to their partners in the other boat to come and help them. And they came and filled both the boats, so that they began to sink.
> When Simon Peter saw it, he fell down at Jesus' knees, saying, Depart from me, for I am a sinful man, O LORD!
> For he and all who were with him were astonished at the catch of fish which they had taken;

And so also were James and John, the sons of Zebedee,
who were partners with Simon. And Jesus said to Simon,
Do not be afraid. From now on you will catch men.
So when they had brought their boats to land, they
forsook all and followed Him.

(Luke 5:5–11)

LAUNCH OUT INTO "THE DEEP"

There are several relevant messages for the church hidden in this account of Peter's call into the ministry. First, Jesus is still commanding His people in a spiritual sense to *"launch out into the deep."*

Especially for those who are studying this series on the names and titles God has given His offspring, such a command could mean *launching out* into the *depth* of God's Word and the *depth* of His Spirit in order to discover our spiritual identity and our full sonship potential.

Of course, if this is to happen we must first push away from the sandy shore of a comfortable, self-serving, self-centered life. Only then can we plumb the depths of **Our Glorious Inheritance**. The Holy Spirit will help us in this endeavor, because—

...As it is written, Eye has not seen, nor ear heard, nor
have entered into the heart of man the things which God
has prepared for those who love Him.
But God has revealed them to us through His Spirit.
*For the Spirit searches all things, yes, THE **DEEP***
THINGS OF GOD.

(1 Corinthians 2:9–10)

Absolutely every aspect of what God has called His people to receive or to be, He has indicated by a wonderful name or title. God identifies Himself this way; naming and titling Himself many ways in Scripture, to reveal who He is and what He can do. He is named Yahweh-Jireh (the LORD who sees and provides), Yahweh-Tsidkenu (the LORD our Righteousness), El Shaddai (the Almighty God), the Rock of our Salvation, a Sure Foundation and so on. Using this same method God has identified His people.

The Holy Spirit searches out the *depth* of this revelation and then—if we ask, seek and knock—He rejoices to communicate this identity-revealing truth to us. This is not something we have to beg the Holy Spirit to do. As "the Spirit of wisdom and revelation," His very ministry is to open the eyes of our understanding that we might know the hope of our calling, the exceeding greatness of God's power toward those who believe and "THE RICHES OF THE **GLORY** OF HIS **INHERITANCE** IN THE SAINTS." (See the prayer of Eph. 1:17–19.)

This last quote could be referring to the saints being a **glorious inheritance** to God or God being a **glorious inheritance** to them—or both. Either way, it is **the deep calling to the deep.** The Holy Spirit, having full access into the infinite depths of the Father's heart, long ago felt the strong pulsation of the divine purpose toward His people. Through the centuries, from time to time, He moved on holy men of God with the revelation of this purpose. As they recorded these inspired words for future generations, the formation of what we call "the Holy Scripture" took place. Now, when we read the Scripture, the Holy Spirit continues His ministry, quickening to our minds the revelation of what we read.

As this impartation takes place, we begin to feel the pulsation of the divine purpose beating hard within us. We find out who we are. We find out what we possess spiritually. Then we discover our destiny. *"The deep"* in God—the deep longing He has concerning His offspring—is revealed to us. This discovery opens up *"the deep"* in us—for we see our potential and begin pursuing it with *"deep"* desire.

Once we discover God's declaration concerning the reason for our existence, we can each affirm these truths with all confidence, saying:

> *I am what God says I am—I have what God says I have—and I will be what God says I will be.*

Some of the names and titles chosen for this book reveal the great benefits that belong to the children of God such as **the Blessed of the Father** and **the Just**. Others primarily reveal the calling we have to be Christlike in character, such as **Peacemakers** and **the Pure in Heart**. Still others unveil the sweetness and beauty of our relationship with God, like **His Garden** and **a Well of Living Waters**. Many other titles, like **the Anointed of the LORD** and **Children of the Kingdom**, focus on the awesomeness of our inheritance and eternal destiny.

Regardless of the category these God-given titles fall under, all of them are vital and all are God's way of expressing His love for us. They are prophetic announcements over our lives.

Prayerful parents often give their children meaningful names at birth in the hope they will eventually grow up into the reality of what those names declare. On a much grander scale, this is exactly what our heavenly Father did for us when we were born again. He gave us a whole new, wonderful identity. Daily—from the very depth of His loving heart—He calls to the deeper part of us (the inward, new creation part) to manifestly become what He has called us to be.

To pursue the world and its lusts is vain and evil and ends in death. To pursue that which is heavenly is glorious and good and leads to life. The flesh part of us is at home with evil. The spirit part of us—that cries out to know God—is only satisfied with being **good**. For this reason certain titles have been chosen for this third volume of **OUR GLORIOUS INHERITANCE** that include the word **good** and that reveal the **goodness** to which we are called. They are: **the Good, Good Fish, Good Ground, Good Seed, Good Soldiers** and **Good Trees**.

3 John 11 says, "He who does good is of God," so it must also be true that those who are of God long to do that which is good. This is also *the deep calling to the deep,* for God is good and He longs to see His goodness reflected in His people. There is, however, a tremendous obstacle. Describing man, Romans 3:12 declares, "There is none who does **good**, no not one."

Left to itself, the flesh will not seek after God. It is at enmity with God and, therefore, at enmity with goodness. Mankind would be locked in this prison of sin were it not for grace. God first graces us to long after Him, to hunger for Him—then He gives grace for grace:

> For He satisfies **the longing soul,** and fills **the hungry soul** with goodness.
>
> (Psalm 107:9)

Once God fills **the Hungry** with His **goodness**, He also graces them to be "zealous of **good works**" (Ti. 2:14). Being "zealous of good works" involves imparting the goodness to others that God imparts to us. This is the normal evolution of God moving in our lives. The divine purpose not only flows **to** us; it then flows **through** us (which actually leads us to the next aspect of this biblical analogy).

"LET DOWN YOUR NETS"

After Jesus told Peter and his associates to *"Launch out into the deep,"* He urged them, *"Let down your nets for a catch."*

What does this mean to us? Once God launches us into *"the deep"* spiritually, our goal should be to reach the needy in this world, to retrieve the souls of the lost. Every tool God gives us to achieve this goal is, as it were, a separate net that we can drop into the ocean of humanity. *"Launching out into the deep"* is somewhat useless and even self-centered, unless we do so in order to *"let down our nets."*

This is the goal. This is the God-given purpose. The one leads to the other. If we find out who we are in Christ and just glory in it—we are selfish. But if we find out who we are in Christ and do something about it, we are doers of the Word and not hearers only. This pleases God.

When Jesus urged the disciples to let down their nets, Peter said, *"Master, we have toiled all night and caught nothing: nevertheless at Your word I will let down the net."* The man who was about to become a fisher of men made three basic mistakes:

(1) *"Master, we have toiled all night and caught nothing"*—Peter judged future possibilities by past failures, when God is never limited by the past.

(2) *"At Your word"*—Peter had a definite word from God, yet he did not realize its power.

(3) *"I will let down the net"*—Peter only partially obeyed. Full obedience would have brought much greater results.

Jesus had said "Let down your nets" (plural), Peter responded, "I will let down the net" (singular). When he began to pull that lone net in, there were so many fish, it began to break. Proper preparation results in readiness to receive the full benefits of a God-ordained miracle.

In a similar way, God is also commanding us to *"launch out into the deep,"* but not just for the purpose of finding out "who we are." He wants us to put this discovery into action. For instance, if we discover the glorious depth of what it is to be **the Anointed of the LORD**, this pivotal revelation should propel us into the glorious release of **the anointing of God** in our lives—that the needs of others might be met. Then we don't just **know** who we are, we **become** who we are.

We already have the written Word to go by. It clearly declares our calling to be **"Fishers of Men,"** throwing out the net of the Gospel to capture those who are lost (Mt. 4:19, Mk. 1:17). This in itself is a sufficient revelation to provide motivation and direction. When we receive a living Word communication from God concerning our purpose in the body of Christ, even more so, we should act on it immediately. We should never measure our future potential by a standard of past failures. Neither should we let any dark memories from yesterday cause us to think small when it may well be time to think big!

If God says, *"Let down your **nets**,"* we should never let down one net half-heartedly. Instead, we should lunge forward in faith—using every means we have to accomplish our God-given goal in the kingdom of God. We must purpose to be EVERYTHING we can be in God, and to do EVERYTHING that we can do—in His name and for His glory.

The Scripture commands every one of us, "This book of the law shall not depart from your mouth, but you shall meditate in it day and night, that you may observe to do according to all that is written in it. For then you will make your way prosperous, and then you will have good success" (Js. 1:8).

So with a heart full of faith in the Word, let us prepare for success! Plan for success! Speak success! Praise God in advance for success! If God says it, He will surely do it. He is not a man that He should lie! If God has spoken, it will surely come to pass!

The fish are waiting. The nets are ready. So when God's timing arrives—act on it! And watch the 'boats' of your dreams fill up and overflow.

Though some sincere ministries may have 'toiled all the night' with only minimal results, God can change circumstances in a moment. His command of abundance can take effect—with nets almost breaking and sanctuary-boats loaded to capacity. Some may have even unknowingly or unselfishly sown seed, on a small scale, that is about to bring a bountiful and blessed return (just like Peter).

We know that any visitation or spiritual awakening can only transpire 'at His Word.' It can only happen in God's perfect timing and at His decree (Peter certainly learned this lesson well). Yet we know, by the prophecies of the Bible and by the signs of the times, that this is the hour! So it is definitely not a time to let down 'one net'—rather, it is time to drop every net available, for the abundant catch is predestined, prophetic and inevitable.

Likewise, it is definitely not a time to be satisfied with just a shallow and meager measure of our sonship abilities and privileges (our title-rights). Instead, it is time to diligently search out every name and title applied to the children of God and pursue, with equal diligence, the manifestation and fulfillment of these God-given callings.

ATTAINING THE FULLNESS OF CHRIST

It seems logical that the more we discover who we are by God's design, the more functional and fruitful we will become as God's representatives in this world. According to Ephesians 4:11–13, God has given to His body the five-fold ministry gifts (apostles, prophets, evangelists, pastors and teachers) "to prepare God's people for works of service, so that the body of Christ may be built up until we all reach unity in the faith and in the knowledge of the Son of God and become mature, attaining to the *whole measure* of the *fullness* of Christ" (NIV).

Every significant and Spirit-breathed revelation promoted in the body of Christ is sent forth to lead us to this goal of Christlike maturity. We know we can attain this goal for John 1:16 speaks in the present tense that "of His fullness we have all received."

However, those who are realistic must admit that this *fullness*, this *whole measure* will never be completely apprehended until the resurrection. It is also just as sure that as we journey that direction we can expect to pass from glory to glory.

Discovering 'who we are' and 'what we have' as heirs of God and joint-heirs with Christ creates an aching in the inner man—for we long to truly become what we see. We walk in this attitude of heart, we fulfill the calling to be **the Hungry** and **the Thirsty**—for our souls hunger and thirst after the truth and after the living God.

This passion of spirit, this aching, inner desire, was first an emotion generated in the bosom of the Father toward His beloved offspring before it was ever brought to birth in our hearts and directed upward toward His throne. In the beginning, the Creator and Sustainer of all men longed with a longing far deeper than words—to make man in His own image and to enjoy sweet fellowship with him. Now we long, with a longing in some ways just as infinitely deep, to successfully arrive at such an exalted stature in God.

Surely, this union of purpose is the very thing David was referring to when He penned Psalm 42:7 (KJV):

> *Deep calleth unto deep* at the noise of *Thy waterspouts: all Thy waves and Thy billows are gone over me.*

For the very waves and billows of longing that have always flowed— from everlasting to everlasting—over the heart of the Almighty, now constantly flow over our hearts as well, as *"deep calls unto deep."*

Here at this statement—at least for the time being—we must pause and go no further. For the very Scripture we are beginning to expound contains one of our God-given titles.

Therefore, its explanation is reserved for the last chapter of this book.

HIS ANOINTED

---

*The LORD is their strength, and He is the saving refuge of **HIS ANOINTED**.*
(Psalm 28:8)

*...And he said to his men, The LORD forbid that I should do this thing to my master, **THE LORD'S ANOINTED**, to stretch out my hand against him, seeing he is **THE ANOINTED OF THE LORD**.*

(1 Samuel 24:6)

*The breath of our nostrils, **THE ANOINTED OF THE LORD**, was taken in their pits, of whom we said, "Under his shadow we shall live among the heathen."*

(Lamentations 4:20 KJV)

*Now these are the last words of David...the man raised up on high, **THE ANOINTED OF THE GOD OF JACOB**, and the sweet psalmist of Israel...*

(2 Samuel 23:1)

THE LORD'S ANOINTED

THE ANOINTED
OF THE LORD

THE ANOINTED OF
THE GOD OF JACOB

HIS ANOINTED ONES

HIS ANOINTED ONE

SONS OF OIL

SONS OF FRESH OIL

He permitted no one to do them wrong; Yes, He rebuked kings for their sakes,
*Saying, "Do not touch **MY ANOINTED ONES**, and do My prophets no harm."*
(Psalm 105:14–15)

*You came out to deliver Your people, to save **YOUR ANOINTED ONE**. You crushed the leader of the land of wickedness, You stripped him from head to foot. Selah*
(Habakkuk 3:13 NIV)

*And he said, "These are the two **SONS OF OIL**, [**SONS OF FRESH OIL**], that stand before the LORD of the whole earth."*
(Zechariah 4:12 Dar, MKJV)

His Anointed

*The LORD is their strength, and He is the saving refuge of **HIS ANOINTED.***

(Psalm 28:8)

*I*n a natural sense, to **anoint** means *to smear or rub something or someone with an oily substance.* In a religious sense, it means *to apply or pour out oil in the act of consecration.* In a spiritual sense, it means *the enduing of certain persons with a measure of God's Spirit to fill a certain office or to fulfill a certain divine purpose.*

The word *anointing* is more than just another term for the Holy Spirit. It is rather the specific application of the Holy Spirit. Apparently, this 'application of the Holy Spirit' can take place either individually or corporately. There is an individual anointing that God gives to each born-again child of God and there is a corporate anointing that He sends on groups of believers who gather to worship, study His Word or do His work.[*1]

The anointing is referred to as our **light** (Pr. 13:9) our **peace** (Mt. 10:12–13, Lk. 10:5–6) and our **glory** (Ps. 3:3; 16:9; 30:12; 57:8). Concerning this last term, David claimed, "I will sing and give praise, even with my **glory**" (Gr. *kabowd*, Ps. 108:1). In other words, he was saying, "I will worship God by means of the glory of God, the anointing of the Holy Spirit, that has been placed on my life." Actually, this is the only kind of worship that qualifies as true worship, acceptable to the Most High God. 1 John 2:20 (KJV) also calls the anointing an "**unction** from the Holy One." (The same Greek word *chrisma*, translated **unction** in this verse, is also translated **anointing** in 1 John 2:27.)

The anointing moving on Ezekiel was spoken of as "**the hand of the LORD**" resting upon him (Ezk. 1:3; 3:14, 22; 8:1; 33:22; 37:1; 40:1). This is promised to all those who have a heart to serve God (See Is. 66:14). For the prophets Elijah and Elisha, the anointing was represented as a **mantle** that passed from one to the other. (See 2 Kgs. 2:1–15.) But when the anointing flowed through Jesus, it was called "**the power of the LORD**," "**virtue**," "**the oil of gladness**" and "**the oil of joy**" (Lk. 5:17; 6:19 KJV; 8:46 KJV; Ps. 45:7, Is. 61:3).

Psalm 45:7 prophesied that the Son of God would be anointed with the "oil of gladness" above His fellows because He would love righteousness and hate wickedness. It follows that if we emulate His example—loving righteousness and hating wickedness—the "oil of gladness" will abound in us as well.

THE OIL SYMBOL

Oil is one of the predominate, biblical symbols of the anointing of God. Throughout Scripture, we often see both men and objects being consecrated to the LORD by the ritualistic application of oil. Such an 'anointing ceremony' usually took place either in direct obedience to God or as a fervent and symbolic prayer. This natural, visible, religious observance represented a far more important, invisible, spiritual reality: the outpouring of the precious oil of God's Spirit. It is this outpouring of God's presence that renders any person, place or thing sacred unto the LORD—set apart for His service.

Why oil? Possibly because the Jews considered oil one of the main staples of life. They used it for food, for medicine, for personal hygiene and cosmetic care, for light and even for the funeral preparations of the dead. Oil, to one degree or another, fed them, sustained them, healed them, cleansed them, beautified them, illuminated their way and prepared them for burial. So it became, in their minds and ours, a perfect candidate for the resulting spiritual type. Because, in a far more profound, spiritual way, the oil of the sweet anointing of God sustains us, feeds us, heals us, cleanses us, beautifies us, illuminates us and prepares us for death (and eternal life beyond).

The anointing of the Holy Spirit is the manifestation of the very life of God, containing the richness of His character and all His flawless and glorious attributes. It is this divine life that meets every need we have. Therefore, scripturally speaking, the possession of oil can be representative of spiritual abundance and the lack of it, representative of spiritual poverty or a state of want. Job, in the midst of his hard trial, reminisced of the time when God had soaked his life with prosperity and blessings. He described this as a time when "the rock poured out rivers of *oil* for me" (Jb. 29:6).

In a similar, though negative use of the type, Joel described an era of great spiritual dearth by prophesying "the new wine is dried up, the *oil* fails." He also predicted that certain ministers would weep over this awful condition, saying, "Spare Your people, O LORD, and do not give Your heritage to reproach" (Jl. 1:10; 2:17). The result of this kind of intercession will be a time of great restoration in the last days when the "vats shall overflow with new wine and *oil*" (Jl. 2:24).

To those who understand biblical symbolism, this kind of language indicates a time of great supernatural manifestations for the church of the living God. As we draw closer to the return of Jesus, the anointing is going to flow down from heaven, and out of our hearts, in a bountiful and unprecedented way. Let us enter this last great era of revival and restoration with joyous anticipation.

THE FIRST BIBLICAL ANOINTING CEREMONY

In Genesis 28, we find the first recorded biblical instance in which oil was worshipfully and ceremonially used. Having just received his first major supernatural visitation from the LORD, Jacob reared up the stone on which his head had been resting and poured oil over it. He then named the place **Bethel**, meaning *house of God.*

Apparently, this was a formal consecration, not only of the physical place, but of Jacob himself. From that day forward it appears the *oil* of the anointing was poured out on his life in a profound and manifest way. About twenty-five years later, Jacob repeated this ritual of pouring oil on a rock-pillar at Bethel, rededicating himself to the original visitation. (See Gen. 35: 9–15.)

The rock-pillar is representative of God, the One who is called "the Rock of our salvation." (See Ps. 89:26.) Though asleep on "the Rock," Jacob was awakened to the glory and importance of "the Rock"—and a pillow became a pillar. How many of us, at one time or another, have also been asleep on "the Rock"! How often we temporarily soothed our aching consciences by resting our minds on what was primarily an intellectual approach to God: mere theology and church tradition. Thank God for the day when we were awakened, not only to the reality of God, but also, to the place of honor and dominion He must occupy in our hearts!

The fact that Jacob poured oil over the rock represents how any person, having received the personal outpouring of God's manifest presence, should then use that same anointing to return worship to God. Our Father has graciously revealed Himself as a pillar of strength in our lives. We are no longer asleep spiritually. We have been awakened. So let us return thanks by pouring out the oil of adoration upon our Creator—with every breath we take.

THE HOLY ANOINTING OIL

The next reference to the religious application of oil is found in Exodus 30:22–33. At the institution of the law, we find Moses initiating Aaron and his sons into the priesthood by anointing them with holy oil.

God Himself gave detailed instructions concerning the ingredients of this holy oil. It was to include a unique blend of *principal* spices *(quality* spices, the *finest* of spices): *pure* flowing myrrh (a liquid myrrh made from the gum resin of a tree that grows in Arabia), *sweet* cinnamon (a spice made from the sweet-smelling bark of several trees belonging to the laurel family), *sweet* calamus (also rendered sweet-smelling cane or fragrant cane), and cassia (also made from an aromatic bark).

All of these were to be mixed with *pure, beaten* or *pressed* olive oil after the art of the apothecary (one who compounds perfumes). (See Ex. 27:20;

30:22–33 NKJV, KJV, Amp, NIV, NAS, UBD.) The various details of this mixture (especially those words emphasized in italic print) speak of the *purity* and *sweetness* of the true anointing, how it is truly our *principal* need and heaven's *finest* attempt at meeting that need. Other correlations contain further insights. The following are quite possibly the most profound.

- **Myrrh** was a major ingredient used in embalming the dead. The inclusion of this ingredient in the holy oil speaks of how the anointing preserves us in a crucified state, compelling us to die daily to the evil influence of this fallen world.

- **Cinnamon** and **cassia** are similar, related spices. Both are obtained from bark, the sometimes thick and tough outer covering of a tree or shrub that protects its sap and preserves its life. Therefore, these ingredients speak of how the anointing powerfully preserves us in a spiritually 'alive' state. It protects the life-giving, sap-like flow of grace that continually pours through our inner being.

- **Calamus** (also called **fragrant cane**) is a reed with a pleasant odor that grows in well-watered areas. This speaks of how the fragrant and beautiful anointing of the Spirit keeps a child of God planted by "the still waters." These are the tranquil, spiritual, living waters that sustain us and quench our deep thirst for intimate communion with God.

So the message is clear. By the true oil of the anointing we are consecrated to God; we are set apart; we are holy. We are preserved in death and we are preserved in life. Daily we are led beside the still waters of grace as *"deep calls unto deep."*

Being anointed with this precious holy oil was necessary if the Old Testament priests were to obtain access into God's holy place. So it is with us in a much higher sense. Also, this holy anointing oil was used to anoint practically everything in the tabernacle. This speaks of the fact that anything having to do with true religious worship must be of the anointing or it is unacceptable to God.

Possibly, God determined that the strong fragrance of the holy oil would counteract the awful stench that resulted from the slaughter and burning of all the animal sacrifices. In like manner, the sweetness of the anointing in our lives (the loving, personal, comfort of God's outpoured presence) more than sufficiently compensates for the crucifixion of the flesh we must all go through in order to maintain intimate communion with heaven.

Noteworthy also is the fact that only the consecrated priests could use this holy oil and that they were only allowed to use it after the prescribed manner. Those who tried to make similar oil for personal use were cut off from Israel. (See Ex. 30:32–33.)

In a similar way, God's anointing only comes to those ordained to receive it. Moreover, those who try to deceitfully mimic the true anointing, or those who attempt to use the anointing for selfish, personal gain, may soon discover that they have signed their own spiritual death warrant.

Inclusion in the anointed priesthood was and is a sacred responsibility. Only a certain tribal family obtained the rights to the priesthood in the Old Testament. Now all believers have this privilege. But with privilege comes responsibility, for "to whom much is given, from him much shall be required" (Lk. 12:48). If the natural symbol was called *"holy* anointing oil," how much more *"holy"* is the spiritual unction it represented. Also, how *holy* must those persons be who receive such a gift from the "high and lofty One...whose name is *Holy"* (Is. 57:15).

SEVEN OLD TESTAMENT ANOINTINGS

Under the Old Covenant standard, seven classes of individuals were included, at times, among "the anointed of the LORD": patriarchs, judges, kings, governors, prophets, priests and soldiers.

Although the entire nation of Israel was chosen to fulfill a certain divine purpose, individual Israelites only rarely received a personal outpouring of "the holy oil" from above. The following unique examples are worthy of our consideration:

(1) Patriarchs—As God watched over the patriarchs (Abraham, Isaac and Jacob, etc.) the Bible declared that He "suffered no man to do them wrong: yea, He reproved kings for their sakes; saying, TOUCH NOT **MINE ANOINTED [MY ANOINTED ONES]**, AND DO MY PROPHETS NO HARM" (Ps. 105:14–15 KJV, NKJV).

(2) Judges—When God ruled Israel by judges, the anointing would move upon them in order to execute the supernatural. For instance "the Spirit of the LORD came upon Gideon, then he blew a trumpet; and the Abiezrites [Gideon's tribal family] gathered behind him" (Jd. 6:34). Soon after, Gideon defeated the huge Midianite army with only three hundred men and became a judge in Israel. Another prime example is Samson who judged Israel twenty years. When the Spirit of the LORD moved upon him, he would perform great acts of supernatural strength. (See Jd. 15:14–16, 20.)

(3) Kings—Later on, when kings were anointed, "Samuel took a vial of oil, and poured it upon [Saul's] head, and kissed him, and said, Is it not because the LORD has *anointed* you commander over His inheritance?" (1 Sam. 10:1). When the Spirit of the LORD came upon Saul, he was given "another heart" and turned into "another man" (1 Sam. 10:6–9). At a later time, when Jabesh-

Gilead was threatened, "the Spirit of God came upon Saul...and his anger was greatly aroused" (1 Sam. 11:6). This reveals that the anointing transfers to us divine emotions. As we flow under the anointing, we will be angry over the things that anger God, we will grieve over the things that grieve God and we will be joyous over the things that give God joy.

At the prophetic announcement of David's royal calling, "Samuel took the horn of oil, and *anointed* him in the midst of his brothers: and the Spirit of the LORD came upon David from that day forward" (1 Sam. 16:13). The lion, the bear and even huge Goliath were no match for David once he received this "holy oil" at God's appointment! Even his harp music was so soaked with the anointing that an oppressive evil spirit was driven from Saul when this anointed psalmist played. After several years David was anointed king over Judah (2 Sam. 2:4) and then, over all of Israel (2 Sam. 5:3). This communicates that any anointed person may, at God's will, move upward in successive degrees of the anointing.

In 1 Samuel 24:6 King Saul is referred to as **the LORD'S anointed.** In Lamentations 4:20 King Zedekiah is called **the anointed of the LORD.** In 2 Samuel 23:1 David is called **the anointed of the God of Jacob.** These three variations of this title can certainly be claimed by any anointed individual. One of the most peculiar kingly examples of the Old Testament is Cyrus, ruler of Persia, who was also numbered among the anointed. Even though he was a Gentile—and possibly did not adhere to monotheism—still it seems God specifically *anointed* him for a certain task: to release the captive Jews in Babylon so they could return to Jerusalem and rebuild their city and their temple. (See Is. 44:26–28; 45:1–3.)

(4) Governors—In the days of the reconstruction and restoration of Solomon's temple, Joshua, the high priest, and Zerubbabel, the governor of Judah, were called "the two **anointed ones [sons of oil** - Dar, **sons of fresh oil**–MKJV] who stand beside the LORD of the whole earth." They were also described as being "the two olive branches which through the two golden pipes empty the *golden oil* out of themselves" (Zec. 4:12–14 NKJV, KJV).

(5) Prophets—One prophetic example is found in 1 Kings 19:16, where the Scripture records the prophet Elijah being commanded by God to *anoint* Elisha to be prophet in his place. The mantle of the anointing passed to Elisha about ten years later when Elijah was carried up to heaven.

(6) Priests—In Exodus 30:30 God instructed Moses to "*anoint* Aaron and his sons, and consecrate them, that they may minister to Me in the priests' office." Notice that they were anointed, not just to minister to the people; they were anointed, first and foremost, to minister to God.

(7) Soldiers—The primary biblical examples in this category involve certain anointed judges or kings who, as soldiers, went out to fight against the enemies of God's people (e.g., Samson - Jd. 15:14–16, Gideon - Jd. 6:34, David - 1 Sam. 17:37–51, Ps. 18:28–40, Jonathan - 1 Sam. 14:1–15, Jehu - 1 Kgs. 19:15–21, 2 Kgs. 9:2 etc.). It is also true that the entire Israelite army was at times endowed with such supernatural power that they often won against insurmountable odds. Deuteronomy 32: 30 speaks of one Israelite putting a thousand to flight and two putting ten thousand to flight. And we are all well familiar with the anointed shouts of the army of God causing the fortress at Jericho to collapse.

THE SYMBOL FULFILLED

All of the preceding categories of God's "anointed ones" under the Old Will—patriarchs, judges, kings, governors, prophets, priests and soldiers—not only served the purpose of God in their day; they also prefigured and foreshadowed the Savior who was yet to come.

How significant it is that the Hebrew title for Jesus—*Messiah*—and the synonymous Greek title—*Christ*—both mean **the Anointed One!** (See Jn. 1:41; 4:25.) The Hebrew word *mashiach* is translated *Messiah* in Daniel 9:25–26. Many other times it is translated *anointed* (e.g., "Do not touch my *anointed ones*," Ps. 105:15). So every Old Testament anointed person was, in a sense, a lesser "messiah" pointing to that greater "Messiah" who was yet to come.

The bestowal of this excellent title on the Son of God speaks of the various callings that Jesus wonderfully and gloriously fulfilled. All seven offices of the anointing, filled by imperfect men under the Old Will, were filled to perfection by the LORD of glory. He was, and is and ever will be the Supreme Patriarch of all ages (the Ancient of days Himself), the Judge of all the earth, the King of kings, the Governor among the nations, the notable Prophet that Moses said would come, the Great High Priest and the soldier-like Captain of our Salvation. He is the Anointed One; simultaneously occupying a position of royal, kingly dominion; mediatorial, priestly service; oracular, prophetic authority and warring, soldier-like courage.

He came to bear witness of the truth, for the anointing is truth. (See 1 Jn. 2:27.) The anointing came to the Son of God when the Holy Spirit descended upon Him as a dove in the river Jordan. Possibly, the Holy Spirit was represented this way because doves have a continual flow of oil from their pours that cleanses their feathers. The first direct result of this flow of the anointing through Jesus was being led by the Spirit into the wilderness for a forty day fast, and the conquering of temptations from the devil. Shortly afterward, this empowered Messiah announced His ministry in the synagogue of Nazareth by quoting from Isaiah 61:

"The Spirit of the LORD God is upon Me; because
*He has **anointed** Me to preach the gospel to the poor; He*
has sent Me to heal the broken-hearted, to proclaim liberty
to the captives, and recovery of sight to the blind, to set at
liberty those who are oppressed,

To proclaim the acceptable year of the LORD."

(Luke 4:18–19)

Isaiah 61:3 went on to explain how the Messiah would impart to His followers *"the oil of joy* for mourning." A very similar expression is found in Psalm 45:7, a prophecy that the Messiah would be anointed with *"the oil of gladness"* above His companions.

Joy and gladness—these words are especially descriptive of the anointed ministry of the Son of God. What joy, what gladness He must have experienced as the oil of the anointing flowed through Him to deliver the oppressed (for the Spirit was poured out on Him without measure—Jn. 3:34)! What joy, what gladness the people must have felt who were privileged to be a part of such a heaven-sent visitation.

Later on, Peter explained to the household of Cornelius, "How God *anointed* Jesus of Nazareth with the Holy Spirit and with power, who went about doing good and healing all who were oppressed of the devil, for God was with Him" (Ac. 10:38). How powerfully this *anointing* destroyed the works of the evil one as it flowed out of the Christ of the New Covenant! Great multitudes of those who were diseased and vexed with unclean spirits pressed around Him and "there went *virtue* out of Him, and healed them all" (Lk. 6:19 KJV). (*Virtue* is a unique KJV rendering of the Greek word *dunamis*, normally translated *power* or *ability*.) Though we never experienced the blessing of walking with the Messiah in the flesh, this glorious *virtue* is still flowing—for it has flowed into our lives healing us of sin's effects and granting us the *power* and *ability* to live *virtuously*.

In Lamentations 4:20 Jeremiah referred to Zedekiah, king of Judah, as **the anointed of the LORD**. He also called him **"the breath of our nostrils"** (**"the source of our life"**—TEV) and explained how the Jews intended to live "under his shadow" among the surrounding heathen nations. If this could be said about an earthly ruler who was full of error, how much more can it be said of the flawless King of kings Himself. He is the Messiah, the Anointed of the LORD. We confess that He truly is "the breath of our nostrils": the "source of life" for us both naturally and spiritually. We will live "under His shadow" all the days of our lives. This in itself is gladness and security—just knowing the Anointed One. How much more glad and secure we should feel when we realize His main purpose in coming was to share His anointing with us!

THE SUPERNATURAL TRANSFER

The eventual transfer of the anointing from Jesus to His followers was profoundly and symbolically depicted by what took place in Gethsemane. The word **Gethsemane** actually means *oil press*—and for a very simple reason. At certain seasonal times of harvest, the olives were gathered from the trees that covered the Mount of Olives (ironically called **the Mount of Anointment** by the Jews) and brought to the garden located near the base. In that garden, called Gethsemane, there was an oil press. This press most likely consisted of two massive, round stones (one stationary and the other moveable) that were made to grate against one another, crushing the olives in between. This process extracted the oil, which then flowed into waiting containers or a reservoir near the bottom of the press.

This Gethsemane process of oil-extraction was the very thing that happened to Jesus in a spiritual sense. During that intense struggle and blood-sweating agony of prayer in the same garden, the Son of God was fiercely crushed between the two great spiritual stones that have always grinded and grated against one another—the immovable and unchangeable foundation stone of the will of the Spirit striving against the easily moved, unstable, rolling stone of the will of the flesh.

In the flesh, Jesus desperately desired to escape the Father's demand that He become a sin offering, tasting death for every man. But in His spirit, the Messiah was gripped with a far more intense desire to fulfill the will of the Father and deliver humanity. The flesh part compelled Jesus to haltingly plead, "O My Father, if it be possible, let this cup pass from Me." But the Spirit within constrained Him to affirm, "Not as I will, but as You will" (Mt. 26:39).

As the hot, bloody sweat oozed out of His straining pores, in a symbolic sense, *golden oil* was issuing forth from His churning, fervid spirit. As olives in an olive press, Jesus was crushed—severely and fatally crushed. But as a result, from the depth of His impassioned heart, the sweet oil of the *anointing* began its journey toward an upper room, where a little over seven weeks later, about a hundred and twenty vessels would be filled to the brim. On the day of Pentecost, when the disciples were baptized with the Holy Spirit, each one immediately became a reservoir of the life of God, a sanctified and fit container of His anointing.

It is a faithful saying that every true believer from Pentecost onward has inherited 'holy oil' from above. No longer is the anointing reserved to a few elite persons. Now every born-again child of God can claim this choice spiritual heritage. 1 John 2:20 (KJV) declares to every son and daughter of God:

> ...*Ye have an* **unction** *from the Holy One, and ye know all things.*

Then verse twenty-seven goes on to explain:

> *But the* **anointing** *which you have received from Him abides in you, and you do not need that anyone teach you; but as the same* **anointing** *teaches you concerning all things, and is true, and is not a lie, and just as it has taught you, YOU WILL ABIDE IN HIM.*
>
> (1 John 2:27)*²

Several important truths are conveyed by these two passages.

❧ **First, the anointing** *abides in us.* It is intended to be a permanent gift, represented, not by water that quickly evaporates, but by oil that clings and penetrates.

❧ **Second, the anointing instructs us how to** *abide in God,* how to maintain intimacy with Him. The anointing witnesses within us what is pleasing and displeasing to God, constantly convicting and constraining us to do what is right.

❧ **Third, the anointing is our teacher:** "the Spirit of truth" who guides us into ALL truth. He makes our spiritual discernment keen. As "the spirit of wisdom and revelation," He unveils the mysteries of the kingdom of God (Jn. 14:26; 16:13, Eph. 1:17). Because of this, we are not totally dependent on human leadership. While honoring all God-placed authorities in the church, still, our greatest dependency is upon the Spirit of God Himself.

Interestingly, the synonymous words *unction* and *anointing* are both translated from the same Greek word *chrisma.* Also, notice the following similarity in the New Testament.

The word *grace* comes from the Greek word *charis.*
The word *gifts* is often translated from the Greek word *charisma.*
The word *anointing* is so rendered from the word *chrisma.*

These three similar-sounding words are inseparably related—for all of God's *grace* (His *charis*) and all of His *gifts* (His *charisma*) flow into our lives and manifest out of us by means of the anointing (His *chrisma*).

We can indulge in all kinds of religious activity, but the important thing is possessing and imparting to others this anointing of the Holy Spirit. As one great revivalist said, *"I would rather have unction than action."* For one Christian deed inspired and empowered by the Holy Spirit is worth more than ten thousand religious activities that are not, no matter how noble the intent of the heart.

FULLY MANIFESTED "SONS OF OIL"

One of the most wonderful aspects of being the anointed of the LORD under the New Covenant is realizing that we, like Jesus, have inherited the potential of filling all seven roles occupied by God's anointed under the Old Covenant.

⌣· As our God is called the Ancient of Days, the Patriarch of all patriarchs, so we, His anointed ones, are called **the ancient people:** for we have been chosen "in Him before the foundation of the world" (Is. 44:7, Eph. 1:4).

⌣· As Jesus is called the Judge of all the earth, so all of His anointed will also eventually fill the role of **judges**, judging angels and judging the nations during the Messianic Age yet to come (Is. 1:26, 1 Cor. 6:2–3).

⌣· As Jesus is named the King of kings, so all who have been 'crowned' with His 'royal oil' are also referred to as **kings.** Even now we reign with Christ, enthroned with Him in absolute triumph and heaven-sent dominion. (See Ps. 8:4–6; 49:14, Ro. 5:17, Rev. 1:5–6.)

⌣· As Jesus will one day be manifested as the Governor of the nations, we as subordinate **governors** will govern the affairs of heaven in this earth, during the Kingdom Age and in the New Creation to come. (See Ps. 22:28 KJV, 67:4, Is. 9:6, 7, 1 Cor. 12:28 KJV.)

⌣· As Jesus was "that great Prophet," all who are in covenant with Him are anointed to prophesy: declaring the Word of God under the inspiration of the Holy Spirit. All children of God, to lesser or greater degrees, are called to be **prophets** and **prophetesses**—for according to 1 Corinthians 14:31, "You can all prophesy." Joel foretold this would be a chief characteristic of the New Covenant Age. (See Num. 11:29, Jl. 2:28, Ac. 2:17–18.)

⌣· As Jesus was the Great High Priest after the order of Melchizedek, so all of His anointed ones are also **priests** after the order of Melchizedek (inheriting the priesthood, not because of natural genealogy, but by the choosing of God). (See Is. 61:6; 66:20–21, Heb. 7:1–28, 1 Pt. 2:5, 9, Rev. 1:5–6; 20:6.)

⌣· As Jesus was anointed to be the Captain of our salvation, so all who receive Him become **good soldiers of Jesus Christ.** As members of the army of God, we fight the good fight of faith. We have weapons of warfare that are "mighty through God" and we are supernaturally anointed to prevail in the battles of life. (See 1 Sam. 17:26, 2 Cor. 10:5 KJV, Eph. 6:10–16, 2 Tim. 2:3–4, Rev. 19:11–14.)

By these scriptural references, it is clear that all of God's offspring will ultimately emerge in the full sevenfold stature of what it is to be the LORD'S anointed. As the chief Anointed One filled these seven ordained positions, so it is for all who make up His body. The golden, holy oil that flowed over the Messiah has also flowed over all His many brethren. (See Ps. 133.) In a spiritual sense, like Zerubbabel and Joshua of old, we are all oil-producing **olive trees**—and through golden pipes we empty the golden oil out of ourselves. (See Jer. 11:16, Ho. 14:6, Ps. 52:8.) This gives us a right to similarly be entitled **"SONS OF OIL"** (Zec. 4:14 Dar).[*3]

Moreover, just as the Father gave His only begotten Son a specific outpouring of grace (or anointing) to fulfill His calling (tasting death for every man), so has He already given grace to us—to fulfill our calling—to achieve our God-given goal in life—to shoulder the spiritual responsibility that rests upon us. (See Heb. 2:9.) So let us arise, find God's will and bear fruit for His glory. We can do it, for God has graced us to do it. As kings and priests, we are anointed to reign and serve with our Elder Brother (the Messiah, the Anointed One) both now and forevermore.

Functioning in this role has been God's choosing for us—from the very foundation of the world. Daily our God *anoints* our eyes with spiritual eye salve that we might see the truth and see the deep things of God. (See Rev. 3:18.) He fights our battles for us that He might **"exalt the horn of His anointed"** (This unique phrase from the Old Testament speaks of God strengthening His anointed, raising them up in His authority, and making them more than conquerors through the outpouring of His power.) (1 Sam. 2:10.)[*4]

Because of the savor of His good ointments, the very name of this Messiah/Bridegroom has become "ointment poured forth" upon His beloved bride (Song 1:3). O, how sweet it is just to mention His name in prayer and feel the gentle oil flow from above! This is the "balm in Gilead" that can heal us of all the wounds we receive here below (Jer. 8:22).

How overwhelming it is, when we realize the price Jesus had to pay for this transfer to take place! Like the resolute salmon that persistently forces its way upstream (so desperate to reproduce, it gives its life in the process), so also, the anointing in the firstborn Son, especially from Gethsemane onward, pushed hard against the strong, hell-bent current of the fallen Adam-nature. In the process of struggling to get to the peaceful and spiritually suitable 'spawning waters,' the Messiah died. But the supreme joy of being able to reproduce a supernatural family of anointed offspring must have far outweighed the agony of the *oil press* and the distressing uphill, upstream journey.

THE TRANSFORMATION: LEPERS TO PRIESTS

We have much to rejoice over. Under the Old Will, in order to be received by God, cleansed lepers had to receive the application of lamb's blood on the tip of the right ear, the right thumb and the right big toe. These three places on the body were then anointed with oil. Afterward, the remainder of the log of oil was poured over the head of the leper.

Strangely, a somewhat similar ritual was associated with the initiation of priests into their sacred office. In consecrating Aaron and his sons into the priesthood, the blood of a ram was placed on the tip of the ear, thumb and big toe; then the initiates were sprinkled with both blood and oil. (See Lev. 8:30; 14:1–57, especially verses 24–29, Ex. 29:20–21.) Surely, the similarity of these two ceremonies was God's way of symbolically foreshadowing what He would do under the New Will. Though we have been covered with the 'leprosy' of sin, God has sanctified us by the blood of Jesus and anointed us with the Holy Spirit, that we might draw near to Him in priestly service. Now we can hear what the Spirit has to say to the church (anointed ears); we can be God's hand extended in this world (anointed thumbs) and we can walk in the light of the truth all our days (anointed toes). Over our heads God has poured out His holy oil that we might think the thoughts of God and comprehend His wondrous mysteries.

Our Redeemer has delivered us from our leper-like past and granted us "the oil of joy for mourning." He has poured into our lives "grace according to the measure of the gift of Christ"—in order to access His throne as priests of the Most High God (Is. 61:3, Eph. 4:7 KJV).

THE PSALM 23 PROMISE

Especially beautiful is the Psalm 23:5 statement, "You *anoint* my head with oil." David was speaking as one of God's sheep. In that day, caring shepherds, sensitive to the needs of the domestic animals under their charge, would anoint the heads of sheep for a specific reason. On this part of the sheep's body, parasites gather to penetrate vulnerable areas: the ears and eyes. Anointing the heads of sheep helps prevent this from happening.

It is also true that parasitical demonic powers gather around the minds of true believers in an attempt to rob them of their spiritual hearing or their spiritual sight. The anointing applied by the Good Shepherd repels these spiritual trespassers and keeps our minds in perfect peace. Knowing we have this hope, we should daily confess, "…*I shall be anointed with fresh oil*" that we might be **"SONS OF FRESH OIL"** (Ps. 92:10 KJV, Zec. 4:14 MKJV).

BEARING THE LAMP/DESTROYING THE YOKE

In Psalm 132:17 (KJV) God said, "I have ordained a lamp for **MINE ANOINTED.**" What is this "lamp"? Psalm 119:105 says, "Your Word is a **lamp** to my feet" and Proverbs 6:23 says, "The commandment is a **lamp**; and the law is a light." Just as a lamp is filled with oil to produce light, so God's Word is full of the oil of His Spirit. We trust in the lamp, this anointed Word, to lead us through the dark valley of the shadow of death. Often in the 'oil lamp' of God's Word, we read accounts of the anointing doing great things for others. This gives us evidence for our faith, helping us to believe that God will do similar things for us. Our hearts should leap within us as we consider the following choice example.

In Isaiah 36 and 37, we find the account of Sennacherib, king of Assyria, bringing Judah under siege. Rabshakeh, his representative, sent messengers with a letter to King Hezekiah saying, "Do not let your God in whom you trust deceive you, saying, Jerusalem shall not be given into the hand of the king of Assyria." Hezekiah, the *anointed* king of Judah, went to the temple and spread the blasphemous Assyrian letter before the LORD. He then prayed, "O LORD our God, save us from his hand, that all the kingdoms of the earth may know that You are the LORD, You alone" (Is. 37:10, 20).

Hezekiah could boldly expect a miraculous and supernatural answer, because three years prior to this event, an awesome and pivotal prophecy was given. The *anointed* prophet, Isaiah, foretold that Assyria would attack Judah, but he also promised:

> ...*Thus says the LORD God of hosts: O My people who dwell in Zion, be not afraid of the Assyrian. He shall strike you...yet...the LORD of hosts shall stir up a scourge for him...*
>
> *It shall come to pass in that day, that his burden will be taken away from your shoulder, and his yoke from your neck, AND THE YOKE WILL BE DESTROYED BECAUSE OF THE ANOINTING...*
>
> (Isaiah 10:24–27)

To fully appreciate this passage of Scripture we must understand the full meaning of the word **yoke**. A yoke is most often defined as a wooden bar or frame by which two draft animals, such as oxen, are joined at the heads or necks for working together. But this can also mean a frame, fitted to a person's shoulders and neck, enabling him to carry a load in two equal portions. Finally, it can be some type of device laid across the shoulders or necks of prisoners of war, both to humiliate them and to prevent them from rebelling or escaping. Either the second or third definition is what Isaiah intended, for the Assyrians definitely planned on making the Jews their slaves.

To those who viewed the ensuing battle through carnal eyes, defeat for the Jews seemed inevitable. But an *anointed* king, who inherited his *anointing* from his forefather David, and an *anointed* prophet, agreed together in supplication to the Most High. God answered miraculously. That night "the angel of the LORD went out, and killed in the camp of the Assyrians a hundred and eighty-five thousand; and when people arose early in the morning, they were corpses—all dead" (Is. 37:36).

The yoke was definitely destroyed because of the anointing—for two men who were anointed of God sought God humbly, fervently and persistently. The awful burden was lifted because, as our title-scripture states, "The LORD is their strength, and He is the saving refuge of **His anointed.**" His ears are always open to their prayers. (Ps. 28:8, See 20:6.)

Now we, as sons of God, experience the fulfillment of these promises in a similar, though spiritual sense. We are presently besieged by an army of evil spirits under the command of the devil himself. Daily these principalities and powers seek to bring us under the yoke of their insidious control. With curled lips and deceitful words, they whisper messages of defeat and enslavement into the minds of God's offspring all over the world. We often hear the echo of Rabshakeh-like words, *"Let not your God in whom you trust deceive you saying He will deliver you."*

The present pressure may seem unbearable, the obstacles of tomorrow insurmountable and the failures of the past inescapable. But again and again, we hear the rumbling echo of Isaiah's prophetic words rolling through the annals of time:

*The yoke will be destroyed because of the **anointing.***

We may grieve inwardly because the glorious son of God part of us is still *yoked* to an iniquity-laden, Adam frame. We may groan at times, so burdened, because our regenerated spirits are still *yoked* to the corruption of the flesh— forcing us to steadily walk the direction of an open grave. But on that great day of restoration and resurrection, surely, we will look back over our earthly battles and, along with multitudes of others, repeat this truth one final time, *"Yes! The yoke truly was destroyed—not because of human will power or human goodness, but because of the anointing of God."* (See Jer. 30:7–11, Ezk. 34:27–31.)[*5]

In that day, the promise initially given to Aaron and his sons will surely be ours as well:

*Their **anointing** shall surely be an everlasting priesthood.*

(Exodus 40:15)

Yes, we really will spend eternity ministering priestly praise to the faithful High Priest, the Messiah-God, who will ever walk before us to receive our anointed worship. (See 1 Sam. 2:35.)

OUR ULTIMATE DESTINY

The anointing is an infinite gift—and we, the anointed, are progressively being shaped into its image. This 'messiah nature' will eventually find fullness of expression in us. Jesus Christ, **the Anointed One**, is totally involved in raising up an eternal family of **anointed ones.** Undoubtedly, God is interested in meeting the present need, but He is also quite engaged in preparing us and equipping us to fill universal and infinite offices of responsibility. We are those chosen vessels who will reign with Him forever. We will judge the earth and judge angels. We will rule the nations with a rod of iron.

Of course, the Kingdom Age will not be birthed into this world without great opposition. Psalm 2:2–3 reveals that the raging heathen of the last days will imagine a vain thing—"The kings of the earth [those allied with the Antichrist] set themselves, and the rulers take counsel together, against the LORD, and against **His anointed**, saying, Let us break their bonds in pieces and cast away their cords from us." In other words, the Antichrist and his world-ruling associates will do their utmost to resist the entrance of the true Messiah. They will attempt to prevent the establishment of the kingdom of God when the LORD comes with ten thousands of **His anointed ones.** How will God react to this future revolt? The same way that we should react now to every one of Satan's plots:

> *He who sits in the heavens shall laugh; the LORD shall hold them in derision.*

> (Psalm 2:4)

There is nothing that can stop the foundational plan of God and His future purposes from coming to pass. Therefore, both God and His people can laugh at all the destroyer seeks to do. We have read and believed Hannah's celebrated song of praise:

> *The adversaries of the LORD shall be broken in pieces; from heaven He will thunder upon them: the LORD will judge the ends of the earth...and EXALT THE HORN OF **HIS ANOINTED**.*

> (1 Samuel 2:10)

We will ultimately triumph and reign with Christ. The God who gave the best of the oil, wine and wheat to anointed ones under the Mosaic covenant will surely grant the best things available in the heavenly realm to us. (See Num. 18:8–12.) Our God has chosen to exalt us to the highest position available in creation. We can be fully confident, therefore, that the Messiah who opened this door of opportunity will triumphantly guide us into the fullness of **Our Glorious Inheritance.** For "He who establishes us…in Christ, and has **anointed** us is God" (2 Corinthians 1:21).

We are ordained to be kings, governors, judges, prophets, oracles and priests forever. We have discovered a simple way of saying all of these things! Eternally, we are **THE ANOINTED OF THE LORD.**

Deep calls unto deep—
For the anointing we plead.
The touch of Your Spirit,
That's all that we need.

'Till Messiah (God's Anointed)
Returns in His glory:
Death's yoke then destroyed—
O glorious story!

This "oil of joy"
Then perfected in all,
Yes, beggars become kings—
Restored from the fall!

Estranged sons of Adam—
Made priests evermore,
Anointed to worship,
With awed access adore—

The King who imparted
Such virtue, such peace—
So awake "Sons of Oil"
His Kingdom—increase.

THREE REASONS FOR THE IMPARTATION OF THE "ANOINTING"

(1) **Cleansing**—There are many instances in which persons were "anointed" with special substances as part of personal hygiene and cosmetic care. (See Rev. 3:3.) Non-use indicated a time of grief or remorse. (See 2 Sam. 14:2.) It was an expected part of showing hospitality to guests. (See Lk. 7:46.)

(2) **Consecration**—Both sacred places (Gen. 28:18; 35:14) and persons chosen for sacred tasks (Ex. 30:23–25; 30–33) were ceremonially anointed.

(3) **Coronation**—It was customary among the Jews to anoint their king as a sign of God's empowerment to successfully fill such a position of responsibility.

So the anointing is for our cleansing, our consecration and our coronation.[6]

Endnotes

[1] In the NIV, Habakkuk 3:13 reads, "You came out to deliver Your people, to save **Your Anointed One**..." This title probably refers to all of Israel. It can be claimed corporately by all redeemed persons under the New Will who are part of the Israel of God (God's princely people who rule with Him). (See Gal. 6:16.)

[2] John wrote these exhortations to Christians who were being wrongly influenced by the teachings of the Gnostics. Two main errors of this sect were corrupting the church: first, the belief that Jesus never really was flesh; He was just a spirit-being, a phantom, who assumed the appearance of flesh; and second, that matter and spirit are separate, so that (as some Gnostics asserted) the flesh can indulge in all manner of licentiousness, yet the spirit can simultaneously be in full and harmonious communion with the Creator. John was exhorting true believers that the anointing within them would sufficiently witness to the error of these and other false beliefs.

[3] **Sons of oil** is a title applied specifically to Joshua, the high priest, and Zerubbabel, the governor, in Zechariah 4:14. It is applicable as well to all who are numbered among God's anointed. The Hebrew is *ben yitshar*, translated **anointed ones** in the KJV, but more literally rendered **sons of oil** in several other versions (Dar, Amp, YLT). The Hebrew word *yitshar* is always translated "oil" in the KJV except in Zec. 4:14 where it is translated "anointed."

[4] Horns in the Scripture are used often to denote strength, conquest, or overcoming power. This is true, presumably, because they are the weaponry given by God to some animals to defend themselves or to attack. An animal whose horns were cut off became somewhat powerless and vulnerable. (See Ps. 75:10.) Horns are also emblems of ultimate triumph in battle, because especially in Bible times, at the conclusive end of some military engagements, the winning side would often signal their victory by the sound of horns being blown. The Amplified Version of Psalm 92:10 states that the horn being exalted is "an emblem of excessive strength and stately grace." Horns and the anointing are symbolically related because, at times, horns were used to hold the anointing oil poured out on key anointed persons who were used of God in significant ways (Js. 6:4–5, 1 Sam. 16:1,13, 1 Kgs. 1:39, Ps. 18:2; 89:17–18, 24; 112:6–9; 148:14, Ezk. 29:21).

[5] These passages in Jeremiah and Ezekiel also speak of the miraculous way God will deal with Israel in the last days. Spiritually they apply to the New Covenant children of God.

[6] Though reworded and stated somewhat differently, this list was drawn from Unger's Bible Dictionary under the word *Anointing*.

THE BLESSED
OF THE FATHER

THE BLESSED OF THE
LORD

THE BLESSED

A BLESSING

*Then shall the King say to those on His right hand, "Come, you **BLESSED OF MY FATHER**, inherit the kingdom prepared for you from the foundation of the world…"*

(Matthew 25:34)

...*You are now* **THE BLESSED OF THE LORD.**

(Genesis 26:29)

BLESSED *is he whose transgression is forgiven, whose sin is covered.*

(Psalm 32:1)

And it shall come to pass that just as you were a curse among the nations, O house of Judah and house of Israel, so will I save you, and you shall be **A BLESSING.** *Do not fear, let your hands be strong.*

(Zechariah 8:13)

THE BLESSED

Blessed *is he whose transgression is forgiven, whose sin is covered.*

(Psalm 32:1)

The word **blessed** has multiple shades of definition. When referring to an object, it means: *something sacred and set apart unto God, to be respected and reverenced.*

When referring to a person in covenant with God, it means: *someone who is supremely happy, enriched with benefits, spiritually prosperous, highly favored, well spoken of and worthy of honor. It also describes a person who possesses qualities of character God considers to be the highest good.*

When referring to God, it means: *worthy of praise, holy, admirable, glorious and exalted—for God is Himself the absolute of what is considered to be the highest good.* He is "the *blessed* and only Potentate, the King of kings, and LORD of lords, who alone has immortality." (1 Tim. 6:15–16, See 2 Cor. 1:3.)[*1]

Webster's Dictionary explains that the word **blessed** means:

(1) (a) held in reverence: VENERATED: the *blessed* saints
      (b) honored in worship: HALLOWED: the *blessed* Trinity
      (c) beatific: a *blessed* visitation
(2) of or enjoying the bliss of heaven—used as a title for a beatified person.
(3) bringing contentment or pleasure.

By this third definition, we can conclude that **the blessed of the LORD** are not only those who experience contentment and pleasure IN GOD; they have also become a source of contentment and pleasure TO GOD. Those who are blessed have not only discovered the source of true happiness; they have become a source of true happiness—to the Father above and to fellow human beings.

One Old Testament Hebrew word, *esher*, translated **blessed** twenty-seven times (KJV), is also rendered **happy** sixteen times. (One prime example is Psalm 144:15, "Happy are the people whose God is the LORD.") Also in the New Testament, the Greek word *makarios*, rendered blessed forty-four times, is translated into the word happy five times (KJV). (For instance, 1 Peter 3:14 explains that we should be "happy" if we "suffer for righteousness' sake.")

So being **blessed** and being **happy** are simply inseparable. True happiness does not rest in the frivolous pursuits of this life; true happiness is inextricably tied in with blessedness. If we can rightfully claim this status, we can expect to experience true, deep and abiding happiness all the days of our lives.[*2]

THE BE-ATITUDES

Probably the most loved verses in the Bible that utilize the word **blessed** are the eight beatitudes Jesus gave in His famed 'Sermon on the Mount.' (Incidentally, three of these beatitudes include titles that are explained in this volume of **Our Glorious Inheritance**.) Listen to the beauty of these poetic phrases authored by the Author of truth:

> *Blessed are the poor in spirit: for theirs is the kingdom of heaven.*
>
> *Blessed are those who mourn, for they shall be comforted.*
>
> *Blessed are the meek, for they shall inherit the earth.*
>
> *Blessed are those who hunger and thirst for righteouness, for they shall be filled.*
>
> *Blessed are the merciful, for they shall obtain mercy.*
>
> *Blessed are the pure in heart, for they shall see God.*
>
> *Blessed are the peacemakers, for they shall be called the sons of God [the children of God].*
>
> *Blessed are those who are persecuted for righteousness sake: for theirs is the kingdom of heaven.*
>
> (Matthew. 5:3–10 NKJV, KJV)

Notice the first seven beatitudes provide a character challenge. The eighth beatitude foretells the kind of reaction this world often returns to those who strive for such divine-like excellence.

We might ask why Jesus repeatedly used the word **blessed** in this passage of Scripture. First, it meant those who manifest such traits pass through the very doors that lead to *supreme happiness*. Second, it meant that such Christlike persons can expect to be *enriched with incomparable benefits* (notice every challenge to blessedness is followed by a promised reward). Third, it meant that those who partake of the divine nature in these areas receive *the favor of God*, having developed traits that God considers to be *the highest good*. They are *blessed* offspring of the *blessed God*. They are *worthy of honor, well spoken of* in heaven and on earth—at least by those who understand what pleases the Most High. Concerning this heartwarming passage of Scripture, F. B. Meyer explains:

The realm of blessedness is all around. It may be entered at any minute and we may dwell in it all the days of our life—Christ's beatitudes give us eight gates, any one of which will immediately conduct us within its confines.[*3]

Of course, Jesus did not initiate this mode of expression with His teaching; He was only continuing in a pattern of language already established under the former covenant. In the book of Psalms especially, we find the announcement of many other "**gateways to blessedness**" such as:

Blessed is the man who walks not in the counsel of the ungodly, nor stands in the path of sinners, nor sits in the seat of the scornful.

(Psalm 1:1)

...Blessed are all those who put their trust in Him.

(Psalm 2:12)

Blessed is he whose transgression is forgiven, whose sin is covered. Blessed is the man to whom the LORD does not impute iniquity, and in whose spirit there is no deceit.

(Psalm 32:1–2)

Blessed is the nation whose God is the LORD; the people He has chosen as His own inheritance.

(Psalm 33:12)

Blessed is he who considers the poor; the LORD will deliver him in time of trouble. The LORD will preserve him and keep him alive and he will be blessed on the earth...

(Psalm 41:1)

Blessed is the man You choose, and cause to approach You...

(Psalm 65:4)

Blessed is the man whom You instruct, O LORD, and teach out of Your law.

(Psalm 94:12)

Blessed are those who keep His testimonies, who seek Him with the whole heart.

(Psalm 119:2)

(See also Ps. 40:4; 84:4–5; 84:12; 89:15; 106:3; 112:1; 118:26; 119:1–2; 128:1, 4, Is. 30:18; 32:20, Jer. 17:7, Dan. 12:12.)

All of us who claim to be "the blessed" should search out not only these, but every "blessed" proclamation in the Scripture—that we might live in our inheritance and fulfill this particular facet of our calling with excellence.

THE DEFINITION AND HISTORY OF THE BLESSING OF GOD

*To **bless** means to make happy, to cause to prosper, or to bestow benefits and blessings upon. When God 'blesses,' He pours out supernatural favor upon His people.*

▒ The Entrance of God's Blessing ————————————————

From the very beginning of creation, we find this concept surfacing in Scripture. Having created the fish and the birds of the air, "God *blessed* them, saying, Be fruitful and multiply." Then when Adam and Eve were created, "God *blessed* them, and God said unto them, 'Be fruitful and multiply, and replenish the earth, and subdue it: and have dominion...over every living thing...' " (Gen. 1:22, 28 KJV).[*4]

In blessing the foreparents of the human race God first gave them a purpose, then God imparted to them the ability to fulfill that purpose. He filled their lives with happiness like that found in heaven. He breathed His very essence into their inner being. Their spirits communed constantly with His—something considered as normal, consistent and perpetual as the beating of their hearts. *God blessed them.* His favor shined toward them more warmly than the fresh, newborn rays of sunlight that penetrated God's garden of delight.

How noticeable it is that for both the animals and man, the first sign of God's blessing was the ability to procreate, to bring forth image-bearing offspring! (And what a blessing this is!) In the case of man, the second sign of God's blessing was dominion: the manifestation of God-given authority. These two signs are still relevant now, especially in a spiritual sense.

We who are blessed of God under the New Covenant are called to "be fruitful and multiply" spiritually by sharing the Gospel with those who are estranged from God, bringing them into His family. We are called to be a people of "dominion" as well, for we possess dominion over sin, dominion over satanic powers and ultimately, dominion over death.

We should also consider that from the onset, God's blessing was imparted only when He spoke it into existence. ("God blessed them *saying....*") If a vocalized confession was the Creator's method, it should certainly be a method His offspring implement as well. (See Ja. 3:8–10.)

THE DEFINITION AND HISTORY
OF THE CURSE OF GOD

When God **curses** *it means to announce or administer the misery, harm, injury, destruction, judgment or death that must necessarily follow sin.*

🕸 The Entrance of the Curse ──────────────

Immediately after the fall, God confronted the serpent and the guilty pair in Eden.

- **To the serpent God said,** "Because you have done this, you are *cursed* more than all cattle and more than every beast of the field; on your belly you shall go, and you shall eat dust all the days of your life. And I will put enmity between you and the woman, and between your seed and her Seed. He shall bruise your head, and you shall bruise His heel."

- **To the woman God said,** "I will greatly multiply your sorrow and your conception; in pain you shall bring forth children, your desire shall be for your husband, and he shall rule over you."

- **To the man God said,**" *Cursed* is the ground for your sake; in toil you shall eat of it all the days of your life. Both thorns and thistles it shall bring forth for you, and you shall eat the herb of the field. In the sweat of your face you shall eat bread till you return to the ground, for out of it you were taken; for dust you are and to dust you shall return" (Gen. 3:14–19).

Notice only the serpent was personally described as being cursed. Adam and Eve were indirectly cursed. God never said to them, "You are cursed" as He said to the serpent. Of course, because the ground was cursed for Adam's sake and his body was of the ground, he and his wife, Eve, received an overflow of the curse that would eventually draw them down into the dust of death. **Death is always the ultimate outcome of sin and the final result of God's curse:** moral death, mental death, emotional death, physical death and ultimately, the "second death": a time when both soul and body will be cast into the lake of fire. This is the inevitable chain of death-dealing events for those who receive God's curse. (See Ja. 1:14–15, Rev. 20:6–15.)

It is a marvelous thought that even in the beginning God intended to turn His curse into a blessing for those He would redeem. If God had not exiled Adam and Eve and destined them to die, they would have been allowed to eat of the tree of life and live on forever. In so doing, they would have become slaves eternally to sin and satanic powers (which would have been a far greater curse indeed!). So the Adamic race must return to the dust to give some of them the blessed opportunity of full recovery. O, the genius of God!

THE SUBLIMINAL INFLUENCE

One of the most convicting and powerful scriptures dealing with this subject is Proverbs 3:33:

> *The curse of the LORD is on the house of the wicked,*
> *but He blesses the home of the just.*

In the very homes of those who are committed to a sinful lifestyle there is a dark, subliminal presence that will eventually produce very destructive results. The vision of Zechariah 5:1–4 elaborates on this truth. The prophet saw a scroll, thirty feet by fifteen feet, flying through the air. God explained, "This is *the curse* that goes out over the face of the whole earth...it shall enter the house of the thief and the house of the one who swears falsely by My name. It shall remain in the midst of his house and consume it, with its timber and stones."

The prophetic picture God paints is ominous. The curse will devour the home of those who are committed to wickedness until that family unit collapses in rottenness. This is not talking about the collapse of a literal physical house, but the collapse of relationships, hopes and anything of value. This is inevitable—for sin is contagious and it always destroys people—mentally, emotionally, spiritually and eventually, even physically. Sin destroys both for time and eternity and often intensifies its evil influence from one generation to the next.

If the negative is true, though, the positive is also true. If men and women are committed to righteous principles, the blessing of God will rest upon that home until it draws every family member under its gentle and pleasant influence. It will command happiness, prosperity and purpose into those lives that are yielded to God's authority. The faithful, covenant-keeping God even promised His blessing would flow down a thousand generations for those who love Him and keep His commandments. (See Dt. 7:9, Ac. 16:31, 1 Cor. 7:14.)

GOD'S ORIGINAL PLAN: CONQUERING HIS OWN CURSE

Although God's justice demanded the entrance of "the curse" into this realm, His love compelled Him to secure a way for men to be delivered and restored to blessedness. This was His plan from the beginning and the reason He began revealing Himself to certain choice individuals out of the human race. The patriarchs of the Old Testament were the first recorded persons to receive the revelation of God. Whenever the Most High revealed Himself to them, *the blessing of God* always followed. Consider the following examples:

- **Noah**—After the devastating, yet cleansing effects of the flood, Noah offered of every clean animal to God on an altar. The Scripture testifies that "the

LORD smelled a sweet savour and the LORD said in His heart, I will not again *curse* the ground any more for man's sake." Apparently, a portion of the original curse was lifted at that point establishing the harvest cycle and making it far easier to produce good crops. Then "God *blessed* Noah and his sons," repeating His original commission to Adam, "...Be fruitful, and multiply, and fill the earth." (Gen. 8:20–9:1 KJV, See Gen. 5:29.)

᭙ **Job**—After his time of great trial and loss, God brought restoration to this great patriarch. "The LORD *blessed* the latter days of Job more than his beginning" (Jb. 42:12). Many students of the Word apply this prophetically, teaching that Job was a prophetic archetype of both Israel and the Church and a revelation of how God will prosper both in an unprecedented way in the latter days.

᭙ **Abraham**—In the first visitation given to Abraham, God pledged, "I will *bless* you and make your name great and you will be a *blessing* " (Gen. 12:2). Of Sarah also, God said, "I will *bless* her and she shall be a mother of nations" (Gen. 17:16). That God would even choose Abraham was somewhat amazing because his family members were all idolaters. According to Deuteronomy 5:7–9, he should have inherited a curse as a result. Instead, through his response of obedience to God, the 'curse line' was broken and a 'line of blessing' was established that would eventually bring God's blessing to the entire world. The Almighty promised this great patriarch, "in you all the families of the earth shall be *blessed*." He also gave the assurance to Abraham, "I will *bless* those who *bless* you, and I will curse him who curses you." (Gen. 12:3, See Gen. 22:18.)

᭙ **Isaac**—To Isaac, Abraham's promised son, God repeated his commitment, "I will be with you and *bless* you...and in your seed all the nations of the earth shall be *blessed*." In another visitation, God said, "I will *bless* you and multiply your descendants for My servant Abraham's sake." Others recognized this special touch of God on Isaac. Abimelech, upon entering a covenant with Isaac, asserted, "You are now **THE BLESSED OF THE LORD**." In his generation, just Isaac and his immediate family filled this role. Now, in this present era, countless thousands who are in covenant with the true and living God are included (Gen. 26:3–4, 24, 29).

᭙ **Jacob and the transferred blessing**—From the very start, one of the most important events in the lives of God's chosen ones was the oral transfer of the blessing of Abraham. There are at least sixteen different facets to the Abrahamic blessing. These cover every area of existence.[*5] Genesis 24:1 reveals that the LORD "*blessed* Abraham in all things." This incredible, all-encompassing blessing did not cease with the passing away of this forefather of all Israelites.

It was passed from one generation to the next. Hebrews 11:20–21 mentions the patriarchal rituals effecting this transfer, emphasizing the faith involved in such an action. "By faith Isaac *blessed* Jacob and Esau concerning things to come. By faith Jacob, when he was dying, *blessed* each of the sons of Joseph, and worshiped, leaning on the top of his staff." (See Gen. 27:1–40; 48:1–19; 49:1–28.)

Imparting the blessing involved faith because those involved had to believe in God's declaration concerning Abraham and his seed in order to effectively reaffirm it. Furthermore, they had to believe in the effectiveness of whatever method was utilized: such as laying on of hands and/or a prophetic word being uttered. This was always a pivotal event shaping the very destiny of the recipients. Before he died, Jacob laid his hands on his grandsons, Ephraim and Manasseh, and blessed them both. He declared that the younger of the two would become a greater and mightier tribe. Before his death, he gathered his twelve sons to his bedside and "*blessed* each one according to his own *blessing*" (Gen. 49:28).

In other words, Jacob recognized a blessing and calling already resting upon each son—then verified and awakened it by his faith-proclamation. Of course, Jacob understood the great value of the patriarchal blessing, for he had even deceived his own father, Isaac, in order to obtain it. It was also Jacob who wrestled with the Angel of the LORD all night, yet when given an opportunity to rest, said, "I will not let you go until You *bless* me" (Gen. 32:26).

➤ **The Nation of Israel**—All godly Israelites were automatically blessed by virtue of being Abraham's offspring, but often this 'blessing status' was reaffirmed and reapplied. For instance, in Numbers 6:23–27 God commanded the Levites to "*bless* the children of Israel," by saying to them:

> *The LORD **bless you** and keep you; The LORD make*
> *His face to shine upon you and be gracious to you; The*
> *LORD lift up His countenance upon you, and give you*
> *peace.*

Then God added, "So they [the Levites] shall put My name on the children of Israel, and I will *bless* them." This divine mandate reveals the power of the spoken word on the lips of God's anointed representatives (something that is still true today) and the power of uttering the name of the LORD. Another prime example of this spoken pronouncement of blessing over the whole nation is found in Deuteronomy 33:1–29. This chapter records "the *blessing* with which Moses the man of God *blessed* the children of Israel before his death."

THE "AMENS" FROM
MOUNT EBAL AND MOUNT GERIZIM

One of the most profound Scriptural examples of this chapter's theme concerns the entrance of the Israelites into the Land of Promise. A grand 'blessing and cursing' proclamation was ordered in advance by Moses and acted out later by Joshua. Having crossed over Jordan, the Israelites gathered together in a valley between two mountains. Half of the tribes of Israel (the offspring of free women—Rachel and Leah) stood on the slopes of Mt. Gerizim to 'Amen' the blessings of God. The other six tribes (four of which were the offspring of bondwomen) stood five hundred yards away on the slopes of Mt. Ebal to affirm the curses. (Notice the evident relation between freedom and blessings, and bondage and curses.)

Joshua, the elders of Israel, the officers, the judges, the priests and the Levites stood between the two mounts around the ark of the covenant, near an altar that had been erected for the occasion. Apparently, in unison they first sounded out the cursings, then the blessings. Thunderclap responses of thousands of 'Amens' were shouted from the tribes on either side.

▓ Deuteronomy 28:1–13 records twenty-six blessing proclamations that we can still claim today ——————————————————————

(1)	The LORD your God will set you high above all nations (v.1).
(2)	All these blessings shall come upon you and overtake you (v.2).
(3)	Blessed shall you be in the city (v.3).
(4)	Blessed shall you be in the country (v.3).
(5-7)	Blessed shall be the fruit of your body, the produce of your ground and the increase of your herds...cattle and...flocks (v.4).
(8-9)	Blessed shall be your basket and your kneading bowl (v.5).
(10)	Blessed shall you be when you come in (on the highest level, this could mean 'coming into' this world at birth) (v.6).
(11)	Blessed shall you be when you go out (on the highest level, this could mean 'going out' of this world at death) (v.6).
(12-13)	The LORD will cause your enemies who rise against you to be defeated before your face; they shall come out against you one way and flee before you seven ways (v.7).
(14-15)	The LORD will command the blessing on you in your storehouses and in all to which you set your hand (v.8).
(16)	He will bless you in the land which the LORD your God is giving you (v.8).
(17)	The LORD will establish you as a holy people to Himself (v.9).

(18-19)   Then all peoples of the earth shall see that you are called by the name of the LORD, and they shall be afraid of you (v.10).

(20)   The LORD will grant you plenty of goods (v.11).

(21-23)   The LORD will open to you His good treasure, the heavens, to give the rain to your land in its season, and to bless all the work of your hand (v.12). (This last one is a repeat of blessing #15, so this blessing is doubly emphasized.)

(24)   You shall lend to many nations, but you shall not borrow (v.12).

(25)   And the LORD will make you the head and not the tail... (v.13).*6

(26)   You shall be above only, and not be beneath...(v.13).

Four other significant promises are found in Deuteronomy 7:14–15, "You shall be *blessed* above all peoples; there shall not be a male or female barren among you or among your livestock. And the LORD will take away from you all sickness, and will afflict you with none of the terrible diseases of Egypt which you have known... ."

🦋 In Deuteronomy 28:15–68, God then lists over a hundred curses in fifty-four verses that will "overtake" those who are disobedient ————

These curses include the most devastating things that could happen in life, including: sickness, pestilence, famine, non-productive crops, turmoil in family relationships, defeat in battle, poverty, confusion, oppression, slavery, insanity, being "the tail and not the head," being "beneath and not above," and finally, utter destruction and death. God foretold these curses would overwhelm the rebellious among His people until they became "an astonishment, a proverb, and a byword, among all nations." He even said they would become "a desolation and a **curse**"—in other words, an example of a cursed people. This was, of course, totally the opposite of what God desired. (Dt. 28:37, 2 Kgs. 22:19, See Is. 43:28; 65:15, Jer. 24:9; 42:18; 44:8, 12, 22, Mal. 2:2.)

After presenting this vitally important and convicting revelation, Moses warned the people of Israel:

> *I call heaven and earth as witnesses today against you, that I have set before you life and death,* **blessing** *and* **cursing***; therefore choose life, that both you and your descendants may live.*

(Deuteronomy 30:19)

GOD'S BLESSINGS ARE CONDITIONAL

It should not be overlooked that in the main 'blessing' verses previously mentioned (Dt. 28:1–13) God also specified some very stringent conditions. The Israelite people had to "diligently obey the voice of the LORD...keep the commandments of the LORD…and walk in His ways" (vs. 1, 9). Moreover God asserted, "You shall not turn aside from **any** of the words which I command you this day, to the right or the left, to go after other gods to serve them" (v.14).

So clearly, under the Old Will especially, receiving God's blessings primarily hinged on human performance. Unfortunately, such requirements were more than demanding; they were impossible. Verse fourteen, mentioned above, stated that the Israelites could not depart from ANY of God's words or commands and still be recipients of His full blessing. How their hearts must have trembled to shout 'Amen' to the following dark declaration that was directed toward Mt. Ebal's congregation:

> *Cursed be he that confirmeth not ALL of the words of this law to do them.*
>
> (Deuteronomy 27:26 KJV)

With one response of resounding agreement, the Israelites that day swore themselves to a life of perfection or suffering the consequences of failing to do so. They soon found this to be an unachievable goal. No wonder, many centuries later, Paul referred back to this incident, explaining, "For as many as are of the works of the law are under the curse; for it is written, 'Cursed is everyone who does not continue **in all things** which are written in the book of the law, to do them'" (Gal. 3:10).

Paul showed us the insurmountable problem. Then, two verses later, the inspired apostle pulled back the veil on heaven's glorious answer—for Jews and Gentiles alike. What a joy it is that:

> *Christ has redeemed us from **the curse of the law**, having become a **curse** for us (for it is written, "Cursed is everyone who hangs on a tree"),*
>
> *That **the blessing of Abraham** might come upon the Gentiles in Christ Jesus, that we might receive the promise of the Spirit through faith.*
>
> (Galatians 3:13–14)

On the strong hinge of this notable event, the ages turned. Now the difference between a cursed and blessed status depends—not so much on human performance (which never ceases to be flawed), but rather, on Jesus' flawless performance (which was and is the epitome of perfection). He who was blessed became a curse, so that we, who are cursed, could qualify to become **the blessed of the Father.**

Delivered from the curse of the sin nature.
Delivered from the curse of satanic control.
Delivered from the curse of death.
And not only that—delivered from the curse of the law.

Of course, certain conditions must still be met if full 'blessedness' is to be enjoyed under the New Will. The 'Sermon on the Mount' proves that—for it is only the "poor in spirit," "the pure in heart," "the meek" and those who "hunger after righteousness" who are rightful recipients of a "blessed" status. Still, recovery from failures, restoration to righteousness and partaking of the divine nature could never be sufficiently acquired by strict adherence to the numerous ordinances and rituals imposed under the Mosaic order. They are acquired—with worshipful wonder—beneath the shadow of a cross on a lonely hill called Calvary. In this holy place, rich forgiveness, boundless mercy and inexhaustible grace are truly given to those who believe. We owe the crucified One an eternity of praise for reversing the curse that we might receive and maintain our status as **the blessed**.

OUR PRESENT "BLESSED" STATUS

The prophet Isaiah saw the outcome of the New Covenant and foretold that God's people of this era would be recognized as **"the offspring whom the LORD has blessed"** (Is. 61:9 NAS).*7

Ephesians 1:3 reveals the awesomeness of our present condition:

> **Blessed** be the God and Father of our LORD Jesus
> Christ, who **has blessed** us with every **spiritual blessing**
> in the heavenly places **in Christ**.

Four very noticeable things about this verse plead for our attention.

(1) Notice the tense—It does not say God WILL bless us: future tense. It announces that God HAS blessed us: past tense. This portion of **Our Glorious Inheritance** is an already established fact as far as God is concerned. So before we even face tomorrow's dilemmas, God has already provided solutions. Before we even recognize our need, God has supplied His abundance. This truth increases in profoundness upon discovering that in the original Greek, verses three and four of Ephesians, chapter one, are actually one sentence. God "HAS blessed us" because we "WERE chosen in Him before the foundation of the world." So before the world existed, God anticipated all that would befall His people and made a way—before the way even needed to be made.

(2) Notice the key word "spiritual" (Gr. *pneumatikos*)—This is a promise that focuses, not on the material, but rather, the *spiritual* needs of men. It concerns that which brings healing and wholeness to the *spirit*. These *"spiritual blessings"* are far too numerous to list fully, but include: salvation, justification, sanctification, redemption, reconciliation, the fruit of the Spirit (the indwelling of the character of God), the gifts of the Spirit (also called *"spiritual* gifts" in 1 Cor. 14:1—the manifestation of God's attributes or abilities) and much, much more. Of course, physical and material well-being often result also from these spiritual blessings.

(3) Notice the location where these blessings are discovered and acquired: "heavenly places"—Having been born again and translated into the kingdom of God, believers are blessed to actually experience a taste of heaven on earth. Ephesians 2:6 claims God has "raised us up together, and made us sit together *in heavenly places* in Christ Jesus." Though this is a constantly available experience of heart, it is usually far more evident during times of worship, Word-study or spiritual fellowship. In Isaiah 57:15, "the High and Lofty One" who inhabits eternity promises that humble and contrite persons will be graced to dwell with Him in "the high and holy place." In this heavenly sphere, they are "revived" (resurrected by the life of God) into all those wonderful blessings provided under the New Covenant.[*8]

(4) Notice the person in whom these blessings reside—They are found "in Christ." This is the position we automatically occupy when we surrender to Jesus' Lordship. Because inexhaustible, infinite resources are found "in Him," unending blessings are available to those who acknowledge Him in His headship role. (See Ps. 72:17–19.)

THE CUP OF BLESSING

Unveiling the meaning and value of the communion ritual, Paul explained:

> **The cup of blessing** *which we bless, is it not the communion of the blood of Christ?...*
>
> (1 Corinthians 10:16)

This term—*the cup of blessing*—is a literal reference to the third cup traditionally drunk during the Passover feast, also called *the cup of redemption*. A special blessing was spoken over this cup, usually by the head of every Israelite family (just as Jesus, the head of the family of God, did during the last supper). Of course, Jesus added the prophetic statement, "This is My blood of the New Testament, which is shed for many for the remission of sins" (Mt. 26:28 KJV).

We begin drinking in this precious blood as soon as we receive Jesus into our hearts. At that precise moment, the lifegiving Spirit of Christ starts flowing into our inner being. Instantly, we are cleansed of all our errors and filled with the very righteousness of God (indeed, the fullness of His divine nature). We are graced to freely partake of "every good thing which is…in Christ" (Phm. 1:6). From that point forward our status as bloodwashed, sanctified persons is renewed day by day and moment by moment. Because of the continual flow of this holy blood through our spirits, we are kept clean and acceptable before His throne—"holy and without blame" (Eph. 1:4).

Drink deeply from this cup, O sons and daughters of God, drink deeply!

THE BLESSEDNESS OF IMPUTED RIGHTEOUSNESS

Imbibing this *"cup of blessing"* mentioned in 1 Corinthians 10:16 has everything to do with the *"blessedness"* of imputed righteousness revealed in Romans 4:6–10. This chapter starts off celebrating the wonderful gift of righteousness God granted to Abraham. It echoes Genesis 15:6, rehearsing how Abraham "believed in the LORD, and He accounted it to him for righteousness." In other words, Abraham invested faith in God, then withdrew righteousness from the same account. So it was by faith, and not by works, that Abraham's sins were blotted out and he obtained a right standing with God.

Paul then reinforces "the *blessedness* of the man to whom God imputes righteousness apart from works" (Ro. 4:6). Psalm 32:2 is restated: *"Blessed* is the man to whom the LORD shall not impute sin" (Ro. 4:8). The question is then asked, "Does this *blessedness* then come upon the circumcised only [natural born Israelites] or upon the uncircumcised [converted Gentiles] also?" (Ro. 4:10).

The answer to this question is a glorious open door. It comes upon all who receive the true revelation of God, all who repent and believe, whether they be Jew or Gentile. Romans 5:17 calls it "the gift of righteousness"—one of the most *blessed* gifts we can ever receive as children of God.

Of course, such an inward impartation of righteousness should automatically result in an outward manifestation of righteous deeds: a desire and an ability to walk in God's commandments. In a sense, this brings 'double blessedness,' for in Luke 11:28 Jesus also said:

> …**Blessed** are those who hear the Word of God, and keep it.

Such persons can doubly expect to be *supremely happy, enriched with benefits and highly favored of God*—especially in the area of divine fellowship. Although access into the Father's presence is a gift of grace (See Ro. 5:1–2), fellowship with Him can be broken by willful acts of rebellion. To prevent this, Psalm 24:3–5 presents the analysis that can still be applied under the New Will:

Who may ascend into the hill of the LORD? Or who
may stand in His holy place?

He who has clean hands and a pure heart, who has
not lifted up his soul to an idol, nor sworn deceitfully.

*He shall receive **blessing** from the LORD, and*
righteousness from the God of his salvation.

One of the most wonderful aspects of this *"blessing"* certainly is sweet intimacy with the Creator. What a blessing it is to receive all of God's benefits and gifts—but what a greater blessing it is to know the Giver Himself, our hearts forever intermingling with His! Those who know such a blessed union have nothing to fear, for our Father is not only fully committed to commanding blessings on His people. He is also a genius at turning curses into blessings in their behalf. (See Num. 22–24, Dt. 23:3–5.)

Though God promised if the Israelites rebelled against Him they would become a "curse and a reproach among all the nations," even in this, He showed His power to reverse the curse and make it a blessing (Jer. 29:18, 44:8). Through the dispersion of the Jews into all the world, two *blessed* things happened: one—the Gentiles became more familiar with Jewish culture and the true revelation of God (which prepared them to later receive the Gospel), and two—synagogues were built in many nations that later became the initial 'contact' for Paul and other early missionaries.

TURNING CURSES INTO BLESSINGS

Because "the gifts and the calling of God are irrevocable," God also refused to allow the seed of Israel to be utterly destroyed (Ro. 11:29). In Isaiah 65:8, He explains why:

Thus says the LORD: "As the new wine is found in the
*cluster, and one says, 'Do not destroy it, for **a blessing** is*
in it' so will I do for My servants' sake, that I may not
destroy them all."

The *"blessing"* is probably, on one level, a reference to the faithful in Israel who remained true to the covenant through the years of apostasy and subsequent oppression and captivity. On a higher level, it was surely a reference to the coming Messiah—for He became the means by which the Abrahamic blessing extended beyond the borders of Judaism into all the world. Because of the incarnation of the Son of God, all "nations" and "families" (cultural people groups or races) of the earth can now be *blessed*. (See Gal. 3:8–14.) Because wine is obtained from grapes, Isaiah 65:8 is probably also a prophetic foreshadowing of the outpouring of the *"new wine"* of the Holy Spirit that fell on the early Jewish church and has since poured out throughout the world in this New Covenant Age.

✸ Zechariah 8:13 echoes a similar message: ─────────────

*And it shall come to pass that just as you were a **curse**
among the nations, O house of Judah and house of Israel,
so I will save you, and you shall be **A BLESSING**....*

There are four valuable interpretations to this verse.

◟· **First,** the Jewish people became a proverb, a byword, and a *curse* in the world when they lost their inheritance to the Assyrians and Babylonians. But after being restored to their homeland, they provided a monotheistic culture, shaped by preparatory doctrines under the Old Will, into which the Messiah could be born, understood and received. *What a blessing!*

◟· **Second,** the beginning church—made up of those disciples who followed Jesus during His earthly sojourn—was for the most part Jewish. As God's remnant in the world they became "*a blessing*" by passing on their knowledge of the Messiahship of Jesus and of true salvation to the Gentile world.

◟· **Third,** this passage is also very applicable to the similar situation regarding the nation of Israel during this present New Covenant era. From 70 A.D. onward, sadly, Israel has been dispersed in all the world, becoming once again (during times of terrible prejudice and cruel anti-Semitism) a byword and a *curse* among the Gentiles. But since 1948 God has been regathering the chosen seed of Abraham to the Land of Promise. This latter day Jewish remnant will ultimately experience a sweeping revelation of the Messiahship of Jesus. The "spirit of grace and supplication" will move upon them and they will look on Him whom they pierced, with hearts full of repentance and trust. (See Zec. 12:10.) When this fully transpires, the dry bones of Ezekiel 37 will be resurrected into a mighty, born again, Spirit-filled army of the LORD—and the ensuing result on the church worldwide will be comparable to exceptional, spiritual "riches" and even "life from the dead" (Ro. 11:12, 15). *What a supreme blessing!*

◟· **Fourth,** Zechariah 8:13 can also be personalized to every believer. Prior to salvation, most believers filled the role of being a "curse." Our lack of moral absolutes was an infectious disease of the soul that we passed on to others. Our carnal attitudes, to one degree or another, harmed and wounded others spiritually. In a very real sense, we were *a curse*! But then God saved us, filling our hearts with godly character and faith in the truth, and we became *a blessing*. Normally, those so transformed are no longer found deceiving others with false beliefs, or injuring others with hurtful attitudes. Instead they are often found bringing healing and blessing to the world around them.

Amazingly, Christians are not only called to bless those who bless them. Jesus even commanded, "Love your enemies and BLESS THOSE WHO CURSE YOU" (Mt. 5:44). If we do so, 1 Peter 3:9 promises that we will "inherit a blessing." In cases like this, we become a doubly blessed people. God blesses us because of the good we do for others—and God blesses us because of the evil others do against us. That sounds like a win/win situation, even for the most persecuted and troubled child of God.

Of course, the final seal on this truth involves the proper understanding of the role of suffering in our lives. Only by going through extreme suffering was the Messiah able to become a source of extreme blessing to the global family. So also, His followers must be crucified with Him to become channels of His blessing. Quite often the two are directly proportional. The more we suffer with Christ the more we are able to bless others. Paul suffered terribly as he followed God's plan for his life, but quite possibly for this reason the apostle could boast to the Roman church, "when I come to you, I shall come in the fullness of the *blessing* of the Gospel of Christ" (Ro. 15:29).

As John Henry Jewett so aptly explained:

> *"As soon as we cease to bleed, we cease to bless."*

THE WINDOWS OF HEAVEN

One of the most intriguing prophecies, in this vein of thought, is Malachi 3:10–12. The prophet rebukes the negligence of God's people in returning the tithe to Him, but promises an awesome blessing if they are obedient:

> *Bring all the tithes into the storehouse, that there may be food in My house, and try Me now in this [prove Me— KJV, test Me—NIV] says the LORD of hosts; if I will not open for you **the windows of heaven** and pour out for you such **blessing** that there will not be room enough to receive it.*
> *And I will rebuke the devourer for your sakes...*
> *And all nations will call you **blessed**...*

The "windows of heaven" being opened speaks of a three things— dramatic, divine intervention, an awesome, supernatural change and an abundant, supernatural supply. (See 2 Kgs. 6:25–7:20.)

After this prophecy was given, the Old Testament writings closed and for four hundred years, Israel was in a time of great political turmoil and oppression (hardly a fulfillment of this word).*9 Then, after this four-century-long 'dry period,' it happened. Three chapters into the New Testament the lowly Nazerene is baptized in Jordan "and the heaven's were opened unto Him." The Spirit of God descended in the form of a dove and the Father announced, "This is My beloved Son" (Mt. 3:16–17).

The "blessing" of the Spirit was poured out on the firstborn Son of God without measure, and in a sense, the river of life began rising. It would soon overflow its banks with the entrance of the Church Age. Prior to this pivotal event, the ministry of the judges and prophets of God could be, for the most part, contained within the boundaries of Judaism. But with the coming of the Messiah, there was not "room enough" within Israel to contain all that God intended to do.

Three-and-a-half years later, from the day of Pentecost onward, the 'blessing' began flowing into every nation, tongue and people. The 'devourer' of the human race was 'rebuked' when Jesus crushed him underfoot. (See Mal. 3:11.) This legally released God to open the windows of heaven over all who call upon His name. (See Jn. 1:48–51.) Such a wondrous, thing is still happening now—and will continue until the end of this age—when an even greater change will take place.

ULTIMATE BLESSEDNESS

When this present age ends, ultimate blessings and blessedness will be the manifest inheritance of the people of God. Titus 2:13 heralds the coming of the kingdom of God with grand words:

> *Looking for the **blessed hope** and glorious appearing*
> *of our great God and Savior Jesus Christ.*

When He returns, the Messiah will unify the brethren worldwide and set up the throne of His kingdom on Mount Zion. It is there, in that sacred location, that Psalm 133:3 states "the LORD commanded the *blessing*—life forevermore." This "blessing of all blessings" (life unending) was "commanded" by God over His people thousands of years ago, but it will be fully manifested when the ever-living, everlasting God will once again visibly walk on the earth. Psalm 37:22 foretells that in that day:

> *...those **blessed** by Him shall inherit the earth, but*
> *those cursed by Him shall be cut off.*[*10]

This 'inheriting of the earth' is the *blessing* handed down from Abraham, the *blessing* that Jacob wrestled with the Angel of the LORD to obtain—and the *blessing* we are striving to obtain as well. Those who comprehend this mystery are often compelled to pray with wording similar to Jacob's celebrated and passionate plea, "*LORD, we will not let you go until you bless us, until we inherit all things, until we reign with you in splendor and glory."* (See Gen. 28:1–15; 32:24–32.)

We can be assured: the grace of God that started this work in us will carry us all the way through to such a glorious destiny! The *blessed* God will fully bring to birth that *blessed* kingdom prepared for those He calls *the blessed of the Father.* Although in these latter days, according to Isaiah 24:6, the "curse" will devour the earth, God's renewed blessing will cause it to be 'reborn' into yet greater glory. When God's glorified king/priests gather to Jerusalem to celebrate the Kingship and High Priesthood of their Savior, God promised:

> *I will make* **them** *and the places all around My hill* **A**
> **BLESSING***; and I will cause the showers to come down*
> *in their season; there shall be* **showers of blessing***.*
> (Ezekiel 34:26)

What a day that will be when the splendor of the celestial pours down into the terrestrial! The Shekinah of heaven's throne room—falling like translucent, golden rain from above—will enliven this realm until heaven-on-earth conditions prevail. In that spectacular era, more than ever before, the LORD will be able to say to His redeemed, **"Blessed** are your eyes, for they see: and your ears, for they hear" (Mt. 13:16).

For the vision afar off will become a face-to-face reality. Just as Ezekiel 34:26 prophesied, God's anointed ones will be a blessing: an everlasting blessing to the Most High God—infinite proof of His power and a source of constant worship ascending before His throne. In that era, we will be able to say even more confidently, "God has blessed us with all spiritual blessings in heavenly places in Christ," for we will have no lack. Abundance beyond our present comprehension will be our everlasting possession.

O, how impossible it is to sufficiently describe in words what our future really holds—the ethereal, Eden-like beauty that will abound in this world during the age to come! In a perfect way, we will then "bless the LORD at all times: His praise shall continually be in our mouths"—for the victory will be fully manifested (Ps. 34:1). Then, after a thousand years, when New Jerusalem descends out of heaven from God, "the throne of God and of the Lamb shall be in it" and "there shall be no more curse" (Rev. 22:3). The cursed shall depart into everlasting destruction, but *the blessed of the LORD* will never know anything but *blessings* and *blessedness* forevermore.

Even the Lamb of God will inherit added blessings as a result of His beautiful, yet difficult sojourn in this vale of tears. Revelation 5:12 reveals heaven will thunder with the proclamation, "Worthy is the Lamb...to receive power and riches and wisdom, and strength, and honor and glory and *blessing*!" What else could this "blessing" be than the end product of the bride of Christ coming forth in His image. She will share His throne and His heart, communing with Him in ecstatic love throughout the ceaseless ages. There is no blessing to God above and no blessing to His offspring below that could ever surpass this wonderful climax to God's redemptive plan.

Therefore, the following promises of **Our Glorious Inheritance** truly sum up those things which sons of God should consider their source of *supreme happiness*, those things which God considers to be *the highest good*:

> *Blessed are those who are called to the marriage supper of the Lamb!*
>
> (Revelation 19:9)
>
> *Blessed and holy is he who has part in the first resurrection. Over such the second death has no power, but they shall be priests of God and of Christ and shall reign with Him...*
>
> (Revelation 20:6)
>
> *Blessed are they who do His commandments, that they may have right to the tree of life, and may enter through the gates into the city.*
>
> (Revelation 22:14)[*11]

No wonder Isaiah 30:18 looks forward into the future with expectancy and announces, *"Blessed are all those who wait for Him."* Those who serve Him and patiently wait for the coming of His kingdom will ultimately receive the best heaven has to offer: infinite happiness... unfathomable benefits...boundless prosperity...indescribable honor...the exalted highness of absolute divine favor...the perfection of character qualities God considers the highest good.

Furthermore they will receive the glorious blessing of hearing the Shepherd/ King say to those sheep on His right hand (the position of intimacy, trust and shared authority), "Come you **BLESSED OF MY FATHER**, inherit the kingdom prepared for you from the foundation of the world" (Matthew 25:34).

Why will He bless His own so abundantly? Not just because we have learned how to *acquire blessings*—but more so, because we have learned how to *be a blessing* to those who need it the most—to the hungry, the sick, the destitute, the imprisoned. (See Mt. 25:31–46.) Yes, this final analysis will shine like a beacon through all of heaven itself, that it really is "more *blessed* to give than to receive" (Ac. 20:35). In a spiritual sense, we stand on the slopes of Mt. Gerizim even now and shout—*"Amen, and Amen"!*

Deep calls unto deep—
"For your **blessing***," we cry,*
Away with the curse
That decreed we should die.

Come upon us, blest showers
of heavenly rain,
So our time-locked souls
Know eternity's gain.

That sin might be conquered
And life reign supreme;
Yes, our shout is "Amen"
To this heaven-sent dream.

But still there is more
(And "the deep" in us knows)
That the highest of callings
From this fertile ground grows:

Being **blessed***—that's the seed,*
The beginning of all good;
BUT BECOMING A ***BLESSING***
Is the blossom that should…

Bring forth glorious beauty
And fruit of great worth,
Being a benefit to God
And others on earth.

THE BURDEN OF BLESSEDNESS

In the psalm-like proclamation Mary made concerning her own calling to be the mother of the Messiah, she boasts, "All generations shall call me blessed" (Lk. 1:48). Commenting on this statement, William Barclay said, "It is the paradox of blessedness that it confers on a person at one and the same time the greatest joy and the greatest task in all the world."

Endnotes

1 Some instances where this word is used of God just in the book of Psalms are as follows: Psalms 18:46; 21:6; 28:6; 41:13; 68:19, 35; 72:17–19*; 89:52; 106:48; 113:2; 124:6. Those emphasized by an asterisk are Messianic prophecies.

*2 *Happiness* may be an insufficient word choice here. William Barclay explains, "The English word *happiness* gives its own case away. It contains the root *hap* which means *chance*. Human happiness is something which is dependent on the chances and changes of life, something which life may give and which life may also destroy. **The Christian blessedness is completely untouchable and unassailable.** "Your joy," said Jesus, "no man taketh from you." (Jn. 16:22 KJV) So quite possibly a better substitute for the word" *blessed*" would be the phrase *"permanently joyous."*

*3 *The Bethany Parallel Commentary on the Old Testament,* (Minneapolis, MN., Bethany House Publishers, 1985) p 1027, Adam Clarke.

*4 The next biblical mentioning of the blessing of God concerned the Sabbath. Genesis 2:3 states that "God *blessed* the seventh day and sanctified it, because in it He rested from all His work which God had created." This seventh day was *blessed* probably for several reasons: first, it is a day set apart for communion with God; second, it was a memorial of the fact that God rested the seventh day and we can enter into His rest; and third, it was a prophecy from the beginning of a divine day of rest, a thousand-year-long millennium that is yet to come. (See Heb. 3:18, 4:10, 2 Pt. 3:7–9, Rev. 20:1–10.) God later instituted, under the Mosaic Covenant, a sabbatical year in which the land was to lay rest. To calm the fears of those who may have felt they would not have enough food, God promised, "Then I will command My *blessing* upon you in the sixth year, and it [the land] shall bring forth fruit for three years" (Lev. 25:21).

*5 The "blessing of Abraham" is fully discussed in Volume One of **Our Glorious Inheritance** in the chapter entitled *The Children of Abraham.*

*6 Our calling to be *"The Head"* is unveiled in Volume Eight of **Our Glorious Inheritance.**

*7 Other versions of Isaiah 61:9 call God's offspring *"a people the LORD has blessed"* (NIV) *the seed the LORD hath blessed"* (KJV) and *"the posterity whom the LORD has blessed"* (NKJV).

*8 This subject is dealt with excellently in Volume Eight of **Our Glorious Inheritance**, in the chapter on *The Heavenly.*

*9 Of course, other books relevant to the history of the era were written, such as 1 & 2 Macabees.

*10 Probably one of the strongest statements in Scripture concerns this final "cutting off" of those who are cursed by God. In 1 Corinthians 16:22 (KJV) the apostle Paul gave the stern warning, "If any man love not the LORD Jesus Christ, let him be **Anathema Maranatha.**" This is a Greek phrase that, in essence, means *cursed at the coming of the LORD.*

*11 These are just three of seven "blessed" statements in the book of the Revelation. Seven is the number of perfection, fullness and wholeness—and these seven proclamations of blessedness will bring us to perfection, fullness and wholeness eternally. (See Rev. 1:3; 14:13; 16:15; 19:9; 20:6; 22:7; 22:14.)

CHILDREN OF THE KINGDOM

HEIRS OF THE KINGDOM

SONS OF THE KINGDOM

A KINGDOM

"The field is the world; the good seed are the **CHILDREN OF THE KINGDOM [SONS OF THE KINGDOM]."**
(Matthew 13:38 KJV, NKJV)

Listen, my beloved brethren: Has God not chosen the poor of this world to be rich in faith, and **HEIRS OF THE KINGDOM** *which He promised to those who love Him?*

(James 2:5)

To Him who loves us and has freed us from our sins by His blood, and has made us to be **A KINGDOM** *and priests to serve His God and Father—to Him be glory and power for ever and ever! Amen.*

(Revelation 1:6 NIV)

CHILDREN OF THE KINGDOM

"The field is the world; the good seed are the
CHILDREN OF THE KINGDOM."

(Matthew 13:38 KJV)

*I*n "**The Parable of the Wheat and the Tares**" the LORD Jesus compared the **CHILDREN OF THE KINGDOM** (our focus in this chapter) to **GOOD SEED** (yet to be explained in this book). (See Mt. 13:24-30.) Why the correlation? Because just as perpetual life and an inherited image are hidden within the heart of every seed, so everlasting life and a spiritual kingdom are hidden within the heart of every child of God. Making this an available experience for all men was the very purpose behind Jesus' incarnation.

The Jews of Jesus' day were, for the most part, expecting a Messiah who would restore a Davidic Kingdom—politically, militarily and spiritually. Their shining hope was that the Romans would finally be subjugated and supremacy would finally be restored to Israel. They must have assumed this all the more upon hearing the message of the Son of God. His main theme for three-and-a-half years was the establishment of the kingdom of God on this earth.

His message was called *"the gospel of the kingdom"* (Mt. 4:23).

His doctrine was called *"the Word of the kingdom"* (Mt. 13:19).

His parables unveiled the laws and the nature of this kingdom, often beginning with the statement, *"the kingdom of heaven is like…"*

After being endued with the power of the Holy Spirit, His first message was "Repent, for the *kingdom of heaven* is at hand" (Mt. 4:17). Not long after that His famed 'Sermon on the Mount' began with the statement, "Blessed are the poor in spirit, for theirs is the *kingdom of heaven*" (Mt. 5:3). He promised His chosen disciples, "It has been given unto you to know the mysteries of the *kingdom of heaven*." Then, finally, after rising from the grave, He spent His last forty days on earth instructing His followers of things "pertaining to *the kingdom of God*" (Mt. 13:11, Ac. 1:3).

So, from the beginning to the end, the establishment of this divine kingdom on earth was Jesus' passion and purpose. It logically follows that if we are His offspring, it will be our passion and purpose as well. To effectively participate in this heaven-on-earth kingdom, though, we must interpret it correctly.

How incredible it is that right before Jesus' ascension, even His closest disciples misinterpreted His purpose in promising to send the baptism of the Holy Spirit. They posed the question, "LORD, will you at this time restore *the kingdom* to Israel?" (Ac. 1:6)[*1]

How difficult it was for them to see that Jesus was not promoting, nor promising, the immediate overthrow of the oppressive Roman government! Rather, His purpose in sending the Holy Spirit was to equip His followers to overthrow the far more oppressive rule of the prince of darkness. The Messiah had already explained to Pilate:

> "My kingdom is not of this world. If My kingdom were
> of this world, My servants would fight, so that I should
> not be delivered to the Jews; but now My kingdom is not
> from here."

(John 18:36)

The last part of this statement implies that there is a time coming when God's kingdom WILL be fully manifested in and from the earth. Until then, God is following a strategy drastically different than what He used under the Old Will. Within the framework of the old order, the kingdom of Israel was established by the defeating of natural armies and the acquisition of a natural land mass. God still moves this way (and the miraculous preservation of the nation of Israel is sufficient proof of that). However, under the new order, God is more interested in advancing His kingdom by enthroning Himself in the hearts of those who believe. When certain Pharisees demanded that Jesus divulge the time of the coming of His kingdom, this great Rabbi of Israel replied:

> "...The kingdom of God does not come with
> observation;
>
> Nor will they say, 'See here!' or, 'See there!' For indeed,
> the kingdom of God is within you."

(Luke 17:20–21)

Such a startling statement was not an admission by the LORD Jesus that the kingdom of God was actually present in the hearts of His opponents. He was speaking hypothetically—in essence, implying "If you ever have an experience of the kingdom of God, it will be internal." Some students of the Word insist that these two verses indicate there will never be a literal, visible, bodily return of the Son of God to this earth. However, once again, this was not Jesus' intended meaning. He was simply revealing that the initial progress of this kingdom was not going to be geograghically trackable.

Notice the key word *observation*. This involves watching something over a protracted period of time. So Jesus was saying that His kingdom would not advance by the overthrowing of one city at a time through military conquest. On the contrary, this unique kingdom was ordained to first manifest in a physically unobservable way: the conquest of men's hearts by the Word and the Spirit. (See Jn. 3:3.)

Finally and climactically, it WILL manifest in a sudden burst of the supernatural at the coming of the LORD. But again, this is not something men will be able to *observe* by watching a progression of events. The suddenness, the intensity and the spectacular splendor of this final, grand event was confirmed by Jesus, three verses after His 'observation' statement:

> *For the Son of Man in His day will be like the lightning,*
> *which flashes and lights up the sky from one end to the*
> *other...*
>
> (Luke 17:24 NIV)

Until that grand day, the advance of the divine kingdom will be gradual and primarily spiritual in nature.

Had all men surrendered to Jesus' Lordship at the very start, theoretically, the rule of heaven could have begun on earth without delay.[*2] But their hearts were blinded to His glory. Multitudes saw Him, yet many of them could not behold the majesty of who He was. They could not comprehend the supreme beauty and depth of what He had to say, nor the profoundness of what He came to do. He did not look or even act like a king. How could they possibly submit to such a questionable kingdom? Little did they know, He was the King of all kings, spoken of as the One whose "kingdom rules over all" (Ps. 103:19).

FOUR IMPORTANT KINGDOM PRINCIPLES

🌸 God's kingdom, in this world, is primarily made up of His people ——

The Greek word for **kingdom** is *basileia* (pr. *bas-il-i'-ah*) meaning *a realm governed by a king—a king's domain*. Therefore, everything in creation submitted to the kingship of the Almighty God is recognizably a part of His kingdom. Because this world for the most part is in rebellion against God's authority, generally speaking, it is presently excluded from His kingdom.[*3] Those individuals in this world who acknowledge Jesus as LORD are included, as well as the parts of this material world that are consecrated to Him. Many versions of Revelation 1:5–6 indicate believers are not only a part of God's kingdom; they actually become a kingdom to Him—for instance:

> *To Him who loves us and has freed us from our sins by*
> *His blood, and has made us to be* **A KINGDOM** *and*
> *priests to serve His God and Father—to Him be glory*
> *and power for ever and ever! Amen.*
> (Revelation 1:5–6 NIV, See NAS, RSV, Amp)

So God's people actually make up His kingdom. We are "**His dominion**," His domain, those chosen ones over which He rules (Ps. 114:2). If this was true under the Old Will, how much more true it is under the New!

✸ The "kingdom of God" and the "kingdom of heaven" are the same ──

The phrase *kingdom of God* is found seventy times in Scripture (NKJV). The similar phrase *kingdom of heaven* is found thirty-two times, all in the Gospel of Matthew. Some Bible teachers assert that this latter phrase would be more correctly rendered *the kingdom of the heavens* or *the kingdom from the heavens* for the Greek word translated *heaven* is always found in the plural.[*4]

Much controversy and complicated arguments exist concerning the correct definition of these two expressions. Some Word-scholars feel that the *Kingdom of God* is a more comprehensive term than the *kingdom of heaven*, the former embracing the entire creation over which God rules, but the latter, just the heavenly portion of the *kingdom of God*.

I feel the following explanation is more logically sound. The term *kingdom of heaven* simply refers to the *place* from which the kingdom is ruled; the term *kingdom of God* instead refers to the *Head* of the same kingdom. This would be like referring to the United States two ways: by naming its capital city or by naming its president. So the two terms are most likely interchangeable and synonymous.

This view is especially supported by the fact that both phrases are used in parallel passages in different Gospels. For instance, in Matthew 13:11 Jesus states that it has been given to disciples to know *"the mysteries of the kingdom of heaven,"* while Luke 8:10 relates the same promise saying, *"the mysteries of the kingdom of God."* (See also Mt. 11:11, Lk. 7:28.) So in the minds of the close disciples of the LORD, there was apparently no mysterious and highly technical division between the two terms.

✸ The coming of the kingdom of God was foreshadowed in advance and prophesied by the prophets ──

The root beginning of the kingdom of God was the emerging of the nation of Israel out of Egypt's bondage, for "the shout of a King" was among them (Num. 23:21). Later, David became God's representative on earth and his kingdom was spoken of as *"the kingdom of the* LORD...*in the hands of the sons of David"* (2 Chr. 13:8). This was a foreshadowing of a more perfect manifestation of God's kingdom that would come under the Messiah.

Isaiah foretold "unto us a Child is born, unto us a Son is given: and the government shall be upon His shoulder: and His name shall be called Wonderful, Counselor, The mighty God, the everlasting Father, The Prince of Peace. Of the increase of His government and peace there shall be no end, upon the throne of David and upon his *kingdom*, to order it, and to establish it with judgment and with justice from henceforth, even for ever..." (Isaiah 9:6–7 KJV).

The angel Gabriel also prophesied of this Wonderful One that "He will reign over the house of Jacob for ever, and of His *kingdom* there will be no end" (Lk. 1:33). So the kingdom of God was foreshadowed by the kingdom of David. (See 2 Sam. 7:13, 16, 1 Chr. 29:1.) This kingdom emerged in fullness in the person of Jesus Christ, who was "the son of David"—rightful heir to his throne (Mt. 1:1; 9:27). Through Him, the kingdom will eventually encompass the globe and fully absorb all nations. (See Ps. 22:28.)[*5]

God's kingdom is expressed when He manifests His power ——————

Simply speaking, the kingdom of heaven is God, through the Messiah and in His people, governing the creation. Wherever and whenever you find God in control, showing His sovereignty and power, you find the kingdom of God manifesting. One Gospel story provides an excellent example of this definition. When exercising His divine authority by healing a blind and dumb man, Jesus said, "If I with the finger of God cast out devils, no doubt *the kingdom of God is come upon you."* (Lk. 11:20 KJV, See verses 14–23.) Matthew 12:22–30 tells the same story stating in verse 28 that Jesus cast out devils by "the Spirit of God." So "the finger of God" and "the Spirit of God" are one and the same. When God decides to reveal and manifest His Kingship, He sends forth His irresistable 'touch,' saturating circumstances with the release of His purpose and presence.

The kingdom of God gripped the scene that day and all of its characters. The King was there, demanding that demonic powers submit to His governing authority. There must have been a wonderful, other-worldly sensation that permeated the atmosphere as heaven came down to earth. And if the kingdom of God, merely *coming **upon** them*, caused a blind and dumb person to see and speak, what glorious overflow of divine power can we expect once the kingdom of God is actually ***within*** us!

The *'deep'* within every child of God should surge just imagining the possibilities.

TWO THINGS THE KINGDOM IS NOT

There are two passages of Scripture that reveal to us what the kingdom **IS,** by telling us what it **IS NOT:** Romans 14:17 and 1 Corinthians 4:20.

❋ Romans 14:17 ————————————————————————

> *The kingdom of God is NOT eating and drinking, but*
> *righteousness, peace and joy in the Holy Spirit.*

Paul was refuting the claims of certain Judaizers who claimed Gentile believers had to keep the dietary laws of the Mosaic order in order to truly be right with God. Though these laws were inspired of God (and they still have great value if good health is to be maintained) they no longer have any bearing on whether or not a person is in a right relationship with God. This is accomplished now through regeneration and the washing of Jesus' blood. Through these experiences God's people are delivered from the power of darkness and *"translated into the kingdom of His dear Son"* (Col. 1:13 KJV).

Experiencing this inner transformation is infinitely more important than an entire lifetime spent in devotion to religious rituals, ceremonies, observances and ordinances. A person can have the latter and not the former, and be without God and without hope in this world. How dreadful!

Jesus certainly shocked the religious leaders of His day when He touched on this issue:

> *...Woe to you, scribes and Pharisees, hypocrites! For*
> *you shut up **the kingdom of heaven** against men; for*
> *you neither go in yourselves, nor do you allow those who*
> *are entering to go in.*
>
> (Matthew 23:13)

Unquestioning allegiance to ceremonialism was more important to them than access into the very presence of God. How tragic! Yet the tragedy is still going on in Christendom. How often leaders, in both the professing and the possessing church, prevent sincere seekers from flowing in God by emphasizing denominational membership, compulsory adherence to questionable ordinances and mandatory participation in non-essential rituals. Usually the cause is spiritual ignorance. Sometimes it is rebellion against the truth. But it always results in 'shutting up' the kingdom of heaven against men.

The passage that we are studying identifies the kingdom of God as "righteousness, and peace, and joy in the Holy Spirit."

Kingdom-righteousness, remarkably, is something we are filled with, not something we earn. It comes first as a gift from God, not an accomplishment on our part. (See Mt. 5:6, Ro. 5:17.) It is far more important to have this kind of imparted righteousness when we stand before God's throne, than to have works of righteousness mounting up to heaven itself. (See Mt. 5:20.) Of course, the automatic result of this inborn righteousness should be righteous thoughts, words and deeds—that we might be a praise to God in the earth.

Kingdom-peace is far more than mere human emotion. It is more than just calmness or tranquility of mind. It is supernatural: not just peace from God, but the "peace OF God which surpasses all understanding" (Ph. 4:7). It is that absolute divine rest that permeates the very heart of God.

Kingdom-joy is also far more than human happiness (which is usually dependent on circumstances). Jesus called it "My joy" (Jn. 15:11)—the same constant, unchanging joyfulness that has always resided in the heart of God. Mere ritualistic observances can never effect this experience within anyone. It can only be discovered "in the Holy Spirit" (Ro. 14:17).

❈ 1 Corinthians 4:20 ────────────────────────

For the kingdom of God is NOT in word but in power.

This passage does not deny the importance of Christian doctrine; it simply reveals that "living, moving and having our being" in God's kingdom exceeds mere doctrine in importance. The kingdom of God is not just words (theology, philosophy, etc.) like so much of what is called religion today. The kingdom of God is most importantly the demonstration of God's power.

The Greek word for *power* in this passage is *dunamis*, which can mean *ability*. So inheriting the kingdom of God automatically involves inheriting God-given *abilities*. This is not a natural, but a supernatural impartation. *Dunamis* is also translated *abundance, might, mighty, miracles, strength* and *violence*—and all of these have relevance. (Notice the following italicized words.) Heirs of the kingdom inherit what Jesus described as *"power...over all the power of the enemy"* (Lk. 10:19 KJV). Through the *abundance* of grace, and the *might* of our God, *miracles* (some subtle, some glorious) are often evidenced in our lives. The *strength* of God is ours—*strength* to rise above adversity and fulfill our God-given destiny. Through us, with a spiritual kind of *violence*, God is in the process of tearing down satanic strongholds in this world.

The original disciples were commanded to go forth and "preach saying, *The kingdom of heaven is at hand*" (Mt. 10:7). What they promoted was so much more than some theoretical, theological concept or some new, intriguing, religious idea. It was divine unction and action: a heavenly kingdom invading the earthly realm to bring persons and events into divine order. (See Is. 9:6–7.)

After commanding His followers to go forth preaching the nearness of the kingdom, in the very next sentence Jesus said, "Heal the sick, cleanse the lepers, raise the dead, cast out demons. Freely you have received, freely give" (Mt. 10:8). In other words, the King was encouraging His kingdom ambassadors, not only to tell men God can victoriously reign in their lives, but to demonstrate it by manifesting His miraculous power.

Paul understood the importance of this. He asserted that his priority was not to preach the Gospel with "persuasive words of human wisdom," but rather in the "demonstration of the Spirit and of *power (dunamis)*" ...that our faith might not rest "in the wisdom of men but in the *power (dunamis) of God*" (1 Cor. 2:4–5).

Let us remember that the kingdom of God is no longer "at hand"; the kingdom has arrived. If Satan fell like lightning from heaven when they announced its soon coming, how much more is he stripped of His power now that the kingdom of heaven has taken up permanent residence in this world— in the hearts of those who believe!

TWELVE ENTRANCE REQUIREMENTS

There are at least twelve biblical requirements placed upon any person desiring entrance into the kingdom of God. The reader should study them all closely, for the things that grant access into God's kingdom also keep us fruitfully functioning in the kingdom with every passing day.

(1) Repentance —————————————————————————

John, the forerunner of the Christ, announced the entrance of the Messiah's reign with the statement, *"Repent: for the kingdom of heaven is at hand."* This same message was echoed by Jesus and then, His original seventy disciples (Mt. 3:2; 4:17; 10:7).

This simply reveals that no one will enter the kingdom, or continue in kingdom-living, without exercising and maintaining repentance: that genuine sorrow, regret and contrition over sin that necessarily precedes salvation. A number of scriptures reveal that repentance is a gift from God (the Puritans called it 'the gift of tears')—so the credit for such an attitude of heart belongs to Him. (See Ac. 5:31, Ro. 2:4, 2 Tim. 2:25.)

(2) A Seeking Heart —————————————————————

In His heart-moving 'Sermon on the Mount,' Jesus urged His followers, "Seek first *the kingdom of God* and His righteousness, and all these things shall be added to you" (Mt. 6:33). The phrase "all these things" certainly included natural provisions as well as spiritual. We need to realize that "seeking the kingdom" means seeking the King and submitting to His regal authority. When fellowship with the King is our priority, the "things" He blesses us with don't get in the way. Therefore, longing for and searching for God's will must be our first priority in life. Only those who seek the kingdom (the King's dominion) find it. So let us cultivate the heart to ask, seek and knock. (See Mt. 7:7–8.)

(3) Poverty of Spirit

Jesus' first beatitude claims, "Blessed are the poor in spirit, for theirs is *the kingdom of heaven*" (Mt. 5:3). 'Poverty of spirit' is the honest acknowledgment that we, as offspring of Adam, are spiritually bankrupt and helpless without Christ. Only those who admit, "Without Him, we can do nothing," can go on to say, "We can do all things through Christ who strengthens us." (See Jn. 15:5, Ph. 4:13.) Only those who admit utter poverty in Adam can enjoy and experience "the unsearchable riches of Christ" (Eph. 3:8). Sometimes those who are literally poverty-stricken tend to manifest 'poverty of spirit' more easily. Possibly for this reason James 2:5 explains that God often chooses "the poor of this world to be rich in faith, and **HEIRS OF THE KINGDOM** which He promised to those who love Him."*6

(4) The Two Births

In John 3:3 KJV, Jesus said to Nicodemus, "Except a man be born again, he cannot see *the kingdom of God*." In other words, the Master was teaching that it is impossible to comprehend the nature of God's kingdom without a spiritual rebirth. Titus 3:5 describes this experience as "the washing of regeneration and the renewing of the Holy Spirit." Jesus then expanded this truth, saying:

> "...*Most assuredly I say to you, unless one is* **born of water and the Spirit**, *he cannot enter the* **kingdom of God**.
>
> *That which is born of flesh is flesh, and that which is born of the Spirit is spirit.*
>
> *Do not marvel that I said to you, 'You must be born again.'*"
>
> (John 3:5–7)

Though water baptism is very important, Jesus' statement concerning being "born of water" is probably not a reference to this ritual of the church. Most likely He was referring to the 'breaking of the water' which signals the birth of a child. This takes place when the amniotic sack breaks and the amniotic fluid pours out. Such an interpretation is likely because in verse six Jesus qualifies what He said in verse five by referring to two births: one of the flesh and the other of the Spirit.

Why is it necessary to be 'born of the flesh' in order to enter the kingdom of God? Because there are certain preparatory lessons we are learning here that will be a seal to our souls for all eternity. First, we are learning the horror of what sin brings and the great value of obedience. Second, we are learning the full glory of the character of God, including His compassion, forgiveness, mercy and grace. Third, that same divine character is being formed in us as we are "changed into the same image from glory to glory" (2 Cor. 3:18 KJV). These are three valuable things that never could have happened to us in a perfected, heavenly state.

(5) Conversion

In Matthew 18:3 Jesus explained, "Unless you are converted... you will by no means enter the *kingdom of heaven*." Conversion is a word with a triune meaning: *to turn from, to turn toward and to return*. Those who are converted *turn away from* this world and its carnality, *turn toward* God and *return* to that place of submission and of intimacy with Him that Adam had in the beginning. A true conversion is not just an initial experience. It is an ongoing process that should be constantly evidenced by an increase of Christlikeness. This should always result in an increase of kingdom-living as well. (See Ps. 51:13; Lk. 22:32 KJV; Ac. 3:19; Ja. 5:19–20 KJV.)*[7]

(6) Childlikeness

In Luke 18:17 Jesus warned "whoever does not receive *the kingdom of God* as a little child will by no means enter it." Developing childlike qualities like simplicity, honesty, humility, unreasoning trust and unquestioning faith is certainly the challenge of this passage. In a childlike way, we must also be submitted to God's authority, confident that He, like a loving Father, will care for us.

Another aspect—children can be caught up in near ecstasy for hours over the simplest things—like chasing a butterfly across a field from one flower blossom to another. So those who are childlike in their approach to God become quite ecstatic over the simplest blessings and revelations that He grants. Those who lose this excitement can become very bored, skeptical or analytical in their approach to the Bible. They may intellectually dissect the Word of God without having a true passion for, and relationship with, the God of the Word. Those who fit this non-childlike description, in the name of theology, often block their own entrance into the kingdom of God.

(7) Righteousness of God

In introducing the New Covenant, Jesus declared, "...unless your righteousness exceeds the righteousness of the scribes and Pharisees, you will by no means enter *the kingdom of heaven*" (Mt. 5:20). Theirs was a righteousness attained by religious works. Yet no one can enter God's kingdom, now or eternally, through the merits of self-achieved righteousness alone. Paul talked about being found in the LORD, "not having my own righteousness, which is from the law, but that which is through faith in Christ, *the righteousness which is from God by faith*" (Ph. 3:9).

Though such imparted righteousness can often be discovered in the Old Testament (for instance, Noah was described as "an heir of the righteousness which is by faith"—Heb. 11:7 KJV, See also Gen. 15:1–6), still, it is much more prevalent and easily acquired through the New Testament (through faith in the death, burial and resurrection of Jesus). In this wonderful era especially, righteousness is a gift. (See Ro. 5:17; 10:9–10.) It is an infilling from God. (See Mt. 5:6.) It is "righteousness... in the Holy Spirit" (Ro. 14:17). It makes us just as righteous in the sight of God as God is Himself. (See 2 Cor. 5:21.) It results in outward expressions of righteous living, because of God's inward influence.

(8) Tribulation

Acts 14:22 cautions that "we must through many tribulations enter *the kingdom of God.*" In Matthew 5:10, the eighth beatitude, Jesus confirmed, "Blessed are those who are persecuted for righteousness' sake: for theirs is *the kingdom of heaven.*" These two scriptures reveal a valuable truth: that part of passing through this world is facing the various tribulations, persecutions, trials and temptations that abound here. However, if we react to these correctly, they work a positive work, not a negative one. They compel us to move into our sonship inheritance by laying hold to all that is rightfully ours as children of the kingdom. Facing tribulations and persecutions in this world also teaches us the faithfulness and unconditional love of our heavenly Father. Such trials are often a preparation for eternity itself and the fullness of the kingdom which is yet to come.

(9) The Conquering of Fear

In Luke 12:32 Jesus assured His disciples with the words, "Do not fear, little flock; for it is your Father's good pleasure to give you *the kingdom.*" The implication is this: that in order to receive of the benefits of the kingdom, we must walk in faith and conquer its opposite: fear. It would do every child of God well to go through the whole Bible and find every instance where God, either directly or indirectly, commands His people "Fear not!" or "Do not fear!" (e.g, Is. 35:4; 41:10,13,14; 44:2, 8; Jer. 46:27–28; Lk. 12:7). Knowing

God's love toward us should give us boldness to walk in courage—because "perfect love casts out fear" (1 Jn. 4:18).

(10) Trusting God Alone

In Mark 10:24 Jesus cautioned "How hard is it for those who *trust* in riches to enter *the kingdom of God.*" This does not mean it is wrong to have wealth; it simply means it is wrong to *trust* in that wealth to supply happiness, fulfillment and purpose in life. Other things could easily be inserted in place of the word *riches* that become the hub of people's lives, like educational pursuits, career choices, sports, hobbies or human relationships. None of these things is bad unless it usurps God's position as being our only source and our highest goal. We can only enter into God's kingdom and function in it daily if the King of the kingdom is exalted on the very throne of our hearts.

(11) Pressing Perseverance and Fighting Faith

Two of the most powerful kingdom scriptures are Luke 16:16 and Matthew 11:12. In Luke 16:16 Jesus explained, "the law and the prophets were until John. Since that time *the kingdom of God* has been preached, and everyone is pressing [forcing his way] into it" (NKJV, NIV). Closely related is Matthew 11:12, "And from the days of John the Baptist until now *the kingdom of heaven* suffers violence, and the violent take it by force."

These scriptures reveal that a drastic and awesome change in the spiritual atmosphere of this earth took place nearly two millennia ago. Until the incarnation, the prince of darkness was in a position of much greater supremacy here. Then the King of heaven arrived, purposing to "overthrow the throne of kingdoms and...destroy the strength of the kingdoms of the heathen" (Hag. 2:22 KJV). He did this effectively through His death, burial and resurrection. Now the dark powers who once dominated the world system are defeated and spoiled: stripped of their authority. (See Col. 2:14–15.) The strength of their control over the human race was the power of sin. Because sin has been conquered, men and women can be "delivered from the power of darkness and... translated into *the kingdom* of [God's] dear Son" (Col. 1:13 KJV). This places God's redeemed in a position of spiritual superiority. (See Col. 2:10.)

The NIV of Matthew 11:12 excellently explains that during this New Covenant era, *"The kingdom of heaven* has been forcefully advancing and forceful men lay hold to it." The establishment of God's kingdom involved a violent overthrow of the satanic government that was formerly in control. So to enter God's kingdom and maintain our position in it, we cannot be passive, tepid individuals. We, too, must be violent, forcefully opposing satanic powers, conquering the power of sin, and subduing the carnality of our own flesh. We must be hard-headed, stubborn-willed faith-fighters: daily fighting the good fight of faith and daily 'pressing' into our inheritance, refusing to live beneath our privileges. Possessing an attitude like this is extremely important to the advance of God's purposes in these last days. For as it was said to Esther, so it could be said to each of us; "Who knows whether you have come to the *kingdom* for such a time as this?" (Es. 4:14).

(12) The Will of God

In Matthew 7:21 Jesus warned, "Not everyone who says to Me, 'LORD, LORD, shall enter *the kingdom of heaven*, but he who does the will of My Father in heaven." This is true on two main levels, because the will of God is revealed by both the written Word and the living Word.

The written Word contains both commandments and promises—revealing the will of God in a dual way: first, His expectations OF His people, and second, His provisions FOR His people. In Matthew 7:21, Jesus' primary emphasis was most likely **the written Word.** For no one can enter God's kingdom, returning to a right relationship with Him, without following the detailed instructions already given in His Word. These commandments and promises explain the correct way to obtain a valid salvation experience. Many supposedly acknowledge Jesus as 'LORD' with only a historical knowledge of Him. This is insufficient. Everything already discussed in this list—repentance, poverty of spirit, the two births, and so forth—comprise "the will of the Father" for those aspiring to kingdom citizenship. So the first eleven requirements are all embraced by this twelfth one in the list.

The second level of discerning the will of God involves **the living Word:** divinely communicated instructions that God, from time-to-time, sends to those sheep who are under His care. The Shepherd of our souls promised, "My sheep hear My voice" (Jn. 10:27). To function effectively in God's kingdom, this is a necessity. Maturity and fruitfulness in God are often directly proportionate to how much believers are truly following God's will—especially His living Word direction for their lives.

FIVE CHARACTER TRAITS OF GOD'S KINGDOM

To successfully live in the kingdom we must adopt the personality of the kingdom as our own. Of course, the character of God's kingdom is the character of God—for the kingdom is permeated by the nature of the royal One who created it. So the more we take on the multi-faceted nature of our God, the more His kingdom manifests in our lives, as simple as that. **Five specific character traits are especially associated in Scripture with God's kingdom: love, forgiveness, humility, authority and stability.**

(1) Love

Mark 12:28–34 records the story of a scribe who asked Jesus to identify the greatest commandment of the law. Sifting through the 613 commandments traditionally associated with the law (the Torah), Jesus quoted Deuteronomy 6:5 saying, "You shall love the LORD your God with all your heart, with all your soul, with all your mind, and with all your strength." Then He added the second, "You shall love your neighbor as yourself." The scribe agreed, stating that fulfilling these two commandments was far more important than all burnt offerings and sacrifices. Commending him for his wisdom, Jesus responded, *"You are not far from the kingdom of God."*

Apparently, Jesus was implying that even though this man had not yet been born into the kingdom of God, he was already embracing its principles. True kingdom citizens are more interested in realism and relationships than rules and regulations. Love is the motivating factor and "the fulfillment of the law" (Ro. 13:10). When love for God and others rules our relationships, laws are no longer needed. When the God-kind of love does not rule our actions and attitudes (when selfishness, pride, anger or lust motivate us), we cease functioning in the kingdom of God and begin functioning under the evil attitudes that rule Satan's dark kingdom.

(2) Forgiveness

In Matthew 18:23 Jesus began by saying *"the kingdom of heaven* is like,*"* then He proceeded to share a parable about forgiveness. One servant who owed the king ten thousand talents (about three hundred million dollars worth of gold, or twenty million of silver) was forgiven of his debt. Unfortunately, he refused to forgive a fellow servant a debt of a "hundred denarii" (about seventeen dollars). Jesus called the unforgiving man a "wicked servant," announcing that he would be "delivered to the tormentors." Then Jesus warned, "So My heavenly Father also will do to you if each of you, *from his heart,* does not *forgive* his brother his trespasses" (Mt. 18:35).

Bitter, unforgiving people are usually very tormented persons; on the contrary, forgiving persons tend to be peaceful and better able to cope with the pressures of life. As Jesus told Peter, those participating in His kingdom must be willing to forgive others seventy times seven times (four hundred ninety times a day, about one time every three minutes—in other words, an unlimited amount). Our Father grants us this abundant pardon; so we must be willing to give it away to others. (See Mt. 6:12–15, Mk. 11:25–26, Lk. 23:34, Col. 1:14, 1 Jn. 1:9.)

(3) Humility

In Matthew 18:1, apparently motivated by prideful ambition, some of Jesus' disciples asked, "Who is the greatest in *the kingdom of heaven?"* Jesus responded by setting a child in their midst saying, "Whoever humbles himself as this little child is the greatest in *the kingdom of heaven*." (See Mt. 18:4, Mk. 9:33–37.) Competitive attitudes, pride of accomplishment, manipulation, domination and selfishness are all opposites of humility and are foreign to the character of God's kingdom.

Only those believers who humble themselves in a Christlike way and take upon themselves the form of a servant can reign as kingdom-kings. (See Ph. 2:5–8.) God's authority manifesting in us is directly proportionate to two things: the level of our submission to Him and our attitude of service toward others. Therefore, the more we humble ourselves before God and man, the more we are exalted in kingdom matters.

(4) Authority

When Peter acknowledged that Jesus was the Son of the living God, the Messiah responded, "I will give you *the keys of the kingdom of heaven*, and whatever you bind on earth will be bound in heaven and whatever you loose on earth will be loosed in heaven" (Mt. 16:19). The idea of 'binding' and 'loosing' was a Hebrew idiom that related primarily to setting religious standards among men.

Traditionally, 'to bind' meant to declare unlawful; 'to loose' meant to declare lawful. Therefore, God's true representatives have the God-given privilege of revealing, in this world, heaven's standard for access into the kingdom of God. Those who bear *"the keys of the kingdom of heaven"* open the door of eternal life to some and close it to others, according to the doctrinal stance they take. (See Ac. 14:27.) The Word they declare is not to be looked upon as the word of men, but the Word of God. (See 1 Th. 2:13.) Such an awesome responsibility rests primarily on the leadership in the body of Christ, yet this impartation is also given to the entire church in Matthew 18:18.

This authority is not to be taken lightly. It can also be abused. Jesus rebuked the lawyers of His day with the words, "Woe to you!...For you have taken away *the key of knowledge*. You did not enter in yourselves, and those who were entering in you hindered" (Lk. 11:52). Of course, *knowledge* is not the only *key to the kingdom*. Prayer, fasting, and all the gifts of the Spirit are keys—for through these things we open the door to the supernatural realm that men might be blessed. Even the fruit of the Spirit and all godly character traits could be labeled *keys*. For every time we return love for hate, manifest hope in the midst of despair, emanate faith in the presence of unbelief or manifest the authority of God in opposition to the authority of Satan, we open a door to the heavenly realm. By manifesting kingdom-life this way, in effect, we *bind* that which is negative, hellish and destructive—and we *loose* that which is positive, heavenly and edifying—into the lives of those we effect.

(5) Stability

The only thing truly stable in this world is the kingdom of God. Everything else is unstable, destined to dissolve into nothingness. Hebrews 12:28 (KJV) says we have received a kingdom which "cannot be moved." Other versions say, "cannot be shaken" (NAS, NIV, NKJV). We are told prophetically that in these last days God will "shake heaven and earth" and "shake all nations" that "the things which CANNOT BE SHAKEN may remain" (Hag. 2:6–7, Heb. 12:26–28). If God's kingdom is described as being unshakable, certainly the people of that kingdom should be unshakable as well. This kind of stability should evidence itself in our day-to-day walk with God, regardless of the pressure we are facing. The Scripture says, "Be stedfast, unmoveable..." (1 Cor. 15:58).

THE GROWTH OF THE KINGDOM

Jesus described the growth of the kingdom of God, in believers and in the world as a whole, by comparing it to the threefold progression of growth in a stalk of wheat:

> And He said, **The kingdom of God** is as if a man should scatter seed on the ground,
>
> And should sleep by night and rise by day, and the seed should sprout and grow, he himself does not know how.
>
> For the earth yields crops by itself: first the blade, then the head, after that the full grain in the head.
>
> But when the grain ripens, immediately he puts in the sickle, because the harvest has come.
>
> (Mark 4:26–29)

❂ The Individual Application of the Parable

With respect to the individual, there are three stages of kingdom growth.

- **The Blade**—First, we are regenerated in the inner man, the hidden man of the heart. Like the life hidden in the blade, so the life of God is mysteriously hidden within us. *This is the stage of new birth potential.*

- **The Head**—Second, the life and character of the kingdom of God begin to take over more territory in our souls (the seat of the mind, will and emotions). As a stalk of wheat begins to develop, putting forth leaves, taking shape and bringing forth the ear or the head, so also children of God should grow in Christlikeness. They should progressively manifest the personality of the kingdom in all their relationships and endeavors. *This is the stage of maturing and growing in God.*

⌣· **The Full Grain**—The third stage can be interpreted two ways. First, it can represent believers who have so ripened spiritually that they are no longer just taking, they are giving. They are ready to become seed sown in the earth, or grain crushed and made into bread, sacrificing themselves for others and for the advance of the kingdom. Second, it can represent the nature of the kingdom coming forth in us in absolute perfection. This will transpire at the resurrection when we will be changed in a moment. Just as the original grain sown in good ground reproduces itself in the full grain of wheat in the head, so Jesus, the original Word, will reproduce Himself in all His many offspring. *This is the ultimate stage of fullness and fruitfulness eternally.*

✹ The Worldwide Application of the Parable ————————

With respect to the world, there are also three stages of kingdom growth.[*8]

⌣· **The Blade**—This first stage represents the entire New Covenant Age when the life of the kingdom is mysteriously hidden in the hearts of men, springing forth all over the world.

⌣· **The Head**—This second stage represents the glory of kingdom-life manifesting visibly in all the earth during the Millennial Reign when both the human race and nature itself will be fully reconciled to each other and to God. This will fall short of absolute perfection, however, for Satan will stir a rebellion at the end of this thousand-year-long era of paradise peace.

⌣· **The Full Grain**—This third and final stage represents the flawless New Creation, the New Heaven and the New Earth—"the dispensation of the fullness of times." If interpreted this way, the "harvest" relates to the full maturing of the plan of God: the renovation and reconciliation of all things when God will finally *reap* a total victory in this realm and once again "fill all things" (Rev. 21:1, Eph. 1:10; 4:10).

With respect to the worldwide application of the parable, it can also be interpreted this way: (1) **The blade**—the Old Testament era of the law; (2) **The head**—the New Testament era of grace; (3) **The full grain**—the Kingdom Age and New Creation beyond.

Though the kingdom of God began in mustard seed smallness—in an obscure manger, in a little town called Bethlehem—it will end up "the largest of all garden plants"—the greatest kingdom ever to rise in the realm of time (Mk. 4:30–32 NIV). Though other kingdoms have arisen with great demonstrations of military might, this kingdom began with a small band of believers whose hearts were full of meekness and hope. Really, it began with what seemed hopeless—a 'grain of wheat' falling to the ground and dying on Calvary.

It was not some huge battlefield soaked with the blood of multiplied thousands, but a lonely hill and one man's blood trickling down from criss-crossed, wooden beams. But because of such a mysterious and wondrous event, the seventh angel will one day sound his trumpet and loud voices in heaven will rejoice to announce:

> *The kingdoms of this world have become the kingdoms of our LORD and of His Christ; and He shall reign forever and ever.*

(Revelation 11:15)

The 'deep' in every true child of God should cry out to the 'deep' in God at the thought of this, praying—

> *"Let it be so, LORD, Your kingdom come, Your will be done, in earth as it is in heaven!"*

Multiplied millions have echoed this prayer. Multiplied millions will be gathered from the four winds of heaven on the day it comes to pass!

Deep calls unto deep,
*For your **Kingdom** we pray.*
Rule over our lives
And use us each day—

To extend your dominion,
Your purpose fulfill,
In a world set against You,
Rejecting Your will—

But we are those seekers
*Who put the **KING** first,*
Enthroned in our hearts,
And continually thirst—

For the Kingdom to manifest,
Not in word, but in power;
For this is 'true Gospel',
What, we need in this hour!

Endnotes

*1 When the disciples asked this question, *"Will you at this time restore the kingdom to Israel?"* Jesus' response was not negative. It was qualified. He said, *"It is not for you to know times or seasons, which the Father has put in His own authority"* (Ac. 1:6–7). In other words, Jesus was implying that the kingdom will eventually be restored to Israel, but only in God's timing. Until that purpose comes into focus, Jesus explained, *"But you shall receive power, when the Holy Spirit has come upon you: and you shall be witnesses to Me...to the end of the earth"* (Ac. 1:8). Since that time the kingdom of heaven has advanced around the globe, and will continue to do so, until the fullness of the Gentiles comes in. Then there will come a time when God will profoundly deal with Israel in the last days. Many Israelites will, at that time, receive the revelation of Jesus being their Messiah (this is already taking place). At His second coming we will then pass into the Kingdom Age when the King of kings will reign from Jerusalem and the Israel of God (which will include the redeemed of both covenants) will be chief of the nations. (See Dt. 28:13, Am. 6:1, Zec. 12:10, Ro. 11:12-25.)

*2 Looking at things idealistically, a statement like this can be made. Practically speaking, though, the full and manifest rule of heaven on earth at that point was not only improbable—it was impossible. Men and women had to have a regenerative experience in order to enter into the kingdom of heaven. So Jesus had to die. He had to shed His blood in order to wash away our sins. This was part of the plan from the start, for Jesus was the "Lamb slain from the foundation" (Rev. 13:8).

*3 Even though this world is in a state of separation from God and the full expression of His kingdom, it must be added that still "the Most High rules in the kingdom of men" (Dan. 4:25, 32).

*4 Unger, Merrill, *Unger's Bible Dictionary*, (Chicago, Illinois, Moody Press) p 632, under *Kingdom of God; Kingdom of Heaven*. Dake, Finis Jennings, *God's Plan for Man*, (Dake Bible Sales, Inc., Lawrenceville, Georgia 1981) p 558.

*5 Though the kingdom of Israel and the kingdom of David were the root beginnings of *the kingdom of God* coming to earth, Jesus said the kingdom Israel should have inherited was instead taken from them and given to a nation (the church) that would bring forth the fruits thereof. (See Is. 9:6–7, Mt. 21:41–46.) Of course, the church is comprised of both Jews and Gentiles who are born again and who accept the Messiah. This truth, however, does not strip natural Israel of its distinct value, purpose and destiny. God has a plan for this elect nation that will surface in these latter days.

*6 See the chapter on *The Poor in Spirit* in this volume of **Our Glorious Inheritance**.

*7 See the chapter on *Converts* in Volume Four of **Our Glorious Inheritance**.

*8 The following is based on the idea that there will be a literal thousand-year reign of Christ on earth before the New Creation comes into being, which the author tends to believe. If this is not the case, the three stages of growth could represent: (1) The Old Covenant Era of the Law; (2) The New Covenant Era of grace, and; (3) The New Creation yet to come.

GOD'S GARDEN

---

*We are only God's co-workers. You are **GOD'S GARDEN**, not ours; you are God's building, not ours.*

(1 Corinthians 3:9 LB)

*...Let my beloved come into **HIS GARDEN**, and eat His pleasant fruits.*

(Song of Solomon 4:16 KJV)

***A GARDEN ENCLOSED** is My sister, My spouse, **A SPRING SHUT UP, A FOUNTAIN SEALED**.*

Your plants are an orchard of pomegranates, with pleasant fruits; fragrant henna with spikenard,

Spikenard and saffron; calamus and cinnamon, with all trees of frankincense, myrrh and aloes, with all the chief spices—

***A FOUNTAIN OF GARDENS, A WELL OF LIVING WATERS, AND STREAMS FROM LEBANON**.*

(Song of Solomon 4:12–15)

*The LORD will guide you continually, and satisfy your soul in drought, and strengthen your bones; you shall be like **A WATERED GARDEN**, and like **A SPRING OF WATER**, whose waters do not fail.*

(Isaiah 58:11)

*My beloved has gone to **HIS GARDEN**, to the beds of spices, to feed His flock in the **GARDENS**, and to gather **LILIES**.*

(Song of Solomon 6:2)

His Garden

A Garden Enclosed

A Spring Shut Up

A Fountain Sealed

A Fountain of Gardens

A Well of Living Waters

Streams From Lebanon

A Watered Garden

A Spring of Water

Gardens

Other related titles contained in this chapter are: **A Garden Fountain** - Song 4:15 NAB, **A Garden Spring** - Song 4:15 NAS, **A Garden Locked Up** - Song 4:12 NIV, **My Beloved's Garden** - Song 6:3 Amp, **A Well-watered Garden** - Jer. 31:12. **The Rose of Sharon** - Song 2:1, **The Lily of the Valleys** - Song 2:1, **Lilies** - Song 6:2, **A Little Rose** - Song 2:1 Amp, **An Autumn Crocus** - Song 2:1 Amp, **A Paradise with Precious Fruits** - Song 4:13 Amp, **Gardens by the Riverside** - Num. 24:6.

Deep calls unto deep
From below to above,
For light and for water—
And the Gardener's sweet love.

He sees our potential
So He 'weeds' us each day,
That His Garden might blossom
In its special way.

Fruit for the Gardener,
So sweet to His taste,
Is praise, then deep worship—
(No, not done in haste).

For we hallow His presence
Which settles like dew,
And like flowers unfolded—
Our hearts are renewed.

GOD'S GARDEN

We are only God's coworkers. You are **GOD'S**
GARDEN, *not ours; you are God's building, not ours.*

(1 Corinthians 3:9 LB)

A garden is usually a rich, well-cultivated area—a plot of ground where herbs, fruits, flowers, or vegetables are carefully nurtured. In certain highly poetical and metaphorical passages of Scripture, the concept of a garden is used to represent the bride of Christ, as well as each individual in that bride.

Much more than a cultivated field, or even a sweet-smelling orchard, the idea of a garden carries with it the strong sense of extreme, personal care and artistic attention to detail. An expertly planted garden always whispers of the simplicity and elegance of perfection—for subtle symmetry and breathtaking balance are always a major emphasis and concern.

A garden is always a place noted for its peaceful atmosphere and its tranquil beauty. A garden well-planned must capture the attention of all passersby and woo them gently into its soothing embrace. What becalming influence is felt there! What a haven from the senseless pursuits that abound in this world! What messages of hope abound there for weary hearts, where newborn butterflies speak of new beginnings, and the small-winged, yet bloated bumblebees testify always that truly *the impossible can be done!*

In the early morning hours, when nature is sighing with relief, and the gleaming dew lies heavy, colored with warm, refracted, rainbow rays of promised light—a garden prophetically speaks of the quiet stability that comes through communion with God and stedfast trust in His timeless Word.

Most of all and above all—whether draped in starlit darkness, or engulfed in penetrating sunshine, *a garden speaks of love.*

—the *love* of the gardener for His work of art, who caresses the ground with each seed implanted.

—the *love* of the earth, drinking in water and soaking in light—then unselfishly giving birth to life and beauty.

—and the *love* that flows from heart to heart of those who often visit this near-heavenly refuge from the ravages of time.

And for those who have ears to hear—a comely, well-watered garden, alive and swelling with nature's activity, is truly an ecstatic and inspiring song of praise to the Creator and a heartwarming, spirit-lifting song of faith to every heaven-bound child of God.

How the entire garden pulsates, as if with one heart, in sublime, harmonious worship of the very One who alone begets all that is harmonious and sublime! What sweet music ascends to heaven as creation celebrates its own existence! What intricate patterns of intertwining melodies!

What grand orchestration and what phenomenal choir accompaniment of thousands of voices combine joyously together to proclaim the goodness and the glory of the Everlasting One! Especially when the sun, like a masterful maestro, arises and sets, announcing the beginning and the ending of a segment of time, the musical menagerie gathers, the air just brimming with excitement.

Feathered flutists, hummingbird harpists, shrill soprano-like sparrows, bass tuba bullfrogs, raspy cricket percussionists, cooing oboe-like doves, and even the droningly monotonous, cello-like locusts—all lift their voices in unison, confidently fulfilling their ordination, more than pleased to play their predestined parts. The hedged-in audience always beams with appreciation—leaves dancing in the wind and flowers gently swaying with every subtle change of rhythm.

Yes, for those who have ears to hear and those who have eyes to see, a pleasant garden is a living and vibrant message of the miracle of life itself—especially when the music pauses, as it often does, and the garden is swallowed up in sudden, holy stillness. For time stands still with reverential hush, and the truth of perpetual life is sermonized over and over again—*every time a seed falls to the ground.*

THE GARDEN-BRIDE

Our title-verse in this particular study is taken from the Song of Solomon. This unique book is undoubtedly the most sublime and poetically inspiring book in the Bible. All eight chapters of this inspired love-song consist mainly of a series of complimentary exchanges shared between a Shepherd/King and his deeply-longed-for bride-to-be. In winged, metaphorical language, this segment of Scripture explores and happily celebrates the soaring, rapturous love-relationship existing forevermore between Jesus, the Shepherd/King/Bridegroom and His beloved, the eternal bride of Christ.

When the Bridegroom speaks of the newly-discovered treasury of emotion abiding in the heart of His espoused bride, He affectionately pours out His praise:

*You are all fair, **MY LOVE**, and there is no spot in
you...How fair is your love, **MY SISTER, MY SPOUSE!**
How much better than wine is your love, and the scent of
your perfumes than all spices.*

*Your lips, O **MY SPOUSE**, drip as the honeycomb;
honey and milk are under your tongue; and the fragrance
of your garments is like the fragrance of Lebanon.*

***A GARDEN ENCLOSED IS MY SISTER, MY
SPOUSE; A SPRING SHUT UP; A FOUNTAIN
SEALED.***

(Song of Solomon 4:7, 10–12)

These wonderfully descriptive verses unveil a great deal of what the bride of Christ is destined to be. Above all other created things, we are His grace-filled haven of visitation, His preferred place of peaceful communion. Therefore, He refers to us as **A GARDEN ENCLOSED**—for we have been exclusively reserved unto our heavenly Husbandman. Even as a virgin reserves herself for her husband-to-be and withholds her love from others, so should we be to Jesus. We should never give our passion, our love, to the world, but rather be—**A SPRING SHUT UP, A FOUNTAIN SEALED.**

As a continually active and energetic fountain, our hearts should constantly overflow with the rippling waters of newborn expressions of doting love that belong to Him alone. Our God has been "a fountain of living waters" to us, so it is only right that we who bear His likeness be "a fountain of living waters" to Him. (See Jer. 2:13; 17:13, Zec. 13:1.)

When we fill up this title-position, we fill up the heart of God as well. We supply His need. We quench His thirst. We become a life-giving spring, "**A GARDEN SPRING, A GARDEN FOUNTAIN, A WELL OF LIVING WATERS**," flowing upward toward the very throne room of the Almighty God. In the eyes of the King of creation we are as "**STREAMS FROM LEBANON**"— for our hearts have been made as white as the crown of snow on these nobly capped mountains. Such a miraculous transformation has naturally resulted in melted down streams of crisp, clear, snow-pure worship rushing happily over the rocky riverbed of life (and, O, how such praise has smoothed over the rough-edged stones—time and time again!) (Song 4:15 KJV, NAS, NAB).

Yes, with the echo of the gurgling waters, we hear within our own hearts, again and again, the echo of truth—the wondrous fact that we have been created, redeemed, cleansed and set aside to satisfy the deep, inward craving of the Creator for loving, spiritual fellowship. *"The deep"* in God flows toward us as a river of living water from His throne. Then, having entered our hearts, it becomes in us a well of living water "springing up into everlasting life" (Jn. 4:14). Out of *"the deep"* in us, this river of God flows back to the very throne from which it came. No wonder the word **Lebanon** can mean *heart-gushings.* For the hearts of God's redeemed constantly swell with *heart-gushings*—as *"deep calls unto deep."*

We are called to be **"a well of living waters,"** not only to the Creator but to those in this world who thirst. 2 Peter 2:17 reveals that the wicked are "wells without water," but Proverbs 10:11 says, "The mouth of the righteous is a well of life." In this sense, *deep also calls unto deep,* from one redeemed heart to another.

Moreover, the Bridegroom says to the bride, "Your lips, O **my spouse**, drip as the honeycomb; honey and milk are under your tongue" (Song 4:11). The thick *honey* of the Holy Spirit and the rich, creamy *milk* of the Word are both very much present under our tongues and in our speech. Our lips drop as the golden garden honeycomb when we slowly, purposefully, and reverently open our mouths to confess God's Word and present our petitions to Him. We taste the sweetness of intimacy with God, the very sweetness which He enjoys as well. This thing called *effectual prayer* is, therefore, a heavenly nectar, patiently gathered from all the many flowers of trust, hope, faith, charity, and praise, that grow in *the garden* of every bloodwashed, heaven-bound soul.

These tender-petaled, spiritual flowers blossom most beautifully when Word-seeds are planted in the fertile territory of life's adversities. Therefore, through these hardships, life is born out of death and something quite beautiful emerges from what seemingly has no beauty at all. This is the plan of God. This is what the Son of God watches over us so intently to perform.

Because such spiritual gardens are rare and costly, we have been securely enclosed. Our gracious Savior and Gardener has erected a strong, protective wall of grace round about His living garden and planted a thick, impenetrable hedge of keeping power on every side.

He has locked the gate to our hearts and He alone bears the key. He has set His angels in the watchtower lest any intruders, any evil principalities, creep in to steal and destroy. Because of these sureties, we can often confess—we are **"HIS GARDEN ENCLOSED"** or, as another translation states, **"HIS GARDEN LOCKED UP"** (Song 4:12 NKJV, NIV).

The Bride is spoken of corporately and collectively as a garden; but we are also spoken of as being individual gardens blended together into one, **GARDENS BY THE RIVERSIDE**, as Numbers 24:6 so beautifully states. The river of life flows past our hearts every moment and when we drink of its nourishing waters, we are quickened by its enlivening influence.

How glorious it is that we are collectively **HIS GARDEN**, but how much more glorious—that we are **HIS FOUNTAIN OF GARDENS**, a multitude of gardens in one—for each member of the bride of Christ has become a garden entire (Song 4:15)! This entitlement speaks of the wonderful truth that we have not been mass-produced in a thoughtless, loveless way. We are all singularly important expressions, *flowing one by one* out of the heart of the Gardener/God.

TWO IMPORTANT FACTORS

It is no coincidence that three of the very spices required as ingredients in the holy anointing oil (calamus, myrrh and cinnamon) are also some of the main spices being grown and developed in this spiritual orchard-garden. Why is this? Because growing in the anointing is necessarily a major part of being called **GOD'S GARDEN**. (1 Cor. 3:9 LB, See Ex. 30:22–33, Song 4:12–15.)

We fill up this *garden-stature* especially when we learn to be channels of the anointing and when we learn how to love. Blossoming as a garden always involves putting others first and showing sincere concern for their needs. The prophet Isaiah presented this truth:

> *If you take away the yoke from your midst, the pointing of the finger and speaking wickedness,*
>
> *If you [draw out] your soul to the hungry, and satisfy the afflicted soul; then your light [shall rise in obscurity] and your darkness shall be as the noonday:*
>
> *YOU SHALL BE LIKE A **WATERED GARDEN**, AND LIKE A **SPRING OF WATER** WHOSE WATERS DO NOT FAIL.*
>
> (Isaiah 58:9–11 NKJV, KJV)

Light and water—these are two vitally important factors.

Where there is no light, color does not exist, for colors are the direct result of reflected light. Also, where there is no light, for the most part, plants cannot grow, for the process of photosynthesis is halted—the process by which chlorophyll-containing tissues, exposed to light, develop much needed carbohydrates. In like manner, where there is no revelation-light from heaven, there can be no lovely, flourishing and color-filled, spiritual garden. 'Walking in the light' always involves walking in the truth and walking in love. When we cease to be motivated by love we immediately pass into the realm of darkness and become a wasteland. (See 1 Jn. 2:9–11.)

A garden also must have its necessary supply of water, so that the plants can remain alive and successfully absorb the necessary nutriments from the ground. In the Scripture, both the Word and the Spirit are represented as an unending, inexhaustible supply of *water*, and both are also represented by *light*—brilliant, warm and heaven-sent. (See Eph. 5:26, Jn. 7:37–38, Ps. 119:105, 1 Tim. 6:15–16, 1 Jn. 1:5–6.) Therefore, this dual symbol doubly emphasizes our utter dependence on God's holy Word and His blessed Holy Spirit, if we are to thrive abundantly.

We must have water and we must have light. They are both essential—absolutely essential. But the only way to keep this light shining, and keep this water flowing, is to "draw out" our souls to meet the needs of the hungry, the thirsty and the afflicted. As we lovingly and faithfully supply water and light to others, God sees to it that the same is maintained toward us. No wonder the Scripture says, "he who waters will also be watered himself." Also, "light is sown for the righteous." (Pr. 11:25, Ps. 97:11, See Is. 27:2–3; 44:3.)

These are laws in the kingdom of God! By this process, not only do we receive water and light, we become what we manifest. We become water and light to others.

CALLING TO THE WINDS

Now we arrive at another important factor that must be included to paint the perfect picture of a pleasant garden—the need of *wind*. The bride pleads for this in Song of Solomon 4:16 (NAS):

> *Awake, O north wind, and come, wind of the south.*
> *Make **MY GARDEN** breathe out fragrance. Let its spices*
> *be wafted abroad. May my beloved come into **HIS***
> ***GARDEN** and eat its choice fruits.*

The **north wind**—that could well speak of the sometimes soul-chilling and sometimes blustery, cold blasts of tribulation-air that swiftly, domineeringly and often unexpectedly, push, pull, and rudely shove a host of dark, foreboding storm clouds into our lives. These northern winds have little gentleness or courtesy about them and certainly no capacity for sympathy.

They often bring rain. They can mercilessly turn a warm day, filled with meaning, into a frigid night, filled with discomfort, and give no warning in the process except the hasty retreat of the sun.

Like a bunch of rough and rowdy herdsmen rounding up a herd of cattle, these contrary, whipping northern winds can rush in unpredictably from seemingly every direction, until the atmospheric corral over our heads is crammed full of fenced-in, frustrated, snorting, hoof-stomping problems.

The **south wind**, though, is quite the opposite—warm, gentle, comforting and refreshing, akin in nature to the very breath of the Almighty—breathing new hope, inspiration and blessed assurance into every heart-garden in its path. These southern-born winds bring wind-borne blessings and always slow down long enough to embrace the weary traveler resting in the shady garden thicket. This is a welcome wind and when it happily departs, on its way to the next needy soul, it always leaves behind sighs of relief and countenances that emanate a fresh supply of faith.

Both of these winds, the *"cold north wind"* and the *"soft south wind,"* are necessary and important (Song 4:16 Amp). Both are complementary and ultimately beneficial. Both are awakened and called upon by the garden-bride who submissively yields to their dual influence. For if we react correctly, the burdens of life only serve to turn our windswept hearts toward heaven in greater trust and surrender—and by these we learn the power of God. The blessings of life, on the other hand, tend to lift our wind-soothed hearts upward in praise—and by these we learn the goodness of God.

By the combined influence and marriage of these two winds our garden can truly—*"breathe out fragrance."* This pleasant fragrance is the sweet-smelling savor of constant, heartfelt adoration—a consecrated life that simply breathes worship with every waking moment. By these winds our garden spices can also be *"wafted abroad"*—profoundly affecting all those around us. Maybe this is part of the reason Jesus explained:

> *The wind blows where it wishes, and you hear the sound of it, but cannot tell where it comes from and where it goes. So is everyone who is born of the Spirit.*
>
> (John 3:8)

THE ROSE AND LILY REVELATION

In Song of Solomon 2:1 the bride declares her identity saying, "I am **THE ROSE OF SHARON** and **THE LILY OF THE VALLEYS.**" Though quite often this statement is assigned to the Bridegroom (Jesus), many respected translations (such as the NKJV and the NAS) attribute this confession to the bride. The Amplified Version quotes her as saying "I am only **a little rose** or **autumn crocus** of the plain of Sharon, or a humble **lily of the valleys** [that grows in deep and difficult places]." This speaks of the bride's tenderness in the midst of a cruel world, her beauty in the midst of an ugly world. It speaks of how vulnerable and insignificant she may feel were it not for the watchful oversight of the Bridegroom.

The "**rose of Sharon**" could be referring to a "bright red tulip-like flower today prolific in the hills of Sharon. It displays a dramatic, deep red mat of color in the grass with the beginning of Spring.'"[1] If this be a correct interpretation, it speaks something similar to Isaiah 35:1, "The wilderness and the wasteland shall be glad for them, and the desert shall rejoice and blossom as **the rose.**" In other words, were it not for the bride of Christ, this desert-like wilderness-world would be devoid of beauty. But our bloodwashed souls, century after century, have provided a "dramatic, deep red mat" of redemption witness and influence worldwide.

There is some controversy over exactly what flower is being referred to as a "lily" in the Song of Solomon. It is translated from one of four Hebrew words: *shuwshan, showshan, shoshan* or *showshannah.* These words come from a root word *suws* that means *bright, cheerful* or *rejoice.* So to be "**the lily of the valleys**" means to blossom in pleasant beauty—bright, cheerful and rejoicing—even in the low places of life. Jesus is certainly the example of that to us—and we who love Him are emerging in His lily-likeness. *Showshannah* is also translated *Showshannim,* a certain kind of trumpet used in temple worship. Apparently, it gained its name because of the lily's tubular, trumpet-like shape. So if we are lilies in God's sight, we should daily trumpet out a song of worship to Him.

In Hosea 14:5 God declared of restored Israel, "**he shall grow like the lily.**" This could be speaking of two things. The first is miraculous productivity. There is no plant more productive. The flower most likely referred to can produce up to fifty bulbs from one root. The second part of the analogy is gentle defiance. Just as the beautiful lily, that appears so defenseless, defies the overshadowing trees and the rough wilderness terrain just to exist, so the Israel of God—with God's aid—has gently and successfully defied this corrupt and godless world.[2]

The bridegroom is described going down to His garden to "gather **LILIES**" (Song 6:2). This could be speaking of the gracious Gardener-God gathering His saints unto Himself, plucking them one-by-one at their departure from this world. While here, they beautified this realm with their blossoming glory and graced this world with the sweet fragrance of devotion to God. In His hands, they radiate, to an even greater degree, their God-given beauty in flowering celestial splendor. (See Song 2:1,16; 5:13; 6:2–3.)[3]

A FEAST FOR THE GARDENER

According to Song of Solomon 4:16, the beloved Bridegroom/Gardener often visits the *garden-souls* of mature divine offspring in order to eat *"His pleasant fruits"* (or *choice fruits* as rendered in the NIV). *Choice fruits* speak of well-ripened, divine-like character traits—like love, joy, peace, longsuffering, kindness, goodness, faithfulness, gentleness and self-control—the very personality of the firstborn Son of God (Gal. 5:22–23). These are *choice fruits,* the fruit of the Spirit, and they are *pleasant* and lusciously inviting. For the LORD of glory finds supreme pleasure in communing with those who take on His image.

Choice fruits also speak of righteous deeds (Colossians 1:10 encourages us to be "*fruitful* in every good work") and ascending praise (Hebrews 13:15 encourages us to continually "offer the sacrifice of praise to God, that is, the *fruit* of our lips, giving thanks to His name").[*4]

All three of these—Christlike character, good works and praise—offer the Son of God a sumptuous feast in which He delights. No wonder the Bridegroom is described as dwelling in the gardens. And no wonder one version of Isaiah 5:7 calls God's people **THE GARDEN OF HIS DELIGHT** (NIV). When we abide in a harmonious, peaceful relationship with Him, we re-experience together the essence of what the first garden, **Eden,** was all about. How ironic it is that **Eden** means *delight,* for in returning to a *delightful,* garden-like relationship with the Creator, in a sense, we return to Eden. In the process, we become to Him **"A PARADISE WITH PRECIOUS FRUITS"** (Song 4:13 Amp).

THE PROGRESSIVE "GARDEN" REVELATION

There are three highly-important, literal gardens mentioned in Scripture: the garden of Eden, the garden of Gethsemane and the garden of Joseph of Arimathaea (where the LORD Jesus arose). All three of these gardens reveal successive steps being taken to produce a fourth garden—that matchless spiritual garden called the bride of Christ.

Because mankind lost access to *the garden of Eden,* Jesus intentionally visited a *lonely garden* of travailing prayer called *Gethsemane,* where His bloody sweat soaked into the ground, so that He could reclaim Edenic bliss for us. And every time His precious blood falls on a plot of Adam-ground, a barren soul is transformed into a hedged-in sanctuary of fruits and flowers. Three days after Calvary Jesus arose triumphantly from a sealed tomb located in yet another garden (*the garden of Joseph of Arimathaea*) so that He could arise victoriously in the *garden-hearts* of His redeemed sons and daughters.

Having come out of the grave, Jesus first appeared to Mary, saying, *"Why are you weeping? Who are you seeking?"* Gazing at Him through her tears, she thought Him to be the gardener. She was more right than wrong. As a gracious and ambitious Gardener, He came forth from the grave determined to sow the seed of His Word in the hearts of receptive men and women worldwide.

We are so blessed and thankful that the Gardener-God included us. We have all, in a certain sense, wept at His gravesite as Mary did, feeling so lost and so alone. But then we met the Gardener and we heard the echo of His question, *"Why are you weeping? Who are you seeking?"*

We responded in faith. He dried our tears. He gave us hope. He brought to pass something in our lives that we could well describe as being more than wonderful! We were nothing but empty tombs, sealed into darkness and destruction. We were spiritually dead in trespasses and sins. But then, by grace, we accepted the crucified One into our hearts and He again victoriously came forth in resurrection power (turning hardened, fruitless ground into a haven of abundant life expressed).

One of our main heaven-sent commissions now is to reach out into the wilderness of sin and draw other barren souls into this transforming experience. We must convince the masses that they too can blossom under the earth-soaking shower of God's anointing. For this living garden must expand and increase until it fully encircles the globe.

> *For as the earth brings forth its bud, as the garden causes the things that are sown in it to spring forth, so the LORD God will cause righteousness and praise to spring forth before all the nations.*
>
> (Isaiah 61:11)

THE KINGDOM AGE AND BEYOND

It is a faithful saying that during the coming Kingdom Age every single inhabitant of the earth will be included in **"GOD'S GARDEN"** (1 Cor. 3:9 LB). God has ordained that creation, as well as His redeemed sons and daughters, be restored back to the original paradise state. Therefore, at the coming of Jesus, the entire world, in a sense, will be 'born again' into the God-breathed perfection of the garden of Eden. The divine presence will be married once again to the trees, the flowers, the hills, the rivers and the creatures of the field.

All things will be permeated with the life of God. The lamb will lay down with the lion. Beauty will abound. Peace will reign in the earth. Sorrow and sighing will flee away.

> *For the LORD will comfort Zion, He will comfort all her waste places; He will make her wilderness like **Eden**, and her desert like **the garden of the LORD**; joy and gladness will be found in it, thanksgiving and the voice of melody.*
>
> (Isaiah 51:3)

Then, as we advance into even greater splendor, the Kingdom Age will give birth to the New Creation. There will be a New Heaven and a New Earth. The supernatural will increase in manifestation. A pure river of the water of life will flow out of the throne of God into every corner of His vast creation.

Then, in a more profound way than ever, we will be "**GARDENS BY THE RIVERSIDE**"—gratefully drinking in this living water and delightfully blooming in infinite fruitfulness (Num. 24:6). Speaking of God's people in the eternal state, Jeremiah prophesied:

> *They shall come and sing in the height of Zion, and shall flow together to the goodness of the LORD...and their soul shall be as* **A WATERED GARDEN**; *and they shall not sorrow any more at all.*
>
> (Jeremiah 31:12 KJV)

O, what beautiful, celestial-like music will surely abound throughout creation in that glorious era (for the musical menagerie, then glorified, will play and sing with flawless ability and absolute concord). What sweet melody, what joyous redemption song, rings in our hearts even now, as we contemplate such a glorious inheritance and destiny!

The inward revelation of this awesome, future possession daily whispers in our hearts of the coming simplicity and elegance of perfection. We are convinced that on our way there, the gracious Gardener will watch over us with extreme personal care and artistic attention to detail. We know that He is deeply involved with those blessed individuals He has elected to include in His garden of delight. This deep emotional involvement is expressed excellently by the following scripture (so filled with figurative language):

> *I have come to* **MY GARDEN, MY SISTER, MY SPOUSE**; *I have gathered My myrrh with My spice; I have eaten My honeycomb with My honey; I have drunk My wine with My milk...*
>
> (Song of Solomon 5:1)

Then the choir of the Song of Solomon encourages both the Bridegroom and the bride:

> *Eat, O* **FRIENDS**, *and drink, drink Your fill, O* **LOVERS**.
>
> (NIV)[*5]

This should be our unceasing prayer: to satisfy His need and be utterly pleasing to Him, to be lovers of God, always providing Him a tranquil, pleasant, rapture-filled *garden-heart* in which to dwell. We recognize that this is our duty, whether we be in season or out of season. We understand that this is our calling, in times stressful and in times blissful. This is our God-given command and, more than that, our great privilege as well: the deepest means of expressing how we really feel toward the heavenly Husbandman.

For, most of all, above all—whether draped in starlit darkness or engulfed in penetrating sunshine—*a garden always speaks of love.*

—the *love* of the Gardener for His work of art (who caresses our hearts with each seed implanted);

—the *love* of these earthen vessels, drinking in spiritual water and soaking in heavenly light—then unselfishly giving birth to life and beauty;

—and the *love* that we feel right now, flowing from our hearts to His and from His heart toward us (like rising vapor, returning as rain).

Yes, it is so very right and will remain so very true forever and always.

*A garden speaks of love—deep love—the deepest exchange of love known in this world. It is the **deep** in every child of God, calling to the **deep** in the heart of our heavenly Husbandman.*

Endnotes

*1 *Harpers Bible Dictionary,* (Harper and Row Publishers, 1985) p 884 under *Rose.*

*2 The symbol of the lily is more fully expressed in the chapter entitled *The Lily Among Thorns* in Volume Two of **Our Glorious Inheritance.**

*3 Other extra-biblical sources use this lily-symbol. It is found in 2 Esdras 5:23–28 in the prayer of Esdras referring to Israel, "O LORD that bearest rule of all the woods of the earth, and of all the trees thereof, Thou hast chosen Thy ONE VINE: and of all the lands of the world Thou hast chosen the ONE COUNTRY; and of all the flowers of the world, **ONE LILY**..." In the Jewish prayer book, at the Feast of Purim, Israel is spoken of as "**the lily of Jacob.**" Also, it is noteworthy that lilies were seen displayed throughout the temple, so we, the New Testament temple of God, should certainly have this lily-symbol engraved in our hearts. (The information in this endnote was gleaned from *The Companion Bible,* App 65 XXI.)

*4 This concept of 'bearing fruit' is covered more fully in the chapter on *Good Ground* in this volume, and the chapter on *Disciples* in Volume Two of **Our Glorious Inheritance.**

*5 Refer to the chapter on *Friends* in Volume Two and the chapter on *Lovers of God* in Volume Five of **Our Glorious Inheritance.**

THE GOOD

Again, the kingdom of heaven is like unto a net, that was cast into the sea, and gathered of every kind:

*Which, when it was full, they drew to shore, and sat down, and gathered **THE GOOD** into vessels, but cast the bad away.*

(Matthew 13:47–48 KJV)

Then He said to them, "Follow Me, and I will make you FISHERS OF MEN."

(Matthew 4:19)

"Behold, I will send for many FISHERMEN [FISHERS]," says the LORD, "and they shall fish them; and afterward I will send for many HUNTERS, and they shall hunt them from every mountain, and every hill, and out of the holes of the rocks."

(Jeremiah 16:16 NKJV, KJV)

Other related titles contained in this chapter (including the Scriptures above) are: **Good Fish**—Mt. 13:48 NIV, **Good Men**—Mt. 12:35, **Fishers of Men**—Mt. 4:19; **Fishermen**—Jer. 16:16, **Fishers**—Jer. 16:16 KJV, **Hunters**—Jer. 16:16.

THE GOOD

Again, the kingdom of heaven is like unto a net, that was cast into the sea, and gathered of every kind:

*Which, when it was full, they drew to shore, and sat down, and gathered **THE GOOD** into vessels, but cast the bad away.*

(Matthew 13:47–48 KJV)

*M*any of Jesus' parables contain a similar, central theme: the unfortunate mixture of good and evil in that which appears to be of God and of His kingdom in this world. The two-verse parable above is no exception.

- **The Net**—In a New Covenant perspective, the "net" being drawn by fishermen represents the Gospel of the kingdom being preached in all the world and gathering "all kinds." Because this is a dragnet— weighted down at the bottom, dragging the sea floor and drawn tight at the top between two boats—it represents the power of the message of Jesus to pervade every level of humankind. The sweep of its influence is felt from the very dregs of society all the way up to the elite, the intellectual and the affluent.[*1]

- **The Sea**—The "sea" represents the entire human race and the dark, turbulent depths to which men have sunk. Isaiah 57:20 explains, "the wicked are like the troubled sea, when it cannot rest, whose waters cast up mire and dirt." (See Rev. 17:15.)

- **The Catch**—The "catch" represents the professing church that has resulted from all such evangelistic activity, those who outwardly profess to accept the doctrines and teachings of Christianity. Notice the catch includes both "the bad" and "the good." How can this be? Because through the centuries, many have claimed to be Christian, who were 'Christian' in name only. Unfortunately, they never fulfilled heaven's requirements for those aspiring to be among "the good."

This last point needs to be re-emphasized: not all who claim salvation really possess salvation. Some do and some do not, for all do not measure up to the Bible-based requirements and standards. Jesus was very blunt in declaring, "You must be born again" (Jn. 3:7). This is not an optional experience. It is mandatory for all who desire to inherit everlasting life and everlasting fellowship with the Most High God.

The Savior also declared, "Not everyone who says to Me, 'LORD, LORD' shall enter the kingdom of heaven; but he who does the will of My Father in heaven" (Mt. 7:21). In the same discourse, Jesus warned that in the Day of Judgment many will claim to have done wonderful works in His name, yet they will unexpectedly and tragically hear Him say, "I never *knew* you: depart from Me." In this very statement, "I never *knew* you," we see the unfolding of the mystery (Mt. 7:23).

John 17:3 declares "this is eternal life, that they may *know* You the only true God, and Jesus Christ, whom You have sent." The Good Shepherd in John 10:14 also explains, "...I *know* My sheep, and am *known* by My own."

This speaks of far more than just an intellectual acceptance of each other's existence. It speaks of spiritual intimacy—spirit-to-Spirit contact. To *know* the LORD is to be personally acquainted with Him. It involves going 'beyond the veil' of flesh consciousness into His divine presence. On the other hand, to be *known* of God is to be filled with His very being and essence, begotten of His Word and born of His Spirit. God, the omniscient One, *knows* every detail about every single human being in this entire world, but He *knows* His offspring in yet a deeper way. Adam *knew* Eve and they became one flesh. In a similar, spiritual sense, the everlasting Bridegroom *knows* each individual member of His bride, for they have become one spirit with Him.

To *know* the Shepherd is to enter into fellowship with Him. To be *known* of the Shepherd-God (Yahweh-Rohi or the traditional, Jehovah-Rohi) is to have Him enter into fellowship with us.

This is the glorious result—*the deep calling to the deep.*

This is the blessed union and blending of hearts that takes place at the moment of salvation. This initial regeneration of the spirit may or may not be physically intense. Though such is often the case, still, the new birth does not necessarily come with any kind of supernatural feeling. It may be simply a faith experience. Without controversy, though, "If anyone is in Christ, he is a new creation" (2 Cor. 5:17). There is definitely a change that takes place— usually quite recognizable—in the heart and life of the newborn believer.

Those who can sincerely claim such a life-transforming experience can also claim a blessed assurance. Romans 8:16 reveals, "The Spirit Himself bears witness with our spirit, that we are the children of God." If we have this Spirit-witness, we can also have the strong confidence that God will keep us in His "**net**" and ultimately draw us to "**the shore**" when His kingdom arrives in fullness. There and then He will separate us utterly unto Himself and forever include us among "**the good**."

GOODNESS DEFINED

To understand this simple, heart-moving title—**the good**—let us inspect the various shades of meaning assigned to this word.

When referring to a person, the word **good** signifies: *one who is wholesome, kind, merciful, loving, benevolent, true, loyal, pure, sincere, honorable, admirable, profitable, praiseworthy and of an excellent character.*

If the word **good** was originally derived, as some suggest, from the word **God**, then it simply means *godlikeness.*

When God is spoken of as being *good*, the meaning is even more lofty—for a *good* God is One who has no capacity for bad. In a supreme and perfect way, He is *kind, merciful, loving, benevolent, honorable, admirable and of an excellent character.* These few descriptive words still do not provide a full view of the personality of the Most High. Actually, the sum total of ALL His wonderful, excellent and praiseworthy attributes can easily come under the heading—*the goodness of the LORD.*

God is *good*. This is such an elementary statement, yet it communicates such a beautiful depth and such a wide breadth of revelation. Seeing it from this broad perspective, we can fully appreciate why David said, "I would have lost heart, unless I had believed that I would see *the goodness of the LORD* in the land of the living" (Ps. 27:13).

When Moses sought the LORD, saying "Show me Your glory," God responded, "I will make all My *goodness* pass before you" (Ex. 33:18–19). When this visitation took place, Moses beheld the glorious form of the LORD passing by and he heard the glorious voice of the LORD proclaiming, "The LORD, the LORD God, merciful and gracious, longsuffering, and abounding in *goodness* and truth, keeping mercy for thousands…" (Ex. 34:6–7).

This entire statement was a revelation of God's *goodness*, for His *goodness* includes His graciousness, His longsuffering, His mercy and His truth. Such splendid divine characteristics are also to be termed *His glory*—for God's *goodness* is His *glory.*

How comforting it is to know that even in a fallen state "the earth is full of *the goodness of the LORD*" (His bounty and blessing poured on both the worthy and the unworthy) (Ps. 33:5). But the *goodness of the LORD* is far more than something outwardly observed. It can be an infilling as well—for those who desire, ask and believe.

*For He satisfies the longing soul, and fills the hungry soul with **goodness.***

(Psalm 107:9)

This is a good God making His people good, just like Him.

Goodness is listed among the nine fruit of the Spirit. It is a natural outgrowth of the indwelling Spirit of God, developed, as all the fruit of the Spirit, primarily for the sake of edifying others. So this infilling of *goodness,* once received, should then be given away. (See Gal. 5:22–23.)

Ephesians 5:9 also declares, "For the fruit of the Spirit is in all *goodness,* righteousness, and truth." In other words, as the Holy Spirit takes over our attitudes, molding and shaping our hearts into the image of Christ, the fruit of the Spirit promotes the truth through us, advances righteousness for us, and evidences the goodness of God in us.

THE CALL TO GOODNESS

All persons claiming to be sons and daughters of God are automatically called to be among **the good**. They simultaneously inherit the related title-callings of being—**good and faithful servants, good figs, good ground, a good harvest, good ministers of Jesus Christ, good seed, good soldiers, good stewards** and **good trees.**

We are commanded to "be of *good* courage" (Ps. 27:14), "fight the *good* fight of faith," "wage the *good* warfare," confess a "*good* confession" and "acknowledge every *good* thing" that is in us (1 Tim. 1:18; 6:12, 13, Phm. 1:6). We are exhorted by God to "do *good,*" "seek *good,*" "love *good,*" "pursue what is *good,*" "cling to what is *good,*" "hold fast what is *good*" and "fulfill all the *good* pleasure of His *goodness*" (Ps. 37:3, Am. 5:14–15, 1 Th. 5:15, 21, Ro. 12:9, 2 Th. 1:11).

It is the "*good LORD'S*" bidding that we hold to a "*good* conscience," "bear *good* fruit," and as *good* men "out of the *good* treasure of the heart," bring forth "*good* things" (2 Chr. 6:27; 30:18, 1 Tim. 1:19, Mt. 7:18; 12:35).

We are also called to "lay a *good* foundation" for eternity by being "zealous for *good* works" and even "rich in *good* works." "For we are His workmanship, created in Christ Jesus for *good* works, which God prepared beforehand that we should walk in them" (Ti. 2:14, 1 Tim. 6:18–19 KJV, Eph. 2:10).

Furthermore, the "*good* Shepherd" urges us to walk in the "*good* way" and to "overcome evil with *good*" (Jn. 10:11, 1 Kgs. 8:36, Jer. 6:16, Ro. 12:21). We are called to daily partake of "the *good* Word of God" that our senses might be "exercised to discern both *good* and evil" (Heb. 5:14; 6:5). If we obey His commandments and confess His promises, we will make our way prosperous and we will have "*good* success" (Js. 1:8). In a spiritual sense, we will possess "an exceedingly *good* land" (the promised land of all the "exceedingly great and precious promises" that we have received) (Num. 14:7, 2 Pt. 1:4).

God's *goodness* is normally linked to His generosity in imparting gifts or help to man. For instance:

> **Good** *and upright is the LORD: therefore He teaches sinners in the way.*
>
> (Psalm 25:8)

> *The LORD is* **good***; for His mercy endures forever.*
>
> (Jeremiah 33:11)

> *The LORD is* **good***, a stronghold in the day of trouble…*
>
> (Nahum 1:7)

Therefore, our *goodness* should also be indicated, not by what we claim to *be*, but by what we actually *do* for others—especially for those who are unworthy. Jesus said it so beautifully in the 'Sermon on the Mount':

> *…Love your enemies, bless those who curse you, do* **good** *to those who hate you, and pray for those who spitefully use you and persecute you.*
>
> *That you may be sons of your Father in heaven; for He makes His sun rise on the evil and on* **the good,** *and sends rain on the just and on the unjust.*
>
> *For if you love those who love you, what reward have you? Do not even the tax collectors do the same?…*
>
> *Therefore you shall be perfect, just as your Father in heaven is perfect.*
>
> (Matthew 5:44–48, See Luke 6:33.)

THE DIFFICULT HURDLE

All of the things spoken so far are lofty and desirable. However, we cannot help but question how any of this can be attained by human beings when Romans 3:12 points out so dogmatically: *"There is none who does* **good***, no not one."*

Jesus expressed the same sentiment, "No one is *good* but One, that is, God" (Mt. 19:17). Paul also, disturbed over his own fallen Adam-nature, confessed:

> *…for to will is present with me; but how to perform that which is* **good** *I find not…*
>
> *I find them a law, that, when I would do* **good***, evil is present with me.*
>
> (Romans 7:18, 21 KJV)

Do these scriptures paint a negative, depressing, pessimistic picture for us all? Is it impossible for sons of Adam to ever attain true *goodness?* No, not at all! The Scripture is simply revealing the utter frailty of the flesh without the intervention of God. Paul argued this point by concluding, "I know that in me (that is, in my flesh) nothing *good* dwells" (Ro. 7:18).

We must admit that within ourselves we are only worthy of separation from God. Within ourselves we have little capacity for good. Compared to the supreme and absolute goodness of the Most High, we have no goodness at all. Besides, without God, any good we can accomplish is only temporary and vain. Isaiah 40:6 laments, "All flesh is grass, and all its loveliness is like the flower of the field." The grass eventually withers. The flower eventually fades.

Had the Messiah refused to intervene in the affairs of men our plight would be hopeless indeed. Thank God, He came! How fitting it was at His birth that the angel of the LORD announced:

> *Fear not: for, behold, I bring you **good tidings** of great joy, which shall be to all people.*
> *For unto you is born this day in the city of David a Savior, which is Christ the LORD.*
>
> (Luke 2:10–11 KJV)

And suddenly, there appeared a multitude of heavenly host saying:

> *Glory to God in the highest, and on earth peace, **good will** toward men!*
>
> (Luke 2:14 KJV)

This *"good will"* of God was the *"good tidings"* that Jesus came to save us from our fallen nature and to make us *good.* His grace not only makes us acceptable in His sight; it empowers us to make *good* choices. These are definitely *good tidings* and this is such a part of the New Will that it has become a sign of true sonship. 3 John 11 succinctly offers:

> *"He who does good is of God."*

THE SYMBOL

It is needful to reemphasize that this title—**the good**—is a reference to fish, good fish as opposed to bad fish. In fact, the New International Version actually translates this title in Matthew 13:48, **good fish.**

As stressed in the beginning of this chapter, the bad fish represent that portion of the human race who are 'caught' in the 'net' of the Gospel (and become professing Christians), but who prove to be unconverted, unregenerated, and therefore, unacceptable to God. "Bad fish" could also be a reference to fish without scales—considered to be unclean and unfit for human consumption according to Old Testament dietary laws. So those persons who are "bad fish" are still unclean. They are unfit for fellowship with God, for they have not been washed from their sin. (See Lev. 11:9–12.)

The **good fish** represent the true sons of God. They are not merely professing Christians. They are possessing Christians. They possess a real relationship with the risen Christ. They have been delivered from an unclean state.

From the start of Jesus' ministry the 'fishing' symbol was evident. It was more than coincidence that the Son of man preached one of His first sermons from the deck of a fishing boat anchored close to the Galilee shore (for He was truly 'fishing' for the souls of men)!

It was also quite fitting that he chose fishermen to be among His most elite disciples! We still hear the echo of his verbal challenge—"Follow Me, and I will make you **FISHERS OF MEN**" (Mt. 4:19). So our highest calling is not only to be **GOOD FISH**, but **FISHERS OF MEN**; helping God achieve His goal in this realm.

Referring to the lost and scattered tribes of Israel (and really all chosen ones who are lost in the 'ocean' or 'forest' of this world) in a good sense, God said: "Behold, I will send for many **FISHERMEN,** says the LORD, and they shall fish them; and afterward I will send for many **HUNTERS**, and they shall hunt them from every mountain, and from every hill, and out of the holes of the rocks" (Jer. 16:16). So all of God's representatives are called to be **fishers** and **hunters**. We are anointed to pursue both Jews and Gentiles—that we might catch them with the 'net' of the Gospel. We can expect success, for God is with us in this endeavor.[*2]

'GOOD' AND FINAL RESULTS

In "**The Parable of the Good Fish**," the net was described as being *full.* This means that the Gospel will produce the *full* results God expected from the beginning. His Word will not return unto Him void of effect. It will accomplish that which He has purposed—for all those 'fish' chosen in Him before the foundation of the world will be successfully caught.

Unfortunately, until that final day of separation there will always be an unavoidable mixture of **good fish** and **bad fish** in the net, just as there will always be wheat and tares in His field. This is just the way things are here in this earth-realm. As Herbert Lockyer so aptly put it—"There was a *Ham* in the Ark, a *Judas* among the apostles; *Esau* and *Jacob* still struggle in the womb of the visible church of Christ. They are not all Israelites who are of Israel."*³

Revelation 7:9 describes this family of God as a great multitude which no man can number. Most likely, this is not because of the large size of the family. It's because no man can say, at this present time, who will be accepted or rejected in the end. This is something only God knows: a knowledge that He will transfer to His separating angels during the Great Ingathering. Though we have often erred in judgment, the angels will make no error when they "separate the wicked from among the just" (Mt. 13:49).

After that fearful, yet glorious day, there will never again be a mixture of good and evil in what appears to be of God and of His kingdom. Neither will there be any mixture of good and evil in us (the flesh at enmity with the Spirit and the carnal mind at enmity with the mind of Christ).

Only that which is pure and sincere will remain. Just as "the evil" will finally "bow before **the good**" (fully submitting to the reign of the righteous), so also the evil that has been in our flesh will finally bow before God's goodness in us and yield to its reign (Pr. 14:19). We will be resurrected into the absolute of goodness, perfected in the image of "the *good* LORD" who will "pardon every one" of His eternal offspring (2 Chr. 30:18 KJV).

Like the God that we serve, we will then be so utterly one with goodness, we will no longer possess any potential for bad. We will be delivered forever and sealed forever in the name of the LORD. In that day, the God who observed "Behold, it is *good*" at the beginning of creation, will most likely declare "Behold, it is *very good*" at the end (Gen. 1:4, 10, 12, 18, 21, 25, 31). Because of "the *good* hand of our God" upon us, we will survive. God will rejoice over us to do us "*good*." (Ez. 8:18, Jer. 32:39–41, See Jer. 24:6.)

We who are entitled **the good** will then grasp all the more clearly that it was not by our might that such a *good work* was wrought in our lives. Jesus always has been and ever will be our source—our only source. Whenever we are gripped with this realization, words of thanksgiving should flow out of our grateful hearts like unto those found in Psalm 144:1–2:

> Blessed be the LORD my strength...**my goodness,** and my fortress.
>
> (Psalm 144:1–2 KJV)

In the end all the glory will be His. As we anticipate such a wonderful destiny, let us speak prophetically to other believers—and to the nation of Israel—that the LORD will "do thee *good* at thy latter end." (Dt. 8:16 KJV, See Ps. 65:11.)

> *Being confident of this very thing, that He who has*
> *begun a **good work** in you will complete it until the day*
> *of Jesus Christ.*
>
> (Philipians 1:6)

In the end, we will be able look back on our earthly sojourn and affirm that all things really did "work together for *good* to those that love God, to those who are the called according to His purpose" (Ro. 8:28 KJV). Like Joseph of old we will be able to say, "What others intended for evil, God meant for *good!*" (See Gen. 50:20.) Until then may we each be bold in claiming:

> *Surely **goodness** and mercy shall follow me all the days*
> *of my life: and I will dwell in the house of the LORD forever.*
>
> (Psalm 23:6)

If we fight "the *good* fight of faith," we will finally obtain "a *good* report" (1 Tim. 6:12, Heb. 11:2 KJV). To our delight we will discover that "*the goodness of God*" that led us to repentance at the start will lead us to New Jerusalem at the end (See Ro. 2:4). So saints of God—

> *Behave courageously, and the LORD will be with*
> **THE GOOD.**
>
> (2 Chronicles 19:11, See Ec. 9:2.)

If we keep our part of this covenant agreement, God will certainly keep His. For "the eyes of the LORD are in every place, keeping watch on "**THE GOOD**" (Pr. 15:3, See Ec. 9:2).

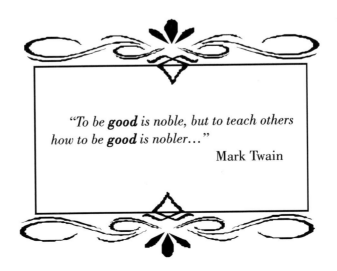

"*To be **good** is noble, but to teach others how to be **good** is nobler...*"
Mark Twain

Deep calls unto deep;
*For Your **goodness** we cry.*
Fill up these vessels,
O LORD, from on high.

Good Soldiers, Good Stewards,
Good Ground and Good Seed;
Good Trees with good fruit—
Stir these callings we plead.

To fight the good fight
Of faith is our goal;
To manifest good works—
Our God-given role.

At the end of the race,
Good reports we'll obtain,
*From the **GOOD LORD** Himself*
When goodness shall reign.

Endnotes

*1 It should also be mentioned that to a lesser degree the "net" of the Gospel was also drawn through the world under the Old Covenant 'catching' a nation called Israel, made up of both false and true Israelites. False Israelites were those who boasted in their natural genealogy, for they could trace their roots back to Abraham, but they had no heart of sincere devotion to the God of Abraham, nor did they walk in the faith of their father, Abraham. They were Israelites in name only, not in truth. True Israelites were the exact opposite, being responsive and submissive to the revelation of the living Word given during that particular era. At the end of this age, the redeemed of both the Old and New Covenants will blend as one and will together make up that eternal family entitled *the Good*. (See also Ps. 66:11, Ro. 9:6, Heb. 4:2.)

*2 Jeremiah 16:16 can be interpreted in a negative sense, if linked to the scriptures that follow it. However, it can be interpreted—as it is here—in a positive sense, if linked to the scriptures that precede it. Only the Holy Spirit knows absolutely the true sense in which it should be taken.

*3 Lockyer, Herbert, *All the Parables of the Bible* (Grand Rapids, Michigan, Zondervan Publishing House, 1963) p. 207, under *The Parable of the Good and Bad Fish*.

GOOD GROUND

---

*But others fell on **GOOD GROUND**, and yielded a crop, some a hundredfold, some sixty, some thirty.*

(Matthew 13:8)

"Now that which distinguished this **good ground** from the rest, was, in one word, **fruitfulness.** By this, true Christians are distinguished from hypocrites, that they bring forth fruits of righteousness: shall ye be my disciples" (John 15:8).

Matthew Henry Commentary on Matthew 13:1-23, "The Parable of the Sower"

GOOD GROUND

*But others fell on **GOOD GROUND**...*

(Matthew 13:8)

*I*n Matthew, chapter 13, we discover eight parables of the kingdom of heaven. Deciphering this first parable is essential for the serious Bible student. In comprehending its symbolic message, Jesus revealed that we lay the foundation for understanding "all parables" (Mk. 4:14).

In this story, Jesus likened the human heart to a parcel of *ground*. (See Mt. 13:1–23, Mk. 4:1–20, Lk. 8:4–15.) How appropriate an allegory this is! For we were originally sculpted by gentle, loving hands out of such base, soil-like substance ("the dust of the ground"—Gen. 2:7). In this same passage, Jesus also likened Himself to a Sower, sowing the seed of the Word into the earthen hearts of men:

> *And as He sowed, some seed fell by the wayside: and the birds came and devoured them.*
>
> *Some fell on stony places, where they did not have much earth; and they immediately sprang up; because they had no depth of earth:*
>
> *But when the sun was up they were scorched, and because they had no root, they withered away.*
>
> *And some fell among thorns, and the thorns sprang up and choked them.*
>
> *But others fell on **GOOD GROUND**, and yielded a crop, some a hundredfold, some sixty, some thirty.*
>
> (Matthew 13:4–8)

Jesus summed up this simple story by saying, "He who has ears to hear, let him hear!" Then to His chief disciples He declared, "It has been given to you to know the mysteries of the kingdom of heaven...For whoever has, to him more will be given, and he will have abundance..." (Mt. 13:9–12).

This 'abundant revelation knowledge,' given to all of God's chosen ones, will necessarily include a strong and even stern message, and an earnest and even urgent appeal, concerning the personal responsibility of those souls who are seeking *gardenhood*. No one will ever fill the title-position of being *the garden of the LORD* except he or she first captures the attention of the gracious Gardener with a life that could be described as *good ground*—fertile, deep, rich soil that potentially can be quite productive.

In a sense, we are courting this heavenly Husbandman, who must marry Himself to the earthen parcels of ground that bear His seed and produce His desired crop. We know God is not interested in merely making men religious. Jesus, the demanding inspector of the 'out of season' fig tree, is still searching for spiritual fruitfulness among those who claim to be His offspring. The King James Version of this parable says that those who are truly "good ground" bring forth "fruit." So the end result of being "good ground" is to become fruitbearers.

Spiritually speaking, fruitfulness falls into four main categories.

(1) **The "fruit" of the divine nature manifesting in us.** (For "the fruit of the Spirit is love, joy, peace, patience, kindness, goodness, faithfulness, gentleness, and self-control." (Gal. 5:22–23 NIV, See also Eph. 5:9.)

(2) **The "fruit" of righteous deeds**: also called "fruit unto holiness," "fruits worthy of repentance" and being "fruitful in every good work" (Ja. 3:18, Ro. 6:22, Mt. 3:8, Col. 1:10).

(3) **The "fruit" of souls being added to the kingdom.** This is described as gathering "fruit for life eternal" (Jn. 4:36).

(4) **The "fruit" of praise**, to be offered to God continually (Heb. 13:15).

Bearing fruit like this is not for our glory, but God's; it is not for our benefit, but for the benefit of others. Jesus even claimed, "By this My Father is glorified; that you bear **much fruit**; so you will be My disciples" (Jn. 15:8).

So if we are to be effective in this world, let us diligently study the four different 'agricultural' conditions of heart we can provide the Savior/Sower. If we are the expert, heaven-bound 'horticulturists' we should be, our response to the first three soil tests should be, *"God forbid!"* The fourth soil test should make us plead every single day and with every breath we take, *"God permit it! God perform it! God bring it to pass!"*

WAYSIDE GROUND

God forbid that the Word declared unto us be like "seed sown by the wayside." This term, "the wayside," refers to the hardened, impacted earth of much-traveled pathways that normally surround cultivated fields. These paths, and the hearts they represent, have been so hardened by life—being trodden down by the foot of men—that they have become impervious to change. What seed happens to fall there is quickly stolen by fiendish, demonic 'birds.'

Sometimes *hardened* by difficult or tragic situations in life, sometimes *hardened* through unbelief or willful sin, hearts such as these are easy prey for the wicked one. 2 Timothy 2:26 says they are "taken captive by him to do his will."

If we are wise, we will diligently watch over the condition of our hearts lest we become insensitive to God and unreceptive to His Word. We will never make directional decisions in life just because 'everybody else takes that route.' This very attitude of mind is dangerous and contagious. It often solidifies impressionable hearts by pouring them into an ill-shaped mold of that which the world terms the 'status quo.'

❧ **A Hard Heart**—If we are to escape this dreadful plight, it would do us good to review some biblical examples of the kind of attitudes that can create a 'hard heart.'

- **Sorrow**—Job, devastated by a series of disasters, lamented over how easy it would be for him to be *hardened in sorrow* (Jb. 6:10 KJV).

- **Rebelling Against God or Forgetting His Power**—The Jews, newly delivered from Egyptian bondage, *hardened* their hearts by rebelling against God's commandments, spoken audibly from Mt. Sinai, and by forgetting His power; displayed so mightily at the opening of the Red Sea (Heb. 3:8–15).

- **Insensitivity to the Needs of Others**—The Israelites were also given the divine mandate not to mercilessly *harden* their hearts against the poverty stricken, but rather to open their hearts and their hands wide unto the poor to meet their need (Dt. 15:7–11).

- **Forgetting the History of God's Judgments**—The lords of the Philistines, plagued by mice and emerods, admonished one another not to *harden* their hearts, as Pharaoh did, against the judgment of God that had fallen on their cities, but rather to repent (1 Sam. 6:6).

- **Pride**—King Nebuchadnezzar, boasting of his earthly accomplishments, was suddenly given over to a spirit of insanity. This severe, though temporary chastisement came because the potentate's mind and heart were *"hardened in pride"* (Dan. 5:20).

- **Religious Tradition**—In the New Testament, we read of Jesus rebuking those Pharisees who "watched Him, whether He would heal...on the Sabbath day; that they might accuse Him." Though they were very religious, they were so rigid in their tradition, they could not receive the very gifts that fell from heaven before their skeptical eyes. The Scripture states that Jesus was grieved because of the *"hardness of their hearts"* (Mk. 3:5).

- **Unbelief**—This was certainly not a condition exclusively reserved to those who blatantly rejected the Messiah. Even Jesus' most intimate disciples had to be reprimanded more than once for allowing their hearts to become *hardened in unbelief* (Mk. 6:52; 8:17; 16:14).

〜・ **Sin**—In Hebrews 3:13 we are commanded to "exhort one another daily" lest any of us be "*hardened* through the deceitfulness of sin."

So whether this compacted condition results from sorrow, rebellion, forgetfulness, coldness, lack of compassion, pride, ignorance, ignoring God's judgments, religious traditionalism, hypocrisy, unbelief or sin, the end result is still the same. Hearts thus hardened cannot effectively receive the implantation of the seed of God's Word. Such is the useless and fruitless outcome of those unfortunate persons that Jesus categorized as being *wayside ground.* We should be driven to our knees at the mere consideration of such an awful prospect.

STONY GROUND

God forbid that the Word received in our spirits be like seed falling on "stony ground." Jesus explained that such a person is one who:

> ...hears the Word, and immediately receives it with joy:
> Yet he has no root in himself, but endures only for a while. For when tribulation or persecution [temptation or affliction] arises because of the Word, immediately he stumbles.
> (Matthew 13:20–21, Mark 4:16–17, Luke 8:13)

The King James Version of Matthew 13:21 says "by and by he is *offended.*" In the hearts of such individuals, there may initially be a thin covering of soil in which the Word-seed can jubilantly grow, but how shallow this surface joy proves to be! In the end, the exposed, rock-like hard-heartedness is more impenetrable than compacted earth.

How often it is discovered (and how deeply heaven grieves) that a hardened backslider is, at times, less affected by the convicting power of the Word than many who have never been enlightened to the truth. No wonder Peter said "it would have been better for them not to have known the way of righteousness, than having known it, to turn from the holy commandment delivered to them" (2 Pt. 2:21).

How tragic it is that the joyous sound of tambourines and the singing and dancing of Israelite women at the edge of the Red Sea could be replaced so quickly by self-centered, unthankful murmurings at the bitter waters of Marah! How quickly God's people forgot (in only three day's time) the God who miraculously delivered them from Egypt's bonds!

But they had no *root* in themselves.

When *tribulation* came, they were quickly offended.

How tragic it is also that the memory of trembling, fiery Mt. Sinai could fade away so easily before the glittering gold of an idolatrous calf and the sensual swayings of lust-filled men and women!

But again—they had no *root* in themselves.

When *temptation* came, they were quickly offended.

And history reveals countless thousands of others who have been offended at God—because of tribulation, persecution, temptation or affliction. But Jesus said, *"Blessed is he who is not **offended** because of Me"* (Mt. 11:6).

We who are born again should of all people be rooted in stability, for within our hearts dwells *"the Root and the Offspring of David"* (Rev. 22:16). We are inseparably linked to the Vine whose roots reach beyond all others. He is the Firstborn of all creation. He is the Beginning and the End, the First and the Last, the Alpha and the Omega—with deep, tenacious roots reaching far beyond the borders of time—penetrating eternity past and eternity future. He is the unchanging One, the epitome of that which is permanent and enduring, the central theme of the forever-settled plan of God.

We are commanded in Colossians 2:7 to be *"**rooted** and built up in Him...established in the faith."* We position ourselves unshakably in Christ this way by simple submission, tender devotion and unswerving trust.

We are also commanded to be *"**rooted** and grounded in love"*: sincere love for God, fervent love for the brethren, and a deep, soul-gripping love for the lost (Eph. 3:17). Furthermore, Psalm 119:165 (KJV) states, "Great peace have they which *love* Thy law; and nothing shall *offend* them." The New King James says "nothing causes them to stumble." The word translated *law* here is *Torah*, which means more than God's laws and commandments. The Torah is the Pentateuch, the first five books of the Bible. These beginning Bible books contain many promises, God's original purpose for man, prophecies of the Messiah and of the glorious restoration He will eventually bring. Deep love for this and the rest of the revelation of God's Word will cause us to rest and trust—for love "bears all things, believes all things, hopes all things and endures all things" (1 Cor. 13:7).

If we are *rooted* in such a two-fold way—"in Christ" and "in love"—we will never be offended at God. We will never stumble over the adverse circumstances of life. Our initial "joy of salvation" will abide with us always—

in victory and in defeat. Even when the "burning sun" scorches us, we will not wither away. We will stand our ground in times of tribulation. We will maintain a winning spirit even when persecution rises. We will never lose our confidence in God even if heart-breaking affliction comes our way. We will never charge God foolishly or allow our hearts to become bitter.

This must be the prayerful longing of our souls if we are to escape the dreadful and unacceptable heart-trap of being *stony ground.*

THORNY GROUND

God forbid that the Word received in our hearts be like "seed falling among thorns." Jesus said that this is representative of the person who hears the Word—

> *And the cares of this world, and the deceitfulness of riches, and the lusts of other things entering in, choke the Word [and it becomes unfruitful].*
>
> (Mark 4:19 KJV, NKJV)

Luke 8:14 declares that such an individual will be *"choked with cares, riches and pleasures of life, and bring no fruit to maturity."* How craftily and subtly these thorns can destroy! (See Pr. 24:30–34.)

❋ The Cares of this Life

The *"cares of this life"* often are not even sinful in nature, yet these thorn-covered branches still seek to encircle us with murderous intent. These "cares" could be all the countless necessities, burdens, conflicts, tasks and time-consuming problems that are a part of living in this world. How often these concerns choke us spiritually until we are drained of energetic faith, sapped of joy and enthusiasm!

To the greatest possible degree, we must guard our hearts from such subtle, pricking intrusions of the enemy. This is accomplished by staying in the Word every day, maintaining a disciplined prayer life and ridding ourselves, as much as possible, of those unnecessary things that steal our attention from Jesus. If we are to bring forth fruit to perfection, we must provide God with the time in which He can manifest Himself to us. We must maintain the attitudes of heart that make us suitable candidates for the inflow and outflow of His power.

❋ The Deceitfulness of Riches

How careful we must be also to avoid being strangled spiritually by *"the deceitfulness of riches."* We know, without a doubt, that God would have His people to prosper, for "He gives us richly all things to enjoy" (1 Tim. 6:17). But we also know this idea can be taken to an erroneous extreme. Abraham was "the father of all them that believe" (Ro. 4:11), an example to us in many ways, and he "was very rich in livestock, in silver and in gold" (Gen. 13:2). Deuteronomy 8:18 also assures that it is God who gives us power "to get wealth," that He may establish His covenant in the earth. However, it is also true that gain is not necessarily a sign of godliness. Neither do godliness and the outpouring of God's blessing have to include the acquisition of material gain. In fact, sometimes the very opposite is true.

Moses, for instance, did not use faith to acquire the riches of Egypt; on the contrary, it was "by faith" that he esteemed "the reproach of Christ greater riches than the treasures in Egypt" (Heb. 11:26). When he forsook Egypt, he was stripped of all material advantage and became a mere shepherd in the desert just because he stood for righteous principles. Later on, God commanded that Moses' tribe, the Levites, were to be given no inheritance of land in Israel, for *the LORD was their portion.* (See Num. 18:20, Dt. 18:2.)

There are other Bible examples in which the acquisition of material riches would have compromised the will of God. Yet, it must be said loud and clear, that if our soul is prospering, God will rejoice to prosper us in other ways as well. (See 3 Jn. 2.)

Many righteous God-fearing men and women have been greatly used of God as channels of finance in the work of His kingdom—and this is a highly important and praiseworthy ministry. Admittedly, the Bible was never meant to be just a "Get-Rich-Quick-Plan" or a "Success and Motivation Handbook." How this holy book is desecrated (and how thorns grope through the darkness to destroy) when men twist the Bible's meaning by taking scriptures out of context and by not building on the proper discipleship foundation! Yet, simultaneously, how often some children of God are stripped of their potential inheritance by falsely equating poverty with humility.

1 Timothy 6:5–12 (KJV) brings balance to this whole discussion. In this convicting passage Paul warned His pastor-protege against *"perverse disputings of men of corrupt minds, and destitute of the truth, supposing that gain is godliness."* From such persons Paul urged Timothy to withdraw himself. Expanding this thought, the apostle argued:

> ***But godliness with contentment is great gain.***
> *For we brought nothing into this world, and it is certain we can carry nothing out.*
> *And having food and raiment let us be therewith content.*
> *But they that will be rich fall into temptation and a*

> *snare, and into many foolish and hurtful lusts, which drown men in destruction and perdition.*
>
> **For the love of money is the root of all evil:** *which while some coveted after, they have erred from the faith, and pierced themselves through with many sorrows.*
>
> *But thou, O man of God, flee these things; and follow after righteousness, godliness, faith, love, patience, meekness.*
>
> *Fight the good fight of faith, lay hold on eternal life…*

According to these writings, some individuals who attempt to use faith to gain wealth may actually be erring from the faith (if their *love of money* is a greater motivation than their *love of God*). Fighting the good fight of faith involves, to such a greater degree, laying hold on those things which last eternally.

Devotion to the will of God must be our first priority. Then, if riches come, those used of God to procure them will have the right spirit. They will consider themselves good stewards over what actually belongs to God. This must have been what Jesus was referring to in His discussion with Peter over earthly riches. Though He explained, "It is easier for a camel to go through the eye of a needle, than for a rich man to enter into the kingdom of God," He also added, "…*with God* all things are possible" (Mt. 19:26). In other words, the key issue is being in cooperation *"with God."* The "eye of the needle" is a small door in the large gates of ancient, walled cities. It is possible for a camel to pass through the "eye of the needle," but it would have to do so on its knees. So those who are blessed materially must stay on their knees as humble stewards over what belongs to God.

It is possible, when covetousness rules the heart of a man, for riches to destroy any possible spiritual fruit. But it is also just as possible that when devotion to God rules a person's motives, riches procured for the kingdom can produce much fruit. God definitely anoints certain individuals to fill this role in the church and without their unselfish and faithful service His work would greatly suffer. Yet on the opposite extreme, sometimes God anoints others to deny self by shunning material possessions. Both paths of service have value, so neither should be excluded from the list of options. The most important thing is the pursuit of the living Word—the perfect revelation of the will of God for each of our individual lives—and let all things be done for His glory and the good of others.

❈ The Lust of Other Things

Finally, how careful we must be also to avoid the deathly, constricting, thorny grip of the "lusts of other things." To understand this statement we must first realize that the word *lust* refers to more than just an out-of-control sexual drive. Lust is *selfish desire.*

Lust can attach its slimy, sinful tentacles to many things.

A person can lust after fame, position, power or recognition.

A person can lust after praise or sympathy.

A person can lust after food or possessions.

A person can lust after an undue amount of sleep, entertainment or certain sinful habits. Of course, any person can also be overtaken with desire through the eyes and through the heart for the gratification of the base, sensual side of the fallen Adam nature—resulting in adultery, fornication, lasciviousness, homosexuality, lesbianism and numerous perversities. This is a serpent with lethal venom.

One area yielded to lust almost invariably leads to another. Those who allow these thorn-like lusts to encircle their spirits, after having once been delivered, often become quite bankrupt spiritually—insensitive to God and uncaring concerning His will. No wonder Peter made the desperate plea, "Beloved, I beg you as sojourners and pilgrims, abstain from fleshly *lusts* which war against the soul" (1 Pt. 2:11). How often even the mighty have fallen into this sensual snare—for she has "cast down many wounded...many strong men have been slain by her" (Pr. 7:26 KJV).

No one is exempt from the possibility. Therefore, we must ever watch and pray, lest we enter into temptation, lest we allow our hearts to fall into the trap of being *thorny ground.*

GOOD GROUND

God permit that we ever be categorized as "Good Ground!" Jesus explained that the seed—

> ...on the **good ground** are they, which in an honest
> and good heart, having heard the Word, keep it, and bring
> forth fruit with patience.
>
> (Luke 8:15 KJV)

So to be good ground we must maintain an "honest and good heart": sincerely loyal to the Word and devoted to its fulfillment.

1 Timothy 1:19 encourages us to hold to "faith, and a good conscience; which some having rejected concerning the faith have suffered shipwreck." Hebrews 13:18 (KJV) asserts that "in all things" we must be "willing to live *honestly.*" To be *honest-hearted* this way is to be a person of scruples, a person

of integrity: honorable, fair, truthful, veracious, candid, open, plain, frank, straightforward, aboveboard and forthright—with God and with men.

David described this good ground condition of heart when he wrote the prayerful words: "Behold, You desire truth in the inward parts: and in the hidden part You will make me to know wisdom" (Ps. 51:6). The Psalmist penned these words after having made some extremely grave errors in his life. But when confronted by the prophet Nathan, he was honest. He did not try to hypocritically or pridefully defend his sin. He rather repented and offered God "a broken and a contrite heart" (Ps. 51:17).

David was restored and the Word-seed was again embedded in the warm, moist soil of his tear-drenched soul. So good ground may not always be a person free from mistakes or failings, but rather a person who chooses to maintain a willing spirit. A good ground believer will often plow and weed the Adam-soil of his human heart. He will constantly inspect his attitudes in order to produce a suitable plot of ground for the heavenly Sower who is so selective. Those who do this are made to know the wisdom of God in that inward chamber called "the hidden man of the heart." Watered by weeping, the seed of the Word germinates there and begins to grow.

In Jeremiah 4:3, God commanded His erring people:

> "Break up your fallow ground, and do not sow among thorns."

Hosea 10:12 (KJV) also similarly warned:

> Sow to yourselves in righteousness, reap in mercy; break up your fallow ground: for it is time to seek the LORD, till He come and rain righteousness upon you.

Fallow ground is land left untilled or unsown after plowing. It has unfortunately become hardened again. Because this unacceptable condition can result in ungerminated seed or weak-rooted plants, the ground must be broken up again.

In like manner, if we are not careful, our hearts newly saved and freshly 'plowed' can again become hardened again. To maintain our status as good ground, we must daily 'cut deep furrows' inwardly with the plowshare of Holy Spirit conviction. We must 'till our souls' with self-examination and travailing prayer.

We must present ourselves suitable candidates for the implantation of the Word-seed, always broken and always ready for the righteousness imparting rain of the Holy Spirit. Then, and then alone, can we bring forth true spiritual fruit: the luscious and precious products resulting from the union of the Word and the Spirit in the inner man.

THE FINAL CHALLENGE

We should also consider another integral aspect of this parable.

It is a great accomplishment to fulfill the calling to be **good ground**. The final challenge, though, concerns not what we are, but what we do. All who are good ground are to be praised, but Jesus said that some of these earthen plots would bring forth *"a hundredfold, some sixty, some thirty."*

We can be satisfied with only a partial manifestation of fruitfulness, or we can fervently pursue the "mark of the prize of the high calling" that God has given to each one of us (Ph. 3:14 KJV).

Possibly, the three levels of fruitfulness Jesus mentioned relate to the temple of God. We can live in the holy of holies, the holy place or the outer court—which speaks of living in the spirit realm, the soulish realm or the fleshly realm in serving God.

The challenge has been presented. Let us be patient and persistent, for fruit never develops overnight. Let us persevere unceasingly, even when the dark, foreboding clouds hover threateningly. "He who observes the wind will not sow, and he who regards the clouds will not reap" (Ec. 11:4).

Let us be as resolute, determined and fervent as the purpose of God that burns within our regenerated hearts. Let us purpose that we must reach our full potential in God (our *hundredfold* measure). For when we finish this race, we will not only review what we did in this life. Most likely, we will be able to also behold what we DID NOT DO and what we COULD HAVE DONE.

We know that dirt is relatively useless unless it successfully brings forth flora-life. In like manner, our sojourn in the flesh is a miserable waste unless we successfully bring forth the fruit-life of the Word and the Spirit. How wonderful, true and important this is!

Some say that the name of **Adam** comes from the Hebrew word *adamah* which quite appropriately means *the ground*. Though he was initially perfect, the first Adam finally proved to be, at least for a season, unfit, infertile soil.

He was "the first man...of the earth, made of dust" (1 Cor. 15:47).

The "last Adam" (Jesus) proved Himself to be good ground in the highest sense. He was "the second Man"— [the second 'perfect' man]—"THE LORD FROM HEAVEN" (1 Cor. 15:45, 47 KJV).

Our challenge now is to identify with Him and become **GOOD GROUND** as He most certainly was. And really there is no other choice to make! So let us be all that we can be for the heavenly Husbandman—then let us "ask of the LORD rain in the time of the latter rain" (for the Word-seed must be watered by the Spirit) (Zec. 10:1). This, too, is *the deep calling to the deep*. For the *deep* desire we have to walk in this identity is only a response to God's *deep* desire for us.

Deep calls unto deep;
O LORD may we be—
Good ground for Your seed,
Bearing fruit unto Thee:

The fruit of Your character,
The fruit of souls won,
The fruit of good works,
And praise to the Son;

Fruit the Husbandman
Yearns to obtain,
So He sends us His Word
As heavenly rain.

It will not return void,
But accomplish His will.
This also is "deep
Unto deep"—calling still.

GOOD SEED

---

*The field is the world; the **GOOD SEED** are the children of the kingdom.*
                                    (Matthew 13:38 KJV)

I tell you the truth, unless a kernel of wheat falls to the ground and dies, it remains only a single seed. But if it dies, it produces **MANY SEEDS ... MUCH GRAIN ... MUCH FRUIT ... A PLENTIFUL HARVEST** *of new lives.*

(John 12:24 NIV, NKJV, KJV, LB)

... The harvest truly is great, but the laborers are few; therefore pray the LORD of the harvest to send out laborers into **HIS HARVEST.**

(Luke 10:2)

And another angel came out of the temple, crying with a loud voice to Him who sat on the cloud, Thrust in Your sickle and reap...for **THE HARVEST OF THE EARTH** *is ripe.*

(Revelation 14:15)

O **MY THRESHING** *AND* **THE GRAIN OF MY FLOOR!** *That which I have heard from the LORD of hosts, the God of Israel, I have declared to you.*

(Isaiah 21:10)

Many Seeds

Much Grain

Much Fruit

A Plentiful Harvest

His Harvest

The Harvest of the Earth

His Threshing

The Grain of His Floor

Grain

His Wheat

Sheaves

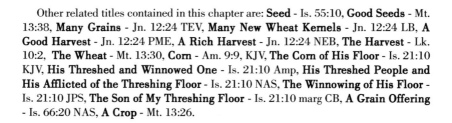

Other related titles contained in this chapter are: **Seed** - Is. 55:10, **Good Seeds** - Mt. 13:38, **Many Grains** - Jn. 12:24 TEV, **Many New Wheat Kernels** - Jn. 12:24 LB, **A Good Harvest** - Jn. 12:24 PME, **A Rich Harvest** - Jn. 12:24 NEB, **The Harvest** - Lk. 10:2, **The Wheat** - Mt. 13:30, **Corn** - Am. 9:9, KJV, **The Corn of His Floor** - Is. 21:10 KJV, **His Threshed and Winnowed One** - Is. 21:10 Amp, **His Threshed People and His Afflicted of the Threshing Floor** - Is. 21:10 NAS, **The Winnowing of His Floor** - Is. 21:10 JPS, **The Son of My Threshing Floor** - Is. 21:10 marg CB, **A Grain Offering** - Is. 66:20 NAS, **A Crop** - Mt. 13:26.

*For surely I will command, and will sift the house of Israel among all nations, as **GRAIN** is sifted in a sieve, yet not the smallest **GRAIN** shall fall to the ground.*

(Amos 9:9)

*His winnowing fan is in His hand, and He will thoroughly clean out His threshing floor, and gather **HIS WHEAT** into the barn; but He will burn up the chaff with unquenchable fire.*

(Matthew 3:12)

Those who sow in tears shall reap in joy.

*He who continually goes forth weeping, bearing seed for sowing [precious seed] shall doubtless come again with rejoicing, bringing his **SHEAVES** with him.*

(Psalm 126:5–6 NKJV, KJV)

GOOD SEED

*The field is the world; the **GOOD SEED** are the children of the kingdom..*

(Matthew 13:38 KJV)

*W*ithin the last few chapters we have been blessed to behold with our hearts the revelation of two very beautiful, important and related title-positions—the calling to be **GOOD GROUND** and the calling to blossom as **GOD'S GARDEN.**

GOOD GROUND is primarily a challenge to every hearer of the Word to offer the Savior/Sower the kind of heart He desires: the kind of earthen plot in which He can effectively plant His seed.

GOD'S GARDEN emphasizes the resulting love-relationship that exists between the heavenly Husbandman and all those redeemed, cultivated and protected plots that together make up His bride and rejoice to bring forth His choice fruit.

In this chapter we will discover yet another excellent, related calling: that of becoming **GOOD SEED.** The exceeding beauty of this title-position is the maturing of the purpose of God that it reveals: the completion of a spiritual cycle. Because if we grow in God as we should, yielding to the nurturing influence of His Word, in the final stage we end up becoming the very thing that was initially sown in our earthen hearts.

We become seed. We become **good seeds** (Mt. 13:38).
We become "**seed** to the sower" (Is. 55:10).
We become individual Word-seeds sown in the earth.
And wherever we are planted, kingdom dominion manifests.

This is to be expected, for we are **children of the kingdom** (a revelation already celebrated in a previous chapter). Through us, the kingdom of heaven manifests in a world very much opposed to its establishment. In us, the life and the values of that spiritual kingdom are perpetuated from generation to generation—as we consistently take over more 'territory' in the name of the LORD.

This is a great privilege and a great mystery. And this is the wondrous seed-potential hidden in the garden-heart of every good ground believer.

THE MYSTERIOUS PARABLE

Jesus' famed parable of "**The Wheat and the Tares**" is the one in which we find several of the main title-callings discussed in this chapter. This symbolic story is the second of eight parables of the kingdom of heaven contained in the thirteenth chapter of Matthew and is as follows:[*1]

> *Another parable He put forth to them, saying: The kingdom of heaven is like a man who sowed **good seed** in his field;*
>
> *But while men slept, his enemy came and sowed tares among **the wheat** and went his way.*
>
> *But when **the grain** had sprouted and produced **a crop**, then the tares also appeared.*
>
> *So the servants of the owner came and said to him, "Sir, did you not sow **good seed** in your field? How then does it have tares?"*
>
> *He said to them, "An enemy has done this." The servants said to him, "Do you want us then to go and gather them up?"*
>
> *But he said, "No, lest while you gather up the tares you also uproot **the wheat** with them.*
>
> *Let both grow together until **the harvest**, and at the time of harvest I will say to the reapers, First gather together the tares and bind them in bundles to burn them, but gather **the wheat** into my barn."*
>
> (Matthew 13:24–30)

After hearing this Spirit-breathed similitude, the disciples requested, "Explain to us the parable of the tares of the field." This is the answer the Teacher of all teachers gave:

> *He who sows **the good seed** is the Son of Man.*
>
> *The field is the world, **the good seeds** are the **sons of the kingdom [the children of the kingdom** - KJV], but the tares are the sons of the wicked one.*
>
> *The enemy who sowed them is the devil, the harvest is the end of the age, and the reapers are the angels.*
>
> *Therefore as the tares are gathered and burned in the fire, so it will be at the end of this age.[*2]*
>
> *The Son of Man will send out His angels, and they will gather out of His kingdom all things that offend, and those who practice lawlessness,*
>
> *And will cast them into the furnace of fire. There will be wailing and gnashing of teeth.*

*Then the righteous will shine forth as the sun in the
kingdom of their Father. He who has ears to hear, let him
hear!*

(Matthew 13:37–43)

THE CALLING TO BE "GOOD SEED"

In this passage of Scripture God's people are referred to as **good seed.**
This particular title contains the revelation of four main aspects of sonship:

(1)   Being buried with Christ (as with the planting of a seed).
(2)   Being resurrected with Christ (as with the germination of a seed).
(3)   Growing in Christ (as with the growth potential in a seed).
(4)   Reproducing and multiplying (as with the perpetuation of seed).

**So simply put, fulfilling the calling to be "good seed" represents, in a
spiritual sense: dying, living, growing and reproducing.**

As usual, in order to fully comprehend the mystery of this title-calling, it
is imperative that we see how it was initially fulfilled in the firstborn Son. In
foretelling the purpose and value of His agony on Calvary, Jesus claimed:

*Most assuredly, I say unto you, unless **a grain of wheat**
falls into the ground and dies, it remains alone; but if it
dies, it produces **MUCH GRAIN**.*

(John 12:24)

Other renderings of this same passage enhance its meaning, while
revealing a number of other related titles for God's people:

*I tell you the truth, unless a kernel of wheat falls to the
ground and dies, it remains only a single seed. But if it
dies, it produces **MANY SEEDS... MANY GRAINS...
MUCH FRUIT...MANY NEW WHEAT KERNELS...
A GOOD HARVEST... A RICH HARVEST... A
PLENTIFUL HARVEST** OF NEW LIVES.*

(NIV, TEV, KJV, NEB, PME, LB)

All sons and daughters of God are the **many seeds** and **the plentiful
harvest** resulting from what Jesus accomplished through His seed-like death,
burial and resurrection.

As harvested grain, we can be used of God two main ways: either to
become *bread* (nourishing the hearts of the spiritually hungry and nourishing
the heart of God) or we can be used as *seed* (producing a new crop of believers
in the world). (See Is. 55:10–11.) Both of these callings speak of total self-

sacrifice and both of these callings are given to every son and daughter of God. We are called to be *bread* and *seed* that we might perpetuate the work of the Holy One of Israel who was Himself both *bread* and *seed*. (See Jn. 6:51.)

In the next two verses after John 12:24, Jesus explains how we become seed sown in the earth, that we may each produce our own 'harvest' unto the LORD. First He warned:

> *He who loves his life shall lose it, and he who hates his*
> *life in this world will keep it for eternal life.*
>
> (John 12:25)

Then he urged:

> *If anyone serves Me, let him follow Me...*
>
> (John 12:26)

In other words, our Forerunner stressed that we will never become **good seed** if we love the natural things of life apart from God and pursue the gratification of the flesh that they offer. In the end, we lose all. We totally miss that which is valuable and sell out for that which perishes. If we instead shun the vanity and futility of living for self and 'lose our lives' in the service of God, Jesus pointed out, "Where I am, there My servant will be also" (Jn. 12:26).

The location Jesus was referring to is not so much a physical position. Rather, it is a position of the heart—an attitude of consecration where we also 'fall into the ground and die,' along with the firstborn Son.

With respect to the children of God, this 'seed-death' is primarily self-renunciation. With Jesus it was literal death as well. As a grain of wheat He was buried in the ground in the tomb of Joseph of Arimathea. Three days later a 'germination' of sorts took place when the Son of God victoriously arose, quickened back to life by the power of the Holy Spirit. Then having emerged from the grave a mature stalk of resurrected wheat—heavy with seed—the triumphant Christ began sowing Himself into receptive hearts. His goal was to reproduce a multitude of offspring *after His kind.*

The phrases—*after his kind* (KJV), *according to its kind, according to their kind, after their kind,* or *after its kind*—are found a number of times in Genesis 1:11–25 and Genesis 7:14. It could well be entitled **God's law of reproduction**: the unchanging truth that the seed of a plant, animal or human being always bears within itself the very image of the original seed. This likeness is then passed down to each succeeding generation.

This is true also with respect to the offspring of the Most High. We have the imprint of His image within our hearts. We have inherited His attributes,

His abilities, His responsibilities and the right to share in His great and glorious destiny. If we dare, in a seed-like way, to identify with the original seed in His crucifixion and self-denial, then we will also be blessed to share in His victory over death, hell and the grave:

For if we have been planted together in the likeness of
His death, we shall be also in the likeness of His resurrection.

(Romans 6:5 KJV)

How true is the statement, "As He is, so are we in this world!" (1 Jn. 4:17). We initially became **good seed** (individual kernels of wheat planted in the world) when we died to the carnal and said 'Yes' to the cross. Then, when we were born again, a 'germination' of sorts took place. We were quickened, made alive with the very life of God. Then we began a growing process—striving daily to fulfill our total potential as "**sons of the kingdom**" (Mt. 13:38).

The more we mortify the flesh with its affections and lusts, the more we are relating to the role of being individual kernels of wheat buried in the earth. The more we walk in the resurrection power in the Spirit—in "newness of life"—the more we are relating to the role of being individual stalks of wheat growing in the midst of a tare-filled world (Ro. 6:4).

Our chief calling, at least in this life, is to complete this spiritual cycle by becoming mature stalks, heavy with golden-ripe grain, ever ready to sow inspired word-seeds into the hearts of those who are receptive. This should be our daily passion—for by doing so, we fulfill spiritually that ancient command:

Be fruitful, and multiply, and replenish the earth, and
subdue it: and have dominion...

(Genesis 1:28 KJV)

By spiritually begetting other sons and daughters *'after our kind'* (reproducing and multiplying) we are actually 'replenishing the earth' with God-fearing, God-loving individuals who will aid in 'subduing' the evil that has taken up its abode here since the fall of Adam. As this transpires, we are simply reclaiming the 'dominion' God imparted at the start. In a manifest way, we become **the children of the kingdom** in the midst of a human race that knows little or nothing of its existence.

THE SEPARATION OF THE WHEAT FROM THE TARES

In the parable we have taken as the foundation of this particular title-study (Mt. 13:24–30), Jesus revealed that there will yet be a time of ultimate separation. Right before the final harvest, all tares must be removed from among the wheat. In this symbolic story, the field—in which both tares and wheat are sown—represents the entire world. It is spoken of, not just as "a field," but as "his field." As full of vice as it is, still, "The earth is the LORD'S and all its fullness" (Ps. 24:1).

The tares are spoken of as being the children of the wicked one. They are purposefully sown by the devil in the midst of the wheat in a desperate attempt to corrupt the final crop.

In order to comprehend the meaning of this scriptural symbol, it is important to first understand what tares are. There are four varieties that grow in the land of Israel. The one most likely referenced to in this passage is a kind of 'bearded' darnel, a poisonous grass, that looks almost exactly like wheat while the two are growing together. The seeds of this noxious plant can cause sleepiness, nausea, convulsions and even death. Therefore, they cannot be left in the field to be harvested along with the good grain. **There must be a separation.** However, it is only when the tares and wheat grow into full maturity that they can be distinguished one from the other without difficulty (the wheat is bent over heavy with grain, representative of humility, while the tares are upright, representative of pride).

In like manner, **children of the kingdom** and **children of the wicked one** at times may resemble one another—especially in the beginning stages of this earthly sojourn. Prior to salvation, unfortunately, most children of the kingdom spend a season of their lives caught up in the spirit of the world and bound by sin—appearing as if they were tares. Some even backslide for a period of time after salvation and indulge again in sin, denying the righteous nature that was birthed in them when they became sons of God. Until they repent and are renewed and restored, their true spiritual identity could easily be mistaken.

In a similar though opposite way, children of the wicked one can at times appear to be very religious, ordering their lives with various disciplines toward godliness, yet all the while they are lost and without God in this world. What a mystery it is that even in the professing church there are many who call themselves Christians and yet are Christless! Because they have never been truly born again or washed in the blood, they cannot be included among the redeemed. Though they appear to be wheat—they are actually tares.

As "The Parable of the Wheat and the Tares" plainly reveals, there are no servants of the householder who can declare ahead of time, without any chance of error, exactly who should or should not be included in the harvest. Therefore, let us "judge nothing before the time, until the LORD comes, who will both bring to light the hidden things of darkness and reveal the counsels of the hearts"

(1 Cor. 4:5). In that day, the angel-reapers will discern all things perfectly and sever the wicked from among the just, the counterfeit from among the true.

THE HARVEST

We have already established that there will be an ultimate harvest. All the redeemed will be gathered unto the LORD of the harvest at the end of this age, 'harvested' into absolute perfection.

It is just as true, though, that a spiritual harvest of the souls of men has been going on constantly for nearly two thousands years. The harvest began formally when Peter thrust in his Word-sickle on the day of Pentecost and reaped three thousand souls into the kingdom of God. A New Covenant time of reaping has been in effect worldwide ever since. God has anointed multiplied thousands of reapers to continue this important task. Jesus urged His disciples:

> *Do you not say, 'There are still four months and then*
> *comes the harvest?' Behold, I say to you, lift up your eyes*
> *and look at the fields, for they are already white for harvest!*
> (John 4:35)

This statement reveals the graveness and urgency of our charge. Ripened wheat is normally golden in color. It turns white right before it falls to the ground and rots. So Jesus was communicating that the time to reap was nearly past—in the day when He walked the earth. How much more urgent it is to 'thrust in the sickle' now!

Incidentally, these words were spoken when the disciples had come back from buying food in a Samaritan town. They said, "Rabbi eat!" Jesus responded, "I have food to eat of which you do not know…My food is to do the will of Him who sent Me and to finish His work" (Jn. 4:31-34). Jesus knew that the door of salvation would not fully open to all races and nationalities until after His death, but He also knew that the Samaritans (many of whom were part Gentile and part Israelite) were ready right then for the Gospel. It was God's timing. Later could be too late. So Jesus abode in Samaria two days and the Bible tells us that many believed on Him.

O, how God needs impassioned men and women who are sensitive to the potential for revival this way—harvesters *par excellence* who know how to even change set plans in order to follow the Spirit and reap in God's perfect timing. We know that great fulfillment and happiness await those who obey the harvest call, for the pledge has been given of old:

> *Those who sow in tears shall reap in joy.*
> *He who continually goes forth weeping, bearing seed*

*for sowing [precious seed] shall doubtless come again with
rejoicing, bringing his **SHEAVES** with him.*

(Psalm 126:5–6 NKJV, KJV)

This joy of harvest surely must be part of the 'wages' Jesus promised to
co-reapers: those who share with Him the responsibility of gathering "fruit for
eternal life." (Jn. 4:36, See Is. 9:1–3.)

BEYOND THE HARVEST

It must be said that gathering "**sheaves**" (bundles of souls won into the
kingdom) constitutes only the first step in the development of those who are
called "**His wheat.**" After being reaped each believer must then pass through
times of threshing, winnowing, then sifting. Each of these steps has its own
unique revelation, which we will now explore.

❧ Threshing the Wheat ────────────────────────

After wheat is harvested, it must be *threshed*—for valuable grain must be
separated from the stalk if it is to be useful to men. Unger's Bible Dictionary
explains that in Jesus' day especially, "The top of a rock was a favorite spot for
this purpose; on this the sheaves were spread out, and sometimes beaten with
flails—but more commonly by oxen. The oxen were either yoked side by side
and driven round over the grain, or yoked to a board or a block of wood, with
stones or pieces of iron fastened to the lower surface to make it rough. This was
dragged over the grain, beating out the kernels."[*3]

Through Isaiah, God lamented over the seed of Israel under his charge,
referring to them as "**My threshing and the grain of My floor**" (Is. 21:10).
Other translations of this title include: "**the corn of My floor**—KJV, **My threshed
and winnowed one**—Amp, **My threshed people and My afflicted of the
threshing floor**—NAS, and **the winnowing of My floor**—JPS." As God's
spokesman, Isaiah was prophesying to the Israelites of the soon-to-come invasion
of Babylon by the Persians. Many would soon be allowed to return home by the
Persians. They had been in bondage in Babylon for seventy years and it served
God's purpose. Their enslavement had been a time of threshing for the Israelites,
separating them from the dead stalk of carnality and idolatry, and the lifeless
chaff of devotionless ceremonialism.

God often uses negative circumstances in our lives to accomplish the same
end. Sometimes He simply uses the preaching of the Word. Paul illustrated this
by comparing ministers of the Word to oxen that thresh or tread out the grain.
(See 1 Cor. 9:9–10.) Of course, God does not overdo this threshing process, lest
the wheat be destroyed. (See Is. 28:28–29.)

🏵 Winnowing the Wheat

The prophet Joel described a time of great revival in these last days by prophesying that "the floors shall be full of wheat" (Jl. 2:24). He was speaking of the *winnowing* process. Once the wheat is gathered in and threshed, it must be *winnowed*: separated from the chaff so that pure grain remains.

In Bible times, this was usually accomplished with a tool called a *winnowing fan* or *a winnowing shovel*. By this device, the threshed wheat was thrown up into the wind. The chaff and remaining bits of straw were then blown to the side. The seed, being heavier, would fall straight down to the ground. John the Baptist spoke of the effect of Jesus' ministry by comparing it to this very process.

> ...He who is coming after Me is mightier than I... His winnowing fan is in His hand, and He will thoroughly clean out His threshing floor, and gather **HIS WHEAT** into the barn; but He will burn up the chaff with unquenchable fire.
>
> (Matthew 3:11–12, See also TEV, NIV.)

🏵 Sifting the Wheat

Sifting is the final stage in the preparation of wheat before it is stored in the garner. Sometimes trays were used which consisted of "meshed material held in wooden rims." More primitive sieves were made of "woven horsehair or other coarse material." This kind of device would purge out all the remaining chaff not blown away by the winnowing process.[*4]

Sifting is also used figuratively to show how God often deals with His chosen. Though God was referring primarily to Old Covenant Israel, the following scripture represents the New Covenant "Israel of God" as well:

> For surely I will command, and will sift the house of Israel among all nations, **as grain is sifted in a sieve**; yet not the smallest **GRAIN** shall fall to the ground.
>
> (Amos 9:9, Also compare Luke 22:31–32.)

🏵 The Revelation of the Symbol

These three processes speak of a progressive separation that must take place in **children of the kingdom** if they are to succeed in fulfilling their calling. "**His wheat**" must be:

(1) Separated from the world.
(2) Separated from that which is carnal and fleshly.
(3) Separated from that which is soulish and selfish.

We must even be separated from traditionalism, ceremonialism and all false religious beliefs and practices. Such a process of separation is effected in sons of God many ways: by the preaching of the Word, by the power of the Holy Spirit, by appropriating promises, by prayerfulness, by fasting, and even by facing tribulations and trials. If reacted to correctly, all these things will ultimately "work together for good to those who love God, to those who are the called according to His purpose" (Ro. 8:28).

The more we pass through the threshing, winnowing and sifting process, the less we are bound to the fallen Adam nature and the more Christlike we become. Then, having gone through this process ourselves we become God's means of continuing this process in others.

In these latter times, more than ever before, God intends to "thresh the mountains" (the kingdoms) by means of a new, sharp, threshing instrument (the church).*5 After the Gospel is preached in all the world for a witness unto all nations, with His winnowing shovel, the Most High will throw the kingdoms of this world up into the winds of tribulations. He will then "sift the nations with the sieve of futility," or, as the KJV puts it, "the sieve of vanity." (Is. 30:28; 41:15, See also 28:28–29, NIV, NKJV, Mt. 24:14.)

As global crises emerge that bring the world to the brink of destruction, all of men's answers will prove to be futile or vain—the "sieve of futility and vanity" will have its intended effect. All of this will serve only to *separate* the children of darkness from the children of light. That which is of vanity will be cast out, while the pure grain will be gathered to His bosom to enjoy intimate communion with a loving, eternal Father.

Having received this revelation, we should never fear, nor be discouraged if rejection comes. The last days will surely bring to birth an era of persecution against true Christianity. We should react as Jeremiah did (who was rejected and persecuted in his day). During his great time of trial he concluded, *"What is the chaff to the wheat?* (Jer. 23:28, See also Pr. 27:22.) The offspring of God may also be scorned, misunderstood and even wrongly scandalized, but still, we can echo the statement, *"What is the chaff to the wheat?"* If God be for us, who and what can be against us?

CONTAINERS OF LIFE
CO-LABORERS IN HARVEST

We must remember that life is resident in the grain. In the beginning, the stalk, the chaff and the grain all shared a common identity. However, once separated from the grain, the stalk and the chaff are relatively useless and go back to the dust. In like manner, until we are separated from the stalk and chaff of that which is worldly and carnal, we cannot perfectly be entitled **His Wheat.** We know the life of God is in us—and this life is far more valuable than the stalk-like, chaff-like carnality and worldliness that surrounds us.

We know that heaven and earth will pass away. The political institutions of this world will pass away. Social orders as we know them will pass away. Religious systems will pass away. That which is of darkness will pass away. Rebellion and unbelief will pass away and be no more. For all of this chaff must be burned with unquenchable fire. (See Heb. 12:25–29.)Those who are of God and of life will endure. They are destined to grow in God forever (for endless growth potential is hidden in the heart of every wheat kernel).*6

Taking this truth as our blessed hope, let us purpose not only to endure with grace the threshing, winnowing and sifting stages of life. Let us rejoice that the LORD of the harvest has included us in **His harvest.** He was the Firstborn, the original grain of wheat falling to the ground, in order to bring forth **many grains** in His image.

We, His many brethren, are the result.
WE ARE GOOD SEED, THE CHILDREN OF THE KINGDOM.
As He was grain, so we are grain.

As He was sent forth as a laborer into the harvest, so we are sent forth as laborers—for the fields are more ripe and more ready than ever. In Luke 10:2 Jesus lamented, "**THE HARVEST** truly is great, but the **LABORERS** are few." Then He requested of His disciples, "Pray the LORD of the harvest to send **LABORERS** into His harvest."

We can be bold in believing that this petition will soon be answered in an unprecedented way. The prophetic moment is drawing near when the Son of man will sit on a white cloud "having on His head a golden crown, and in His hand a sharp sickle" (Rev. 14:14). An angel will then come out of the temple in heaven, crying with a loud voice:

> *Thrust in Your sickle and reap: for the time is come*
> *for You to reap: for* ***THE HARVEST OF THE EARTH***
> *is ripe.*
>
> (Revelation 14:15)

We are "**LABORERS TOGETHER WITH GOD**"—"**GOD'S FELLOW WORKERS**" (1 Cor. 3:9 KJV, NKJV).*7

Let us, therefore, become one with the vision, considering it a 'labor of love.' May we be gripped with the realization that this "gospel of the kingdom" must be "preached in all the world as a witness to all the nations; and then the end will come." (1 Th. 1:3, Mt. 24:14, See Pr. 10:5; Jer. 8:20.) In that notable day, we who are entitled **GOOD SEED**, will be planted in a new and glorious age—a time when all God's royal offspring will blossom in matchless splendor and manifest spiritual fruit that will endure forever.

A FINAL THOUGHT

After wheat is threshed, winnowed and sifted, if not used as seed to produce a new crop, usually it is ground up to produce bread. This speaks of total self-denial, for the benefit of others and for the benefit of God. It speaks of sacrificing our lives to satisfy the starving hearts of those who hunger for the truth, and to satisfy God's hunger to be served and worshiped.

Ignatius, one of the early church fathers, made a reference to this concept when he was led, along with a number of other believers, into an arena to be devoured by wild beasts. Just prior to entering, Ignatius—soon to be martyred—made the statement:

> *"I am the wheat of Christ. I am going to be ground by
> the teeth of wild beasts that I may be found pure bread."*

May we always maintain a similar attitude—a willingness to give God our all.

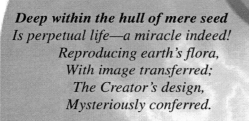

Deep within the hull of mere seed
Is perpetual life—a miracle indeed!
Reproducing earth's flora,
With image transferred;
The Creator's design,
Mysteriously conferred.

Deep in those hearts receiving God's call
Is a holy potential—surviving the fall!
Reproducing His image,
In daughters and sons;
*Yes, **deep calls to deep**,*
In these seed-like ones.

But the seed must be planted
In the 'ground' and then die,
Releasing Christlikeness
That does inward lie.

So yield yourselves now
To the Husbandman's cast.
He'll sow you on earth,
And reap you at last!

Endnotes

---

*1 The first of the eight parables, The Parable of the Sower, and also the seventh, The Parable of the Net, are explained in the chapters entitled *Good Ground* and *The Good* contained in this volume of **Our Glorious Inheritance**. The revelation of the third, The Parable of the Mustard Seed, is explained in this chapter. The revelation of the fourth parable, The Parable of the Leaven, is contained in Volume Four of **Our Glorious Inheritance** under the title *One Bread*. The fifth parable, The Parable of Hidden Treasure, and the sixth, The Parable of the Goodly Pearl, are both unveiled in Volume One under the titles *Treasure Hid in the Field* and *The Pearl of Great Price*.

*2 In Matthew 13:40 the King James Version explains that these things will happen at *"the end of this world."* But the Greek word translated *world* in the King James is *aion*, a word more correctly translated *age*. At the coming of Jesus, the world as we presently know it will end and the "age of grace" will come to completion. But the earth itself will not suddenly cease to exist. Quite the contrary, according to the Scripture, the kingdom of God will be established in this world for a thousand years. Then, after being renovated by fire, a new earth will abide forever. For this reason the New King James Version and other translations substitute the word *age* for *world*.

*3 Unger, Merrill, *Unger's Bible Dictionary*, (Moody Press, Chicago, Illinois) p. 1092 under *Threshing Floor*.

*4 Miller, *Harper's Bible Dictionary*, (NavPress Inc. Colorado Springs, Colorado) p. 682 under *Sieve*.

*5 This scripture (Is. 41:15) will most likely have a dual fulfillment: in the church and in Israel. Zechariah 14:1–3 and other passages clearly indicate that Israel, though a helpless worm in the sight of all nations, will miraculously—by the help of God—overcome them. Thus, she will "thresh the mountains" as she discovers her Messiah. The true Israel of God will then be ushered into her position of headship during the millennial era—just as God originally promised in Deuteronomy 28:13.

*6 It is quite interesting to see that wheat kernels have a triune nature: the outer shell or bran, the white, pulpy 'meaty' part inside called the endosperm, and the wheat germ in which is found the life of the grain. This relates to the triune nature of those who are entitled **His Wheat**—for we are body, soul and spirit. In a similar way, the 'life of God' is not in our flesh; it is not in our souls; it is resident in our regenerated spirits.

*7 The similar title–callings of *Laborers* and *Workers* will be explored in future volumes of **Our Glorious Inheritance**.

GOOD SOLDIERS
OF JESUS CHRIST

———————————————————

You therefore must endure hardship, as a
GOOD SOLDIER OF JESUS CHRIST.
(2 Timothy 2:3)

*Your **TROOPS** will be willing on Your day of battle. Arrayed in holy majesty, from the womb of the dawn, You will receive the dew of Your youth.*

(Psalm 110:3 NIV)

*It is He that buildeth His stories in the heaven, and hath founded **HIS TROOP IN THE EARTH**.*

(Amos 9:6 KJV)

*The LORD gave the Word: great was **THE COMPANY** of those who proclaimed it.*

(Psalm 68:11)

*...What will ye see in the Shulamite? As it were **THE COMPANY OF TWO ARMIES**.*

(Song of Solomon 6:13 KJV)

*So I prophesied as He commanded me, and the breath came into them, and they lived, and stood upon their feet, **AN EXCEEDINGLY GREAT ARMY**.*

(Ezekiel 37:10)

*Who is she who looks forth as the morning, fair as the moon, clear as the sun, awesome as **AN ARMY WITH BANNERS [TROOPS WITH BANNERS, A BANNERED HOST]**?*

(Song of Solomon 6:10 NKJV, Dar, Amp)

HIS TROOPS

HIS TROOP IN THE EARTH

THE COMPANY

THE COMPANY OF TWO ARMIES

AN EXCEEDINGLY GREAT ARMY

AN ARMY WITH BANNERS

TROOPS WITH BANNERS

A BANNERED HOST

THE ARMIES OF
THE LIVING GOD

THE ARMY OF THE LORD

THE LORD'S ARMY

*Then David spoke…"Who is this uncir-cumcised Philistine, that he should defy **THE ARMIES OF THE LIVING GOD**?"*

(1 Samuel 17:26)

*And He said, "No, rather I indeed come now as Captain of **THE HOST OF THE LORD** [Commander of **THE ARMY OF THE LORD**]." And Joshua fell on his face to the earth, and bowed down, and said to Him, "What has my LORD to say to His servant?"*

*And the Captain of **THE LORD'S HOST** [Commander of **THE LORD'S ARMY**] said to Joshua, "Remove your sandals from your feet, for the place where you are standing is holy." And Joshua did so.*

(Joshua 5:14–15 NAS, NKJV)

*"For I have bent Judah, **MY BOW**, fitted **THE BOW** with Ephraim, and raised up your sons, O Zion, against your sons, O Greece, and made you like **THE SWORD OF A MIGHTY MAN**."*

*Then the LORD will be seen over them, and **HIS ARROW** will go forth like lightning. The LORD God will blow the trumpet, and go with whirlwinds from the south.*

(Zechariah 9:13–14)

The Host of the Lord

The Lord's Host

The Sword of a Mighty Man

His Bow

His Arrow

A Polished Shaft

Weapons of Good

His Royal Horse in the Battle

The Violent

Other related titles contained in the chapter are: **His Army** - Ps. 110:3 Har, **His Armies** - Ex. 7:4, **The Armies of Israel** - 1 Sam. 17:10, **The Armies in Heaven** - Rev. 19:14, **Fellow Soldiers** - Ph. 2:25, **Soldiers** - 2 Tim. 2:4, **His Warriors** - Is. 13:3 NIV, **His Mighty Warriors** - Is. 13:3 NAS, **His Host** - Ps. 110:3 RSV, **The Host** - Js. 3:2 KJV, **The Host of the Children of Israel** - Ob. 20, **His Hosts** - Ps. 103:21, **Volunteers** - Ps. 110:3, **The Weapons of His Indignation** - Is. 13:5 KJV, **The Weapons of His Wrath** - Is. 13:5 NIV, **Weapons of Righteousness** - Ro. 6:13 PME, Mon, **His Majestic Horse in Battle** - Zec. 10:3 NAS, **His Goodly Horse in Battle** - Zec. 10:3 KJV, **A Polished Arrow** - Is. 49:2 NIV, **A Select Arrow** - Is. 49:2 NAS, **His Sword** - Zec. 9:13 LB, **A Warrior's Sword** - Zec. 9:13 NAS, **Forceful Men** - Mt. 11:12 NIV, **Daughter of Troops** - Mi. 5:1, **The Valiant of Israel** - Song 3:7, **The Armies in Heaven** - Rev. 19:14.

*"And He has made My mouth like a sharp sword; in the shadow of His hand He has hidden Me, and made Me **A POLISHED SHAFT**; in His quiver He has hidden Me.*

And He said to me, 'You are My servant, O Israel, in whom I will be glorified.' "

(Isaiah 49:2–3)

*...But, like men rescued from certain death, put yourselves in God's hands as **WEAPONS OF GOOD [WEAPONS OF RIGHTEOUSNESS]** for His own purposes.*

(Romans 6:13 PME, Mon)

*...for the LORD of hosts will visit His flock, the house of Judah, and will make them as **HIS ROYAL HORSE IN THE BATTLE**.*

(Zechariah 10:3)

*And from the days of John the Baptist until now the kingdom of heaven suffers violence and **THE VIOLENT** take it by force.*

(Matthew 11:12)

GOOD SOLDIERS OF JESUS CHRIST

You therefore must endure hardship, as a **GOOD SOLDIER OF JESUS CHRIST.**

(2 Timothy 2:3)

A soldier is someone engaged in military service, a professional fighter, A SKILLED WARRIOR.

Normally, any person trained to fill this role is marked by certain valuable character traits as: soberness, self-discipline, unquestioning obedience, a willingness to sacrifice all, and—as Paul exhorted Timothy—a readiness to "endure hardship." To be truly effective as sons of God, it is imperative that we seriously consider this *soldiership* calling and diligently pursue its fulfillment. Especially as we near the end of this age, God needs more than just a church full of self-satisfied, professing believers. God needs *warriors who* are willing to give their all and fight to the end for the cause of right. And if the body of Christ fails to meet this challenge, who will? As Edmund Burke so aptly put it:

"All that is necessary for the triumph of evil is for good men to do nothing."

HEARING THE CLARION CALL

Unfortunately, many soldiers in this world quite often have fought in the name of a questionable and, at times, even damnable cause. There have been far too many instances in which skilled warriors were merely helpless pawns, manipulated by corrupt, cruel men, with hearts as cold as steel, who thought nothing of sacrificing the flesh of thousands on an idolatrous battlefield altar to worship the god of greed.

Of course, this is not always the case. Many wars have erupted, and many battles have been fought, in the name of a righteous and noble cause— defending liberty, delivering the oppressed, or subduing an oppressor. Often those enlisted to achieve such worthwhile objectives are individuals whose lives sound a clarion call to courage and commitment (like sure-footed drummers and high-stepping trumpeters marching at the head of an infantry). Our hearts are often stirred, and never left unaffected, when we hear their voices echoing through the annals of time.

Men like John Paul Jones, the father of the American Navy, whose ship, riddled with cannon-ball holes, was on the verge of sinking, still cried out, *"I have not yet begun to fight."*

Or heroic Nathan Hale, who spoke with remarkable calmness to his executioners as they tightened the noose, *"I only regret that I have but one life to lose for my country."*

Or even the earnest soldier-cry of Patrick Henry, who argued, *"Is life so dear, or peace so sweet, as to be purchased at the price of chains and slavery? Forbid it, Almighty God! I know not what course others may take, but as for me, give me liberty, or give me death."*

Without even stopping to consider the religiousness of these men or the morality of war, courage like this cannot go unheeded. If these notable individuals could be possessed with such zealous devotion for a cause that was primarily temporal and earthly, how much more should we, the sons and daughters of God, be consumed with devotion to the purpose of God! How much more should we be prone to making statements such as these—yet with a religious connotation! For ours is a totally righteous, necessary and eternal cause!

May God help us to be as the men of Zebulun who were **"expert in war"** and were **"not of a double heart"** (1 Chr. 12:33 KJV). May we purpose to fight with all our might for the advancement and establishment of that kingdom which shall never end.

THE WAR TO END ALL WARS

Most of the wars fought in this earth-plane would have been unnecessary, had men only been ruled by reason. It is impossible to read history without grieving. How senseless the carnage that has so grossly marred the history of this planet! What a gruesome picture war paints of the darker side of the human nature! And how men have futilely returned, again and again, to this supposed cure for the maladies of the human race, only to discover it an ineffective antidote. James, the epistle-writer, explained why:

> *From whence come wars and fightings among you?*
> *Come they not hence, even of your lusts that war in your*
> *members?*
>
> (James 4:1 KJV)

So war will never cease until lust is fully rooted out of the hearts of men. Truces may be signed and for a season this temporarily halted disease of the human race deceptively recedes. Yet in hidden places (in man's collective inner being) the hatred, prejudice and greed that causes war still festers silently. Then, like the spirochete bacteria of syphilis, it will insanely erupt, worse than ever, at the next unexpected reappearance. No wonder John Foster Dulles, the Secretary of State under Dwight Eisenhower, concluded:

Wars to end wars are an illusion. Wars, more than any
other human activity, create the conditions which breed
more war.

This pessimistic view may be true concerning conflicts spawned at the will of man—for no war in this world has ever brought warfare to a permanent end. But those who adhere to this line of thought fail to consider the divinely-authored battle plan of the ages.

The Bible verifies that from the fall of Lucifer onward, the forces of darkness and the forces of light have been engaged in unrelenting conflict. It also foretells the end result of this global controversy that rages in realms both natural and spiritual. Ultimate peace that passes understanding will be the outcome, forever reigning in the hearts of God's offspring. His final victory in establishing the New Creation will bring an end to all wars, once and for all. Therefore, this endeavor is of all endeavors most worthwhile, for the praiseworthy results are perfect and infinite!

At the entrance of the coming Kingdom Age, Isaiah 2:4 will be wonderfully fulfilled:

> *...They shall beat their swords into plowshares, and their*
> *spears into pruninghooks; nation shall not lift up sword*
> *against nation, **neither shall they learn war any more.***

Nothing can prevent this triumphant finale, for God has spoken it in His forever-settled Word. So even when the present moment seems terribly unstable, and the future years cloudy and uncertain, we can unwaveringly repeat the words of a former shepherd turned warrior (with a spiritual connotation):

> *The LORD is my rock, and my fortress, and my*
> *deliverer; my God, my strength, in whom I will trust...**for***
> ***You have armed me with strength for the battle;*** *You*
> *have subdued under me those who rose up against me.*
>
> (Psalm 18:2, 39)

In the natural, we may feel vulnerable because of sin's power, but spiritually, we can have absolute confidence. God clothes us with salvation and the strength that comes with it. (See Ps. 132:16.) Because of this, our capacity for winning spiritual conflicts does not rest on human will power or natural abilities. "The race is not to the swift, nor the battle to the strong" (Ec. 9:11).

Often God takes those who feel incapable of facing the enemy and equips them supernaturally. In doing so, He receives all the glory unto Himself. A shepherd's rod, the jawbone of an ass, a stone and a sling, three hundred trumpets: all of these may have seemed like weak and insufficient weaponry.

But when God armed Moses, Samson, David and Gideon with "strength for the battle," these questionable weapons proved to be unquestionably powerful. So it is with us yet, in a higher sense.

In Romans 9:29 and James 5:4, our celestial Commanding General is called **the LORD of Sabaoth**, meaning *the God of armies.* He is the One who marshals a heavenly host to preserve the remnant of His people and champion the cause of the oppressed. This is the equivalent of another Old Testament title: **the LORD of hosts.** This name of God has been interpreted as meaning: *the Supreme Head of a multitude of covenant believers that are mighty through God.* It has also been interpreted to mean *the God of an army of militant angels that are poised and ready for battle.*

So the word "hosts" can refer to both people and angels. In Exodus 12:41 (KJV) it is used of Israel—"at the end of four hundred years...all **the hosts of the LORD** went out from the land of Egypt." This could have meant that all of God's people and all of the angels that were commissioned to protect them left Egypt. In this present covenant, this term can still be used for all those who have come out of the world and acknowledged Jesus as LORD. We are not a natural army, but a spiritual one. We are **"THE HOST OF THE LORD."**[*1]

THE DRASTIC SHIFT
FROM THE OLD TESTAMENT TO THE NEW

The definition of an **army** is a *large organized body of men and women trained for war.* In the Old Testament, the LORD of Sabaoth raised up and commanded a natural Israelite army, which primarily fought natural enemies to secure a natural Land of Promise.

In the New Testament, God is still just as much engaged in warfare, but now the primary arena of battle has moved into the spiritual realm. Therefore, the army of the LORD in this era is essentially spiritual in nature—made up of born again Jews and Gentiles who are daily fighting spiritual principalities and powers to secure a spiritual 'Land of Promise': a 'land' of God's "exceeding great and precious promises" (2 Pt. 1:4).[*2]

Because of the dual Old Will/New Will nature of this conflict between good and evil, it is quite understandable why the following inquiry was made, and answer given, concerning the bride of the Shepherd/King in the Song of Solomon. In response to the choir, the favored maiden, who represents the bride of Christ, sings out the question concerning herself:

"What would you see in the Shulamite?"

(Song of Solomon 6:13)

The choir's mysterious response is immediate:

"As it were **THE COMPANY OF TWO ARMIES.** *"*

(Song of Solomon 6:13 KJV)

What is this "company" and who are these "two armies"? The "company" is the singular bride of Christ, which includes the redeemed of both the Old and New Covenants, all those who ever have, or ever will be married to God in a covenant relationship. These two groups of redeemed people also fill up the ranks of *two* somewhat different, yet very related *armies.* Both have been commissioned by the Most High God and supernaturally empowered to fulfill a highly important, singular task: the conquest of the kingdom of Satan and the reestablishment of the kingdom of God in this world! So we are **one company,** but **two armies,** both of which together could be termed **"THE ARMIES OF ISRAEL"**—for both are eternally a part of "the Israel of God" (1 Sam. 17:10, Gal. 6:16). This is a great truth and a great mystery indeed!*3

Curiously, before the children of Israel were even delivered from slavery, when they had no weapons and were not trained in war, God still called them **"HIS ARMIES"** (Ex. 7:4). He saw them, not as they *were*: weak, oppressed and broken-willed; but as they *could be*—courageous, strong and full of overcoming faith. So it is with New Covenant offspring, even those who are freshly saved. The Father sees us, not in our former condition, enslaved in sin. Rather, He sees us as His champions, raising the banner of truth—and rushing into battle with a war cry that strikes terror in the host of Satan.

THE BATTLE OF THE AGES

Initially, man was not involved in this strange war that has spread from heaven to earth and persisted for centuries. This terrible conflict began the very moment Satan rebelled in the celestial realm. Perhaps the Bible was referring to this uprising when Isaiah described Lucifer's attempt to exalt his own throne "above the stars of God." (See Is. 14:12–19.)

Revelation 12:7 also explains that **"there was war in heaven."** The beautiful, jewel-bedecked cherub that covered the throne of God—at one time full of wisdom and perfect in beauty—received a drastic change in appearance when he resisted the sovereign rule of the Almighty. He became a hideous, red dragon pitted against Michael and the righteous angels. Apparently, a third of the angels fell under the dragon's anarchistic influence for "his tail drew the third part of the stars of heaven and did cast them to the earth." (See Ezk. 28:12–19, Rev. 12:3–4, 10, 15 KJV.)

Many of the details concerning when, where and how all of these things took place are questionable. One thing is quite certain. After Lucifer was exiled to the earth, he began stalking the innocent ones who occupied the garden of Eden. **The first deadly weapons he wielded were words—treacherous, deceitful, deadly words**. In a manner similar to Psalm 55:21:

> *The words of his mouth were smoother than butter, but*
> ***war was in his heart:*** *his words were softer than oil, yet*
> *were they **drawn swords**.*

The serpent first penetrated the woman's heart with his subtle, seductive words; then he viciously sliced it open, as with a razor-sharp dagger. He poured in His poison. Eve was spiritually dead within a mere moment.

The satanic invasion surged forward in full force when Adam's spirit was also successfully corrupted. In a sense, the entire world fell—indeed, all human beings yet to be born fell—when Adam succumbed to the dark power of the evil one. For "by one man sin entered into the world, and death by sin" (Ro. 5:12 KJV).

From that time onward, hordes of evil powers flooded this realm, bent on perverting and destroying all that had initially been the epitome of loveliness. Nothing was exempt from the hellish onslaught. Even nature was gripped with suffocating death and ever-living things began to wither and waste away. The animal kingdom, that had only known the priceless peace of paradise, was suddenly invaded with fear, hate and senseless bloodshed. The hearts of men, though, were the primary target—for Satan had determined that the Adamic race must be kept in a corrupted state.

The next battlefield casualty was Abel, who launched a successful 'offensive thrust.' He broke through 'enemy lines' when he worshipfully offered up to God a bloody, sacrificial lamb. With his sincere act of repentance and devotion, he captured God's attention and drew the favor and presence of Deity back into this dark vale of tears. The light of truth, which had seemingly been put out forever, came back to life and began flickering with redemptive hope once again. (See Heb. 11:4.)

This was too much of a threat to the devil. With great fear he realized that the foundation of his newly acquired kingdom was being shaken. Cursed man was being blessed. This had to be ended before any more positive progress toward restoration could be made. So the demons moved quickly—stirring jealousy and murder in the heart of Abel's brother, Cain. What transpired was so much more than just a strong and hostile rivalry between two brothers, resulting in a fit of rage and a tragic death. This was an attack of satanic powers intent on maintaining control of this realm. They were more than willing, and really quite pleased, to use a human being in bringing to pass their evil design.

More often than not, this peculiar blending of two realms is the cause for the wickedness that abounds here. The following scripture explains why:

The heaven, even the heavens, are the LORD'S: but the earth He has given to the children of men.

(Psalm 115:16)

Because the earth is under man's authority, delegated at the will of God, Satan has no legal right to set up his kingdom here, except he does it in and through men who yield to his diabolical influence. This is the mystery of the matter. The war is still between God and Satan. But in this realm, the battle being lost or won is often determined by the choices men make in either yielding to the authority of God or the authority of the devil and his evil cohorts. Because of this, both God and satanic powers are searching for vessels—for every inhabited soul becomes a soldier in either God's army or the devil's militia.

So the sum of all strife in this woeful world involves much more than just the struggle of flesh against flesh. What we see in the natural is actually an overflow from another sphere, the direct result of the violent clashing of two invisible, spiritual kingdoms. As the continental plates, under the surface of the earth, often collide (resulting in natural disturbances like earthquakes and volcanoes) so the kingdom of darkness and the kingdom of light are continually colliding (resulting in social disturbances like political upheavals, rampant disease, wicked trends in society and, on the positive side, revivals and spiritual awakenings).

An excellent negative example of this subliminal, spiritual activity is found in both Pharaoh and the Canaanites. It wasn't just this evil potentate who desired to keep the Jews bound in Egyptian captivity, neither was it simply the Canaanite tribes who sought hard to keep the Israelites out of the Land of Promise. Behind the scenes, in both of those cases, it was evil principalities determined to do everything within their power to hinder the purpose of God. This overflowed into all the violent opposition that manifested against the Israelites in the natural realm.

It must be reemphasized that until the incarnation of the Son of God, this 'War of the Ages' manifested primarily in conflicts that involved natural armies. Yet how awesomely God intervened—fighting again and again in behalf of His chosen people. When Pharaoh, along with his charioteers and infantry, pursued the Israelites to squelch their rebellion, the Israelites panicked. Indomitable Moses calmed the people and instilled faith in their hearts with words that still echo:

> *"Do not be afraid. Stand still, and see the salvation of*
> *the LORD, which He will accomplish for you today. For*
> *the Egyptians whom you see today, you shall see again*
> *no more forever.* **THE LORD WILL FIGHT FOR YOU,**
> **AND YOU SHALL HOLD YOUR PEACE."**
>
> (Exodus 14:13–14)

How powerfully God fulfilled these words as He rolled back the waters of the Red Sea. Gazing through the cloudy, fiery pillar, He spun the wheels off the chariots of the presumptuous, pursuing Egyptians. Terrified, they cried, *"Let us flee from the face of Israel; for the LORD fights for them…"* (Ex. 14:25).

It was too late. The frothing waters came crashing in, drowning the adversaries. As their bodies floated downstream, what a gala scene of celebration took place! How the presence of God must have permeated the atmosphere as Miriam, the prophetess, and the women of Israel began playing timbrels and dancing with joy across the wilderness sand dunes! And what victorious faith must have flooded their hearts as Moses and the children of Israel sang this song of triumph:

> *I will sing to the LORD, for He has triumphed gloriously!*
> *The horse and its rider He has thrown into the sea!*
> *The LORD is my strength and song, and He has become*
> *my salvation…*
> **THE LORD IS A MAN OF WAR…**
>
> (Exodus 15:1–3)

Yes, as strange as it may seem, this is a true saying—*"the LORD is a man of war."* Were it not for this truth, surely 'the War of the Ages' would have shifted to the side of evil long ago.

A WARRING GOD

Over the next fifteen hundred years, numerous times, this God of armies fought supernaturally to defend His people. His chief purpose was to preserve a covenant nation in which the Messiah could be born—so that His kingdom could then be established on earth.

How thrilling it is to read the account of how God appeared to Joshua with a drawn sword in His hand introducing Himself as "THE CAPTAIN OF **THE HOST OF THE LORD,**" or, as another translation puts it, "THE COMMANDER OF **THE ARMY OF THE LORD**" (Js. 5:14 KJV, NKJV). Soon afterward this heavenly Captain caused Jericho's walls to fall flat. We read also how this warring God "cast down large hailstones from heaven" as He assisted Joshua in defending the Gibeonites (Js. 10:11). How intensely the LORD of glory involved himself in that battle, apparently bringing the entire solar system to a standstill so the sun would obey Joshua's decree!

Many years later, Jonathan took a bold step of faith and single-handedly defied an entire Philistine camp. His shout—*"There is no restraint to the LORD to save by many or by few"*—still lives on. After Jonathan slayed about twenty men, God sent an earthquake to destroy the rest (1 Sam. 14:6 KJV).

David was also supernaturally empowered in battle, bringing Goliath down with just a stone and a sling. He cried out to the fearful Israelite soldiers, "Who is this uncircumcised Philistine, that he should defy **THE ARMIES OF THE LIVING GOD**" (1 Sam. 17:26). It was David also who claimed bending a bow of steel with his hands, and one time, by God's power, running through a troop and leaping over a wall. (See Ps. 18:29.)

These are just a few examples of how the God of war moved on normal human beings and made them agents of supernatural destruction. The classic example is found in 2 Chronicles 20. King Jehoshaphat heard the prophecy, *"The battle is not yours, but God's...You shall not need to fight in this battle."* In response, he sent forth only singers and musicians against the armies of Moab, Ammon and Mt. Seir. Honoring his faith, God sent angelic ambushments against the enemy, routing them mightily as the Jews simply praised God, singing of His ever-enduring mercy.

Are not all of these examples perfect proof that God truly is a God of war and that if He is truly on our side, we have nothing to fear! He promised His covenant warriors, "Five of you shall chase a hundred, and a hundred of you shall put ten thousand to flight" (Lev. 26:8). Whether the struggle is an offensive or defensive one, we still know, "He is a shield to those who put their trust in Him" and in the worst of situations, "the battle is the LORD'S" (Pr. 30:5, 1 Sam. 17:47).

JESUS: THE EXEMPLARY SOLDIER

God's first 'plan of attack' failed to a certain degree because it hinged on human performance without the indwelling of God's Spirit. God knew from the beginning, the Old Covenant pattern would only be an intermediate step. Had the Israelites always obeyed God, they could have easily remained the greatest nation in the world. Politically, socially, economically and spiritually, they would have been "the head and not the tail, above only and never beneath" (Dt. 28:13). But they rebelled and suffered the consequences. About the time of the incarnation, instead of 'ruling with God,'

Israel was instead ruled by man, under the dominion of the heathen. What a terrible tragedy that the Romans had iron-fisted control of the very nation that should have been ruling the nations herself with a rod of iron!

Then Jesus came—bringing to light a revolutionary new 'battle plan.' He knew the only way God's kingdom could be established on earth was to change man from within. Since the arena of battle was to become, more than ever, the human heart, the new enemies targeted must be the things that corrupt men's hearts the most: satanic powers, the deadness of the human spirit, the carnality of the flesh, and that vicious enemy called sin. Many of the Jewish leaders in Jesus' day did not anticipate this radical change in God's methodology. They expected the true Messiah to conform to the set pattern of former liberators, muster an army and drive the Romans out of the holy land. Instead, Jesus ignored this natural approach and launched a major spiritual offensive.

In foretelling this new methodology, Isaiah first described a time of spiritual crisis when truth would fall in the street to be trodden under the feet of men. (See Is. 59:14–15.) Then He strangely depicted the coming Messiah dressed in military regalia:

> *For He put on righteousness as a breastplate, and a helmet of salvation on His head; He put on the garments of vengeance for clothing, and was clad with zeal as a cloak.*
>
> *According to their deeds, accordingly he will repay, fury to His adversaries, recompense to His enemies...*
>
> *So shall they fear the name of the LORD from the west, and His glory from the rising of the sun;* **when the enemy comes in like a flood, the Spirit of the LORD will lift up a standard against him.**
>
> *The Redeemer shall come to Zion, and to those who turn from transgression in Jacob, says the LORD.*
>
> (Isaiah 59:17–20)

Almost two thousand years ago, Jesus, the Redeemer, became **the standard** the Holy Spirit lifted up against the enemy. This word has a dual meaning.

- First, a **standard** can be a conspicuous object, as a banner, carried at the top of a pole and used as a rallying point, especially in battle. It is an ensign that emblematically reveals the nation, or heralds the cause, for which that particular army is fighting.

- Second, a **standard** can also be that which is established by authority, custom, or general consent as a model and an example by which others are measured, compared, or challenged.

Jesus fills up both of these definitions, to the highest degree.

When the Savior was 'lifted up' on Calvary's tree, He became an example of martial courage and commitment—fighting unto death against the enemies of the human race. In exhibiting such lion-like valor, He became for us the established criterion, the exemplary soldier.

As **"a banner to the people"** and **"a banner for the nations"** (the KJV says, "an ensign of the people" and "an ensign for the nations") He has since been raised high above the whole human race (Is. 11:10–12 NKJV, KJV). As the everlasting and living standard—**Jehovah-Nissi, the LORD our Banner**—He has become the rallying point for all God's covenant people in this great battle between the sons of light and the sons of darkness. No wonder Psalm 89:19 NIV prophesied that the Messiah would be **"A WARRIOR."** (See Ex. 17:15 KJV, NKJV.)

VIOLENCE FOR VIOLENCE

The kingdom of heaven had suffered much *violence* with the beheading of John the Baptist and the crucifixion of Jesus. But after the ascension of Jesus and the outpouring of the Holy Spirit on Pentecost, the early disciples dared to rise up in *violent* opposition of the enemy who had come in like a flood. They preached with passion, stirred whole cities, manifested the miraculous, covered the known world with the Gospel, and won thousands into "the Way." Many of these early champions of faith became standards also—exemplary soldiers, a challenge to all who would follow. This should not have taken anyone by surprise for Jesus encouraged such radical behavior on the part of every **"fellow soldier"** in the kingdom of light (Ph. 2:25 KJV). While still in the world, He prophesied:

> *"...from the days of John the Baptist until now the kingdom of heaven suffers violence, and **THE VIOLENT** take it by force."*
>
> (Matthew 11:12)

Of course, the Savior was speaking of a new and different kind of violence: not resulting in a battlefield littered with mutilated corpses, but rather in the humiliation and defeat of dark principalities whose spiritual strongholds had stood practically unopposed for millennia. Yes, this strange band of mercenaries—some of them former fishermen and tax collectors—earned the title right from the start. They were **"THE VIOLENT"**—taking the kingdom of God by "pressing" into it—pressing past all the doubts, fears, depressions, lusts and sins that seek to entrap the souls of men. (See Lk. 16:16.) They were adamant, determined, passionate and intense. They were never intimidated. Political and religious leaders were intimidated by them.

According to Webster's Dictionary, one of the definitions of the word **violent** is:

> *That which is marked by extreme force or sudden intense activity.*

What a fitting description of the characters and events that fill the stage, scene by scene, in the book of Acts! It wasn't a gentle breeze and a warm glow that came from heaven into the upper room and the hearts of the disciples—it was a rushing, mighty wind and a consuming fire. Those who came under this dual influence did not become pew-warmers craving to be religiously entertained. Many of them were the **"DEDICATED WARRIORS"** Psalm 110:3 (NIV footnote) prophesied about—the kind of zealots for truth who wake up fighting and reluctantly go to bed in the same stance.

Though the devil stirred up great hatred against them, resulting in the Imperial Persecutions (by which multiplied thousands were martyred) still— those early believers emerged as **"THE VALIANT OF ISRAEL"** under the New Covenant. (Song 3:7). They returned love for hate and their message lived on (for darkness is always overcome of light). Like Jesus, these early 'soldiers of light' were careful to instruct those who would follow after. In fact, one of their number, concerned for our welfare, recorded his experiential knowledge regarding the armor Christians should wear and the weapons they should bear, in epistles written to the church. You might even label some of his writings: *A New Testament War Manual.*

WEARING GOD'S ARMOR

The apostle Paul, like a general encouraging front-line foot soldiers, presented these important words of exhortation to the Ephesian believers:

> *Finally, my brethren, be strong in the LORD, and in the power of His might.*
>
> *Put on **the whole armor of God**, that you may be able to stand against the wiles of the devil.*
>
> *For we do not wrestle against flesh and blood, but against principalities, against powers, against the rulers of the darkness of this age, against spiritual hosts of wickedness in the heavenly places.*
>
> *Therefore take up **the whole armor of God**, that you may be able to withstand in the evil day, and having done all, to stand.*
>
> *Stand therefore, having girded your waist with truth, having put on the breastplate of righteousness,*

> *And having shod your feet with the preparation of the*
> *gospel of peace;*
> *Above all, taking the shield of faith, with which you*
> *will be able to quench all the fiery darts of the wicked one.*
> *And take the helmet of salvation, and the sword of the*
> *Spirit, which is the Word of God.*
> *Praying always with all prayer and supplication in*
> *the Spirit...*
>
> (Ephesians 6:10–18)

It would be an excellent practice for every Christian soldier to start off each day confessing the spiritual, military regalia described in these verses. It is called "**the whole armor of God.**" This could mean two things—either that the armor comes from God or that it's identical to the armor God wore when He walked on the earth. Probably both are true. It is certain, if we 'dress for the occasion,' no principality, no evil power can ever gain the victory over us. Our faith-shield quenches, not most, but ALL the fiery darts of the wicked one.

If a satanic assault was the only war front, winning would be relatively easy, but we have another adversary, in some ways, more sinister and dangerous. This enemy has always been an ally of the devil. It is our own fallen, unregenerated flesh. Paul talked about this 'Trojan horse' we all have to face with the following words:

> *For I delight in the law of God according to the inward*
> *man: but I see another law in my members, **warring***
> *against the law of my mind, and bringing me into*
> *captivity to the law of sin which is in my members.*
>
> (Romans 7:22–23)

So the war is not only without; it is also within. We are constantly under attack—on the outside and on the inside. (See Ja. 4:1.) Mere philosophy and psychology are insufficient to protect us. We must have "**the whole armor of God.**" Leaving off any piece could make us vulnerable.

David refused to trust in the natural armor Saul tried to give him for he had not yet 'proved' it. Instead he trusted in the armor of God—the anointing— that had enabled him to emerge victoriously from other attempts on his life. (Could it be that the lion and the bear were actually sent by satanic powers to devour the boy-king-prophet before he came into the fullness of his calling?) By experience, David knew the anointing would never fail him. In like manner, we cannot trust in mere religion, theology, or church rituals to be our covering of defense. We must put on God's armor, and that necessarily includes:

⌣· **The Belt of Truth**—Truth is that which is actual and real. If our lives are based on deception—whether it be satanic deception, sin's deception or self-deception—we are bound to be defeated. So being "established in the present truth" must be one of our first priorities. If we have been begotten by "the word of truth," and are under the guidance of "the Spirit of truth," such a goal is absolutely attainable. This world with its false opinions will pass away, but the truth will endure forever (2 Pt. 1:12, Eph. 1:13, Ja. 1:18, Jn. 16:13).

⌣· **The Breastplate**—This piece of armor is called both "the breastplate of righteousness" and "the breastplate of faith and love" (Eph. 6:14, 1 Th. 5:8). The main issue is that the breastplate guards the heart, and these three things definitely do. Proverbs 4:23 (NIV) says, "Above all else, guard your heart, for it is the wellspring of life." The KJV says, "out of it are the issues of life."

⌣· **The Helmet**—1 Thessalonians 5:8 adds that the helmet (the thing which protects the mind) is not just salvation, but the "hope of salvation." Hope is desire mixed with expectation. Salvation means deliverance. So wearing a helmet called "the hope of salvation" means desiring and maintaining the full expectation that God will deliver us from any adversities we face in life. This kind of positive attitude is an indispensable part of God's armor. It is the mind of Christ gaining ascendancy in us. Without this, we would quickly succumb to despairing and fearful mental attitudes.

⌣· **The Shield**—Real faith in God's Word makes us disbelieve satanic or demonic words. This is how we "quench all the fiery darts" (or "extinguish the flaming arrows of the evil one" as the NIV puts it) (Eph. 6:16). The words of Satan and his evil hordes are "set on fire by hell" and like arrows they can pierce us (Ja. 3:6). Of course, they have absolutely no power over us if we trust utterly in our God. Satan is not omnipresent, so he cannot personally attack every Christian daily. He is confined to being in one place at one time. However, his demonic associates do strive against us constantly. If and when they do, Psalm 91:4 reveals that God's truth becomes our "shield and buckler." So the shield is representative of both faith and truth, simply because the truth is the basis of our faith. Our faith is as mighty as the truth on which it rests.

How excellent is God's promise to Abraham, "I am your shield!" This promise belongs to us as well. (Gen. 15:1, See Dt. 33:29, Ps. 3:3; 28:7.) Shields used by soldiers in Bible times often covered about half the body or more. The divine shield surrounds His own entirely. Psalm 5:12 celebrates this truth saying, "For You, O LORD, will bless the righteous; with favor will You surround him as with a shield." Psalm 18:35 also talks about the "shield of...salvation" (NIV— the "shield of victory"). God's offspring can and should don all of these.

⌣· **The Shoes**—The "Gospel of peace" is the good news that formerly estranged men and women, once at enmity with God, can now have "peace with God through our LORD Jesus Christ" (Ro. 5:1). Furthermore, in all the ups and downs of life, we can maintain a harmonious relationship with God (through grace, through the cross and through all God's covenant promises). We can experience the peace of God that passes understanding. To wear this message like shoes is to declare it everywhere we go, fulfilling the call to be peacemakers. By introducing God's peace into strife-filled lives, we teach them how to win the war of the soul—especially as they realize that God is now at peace with man, and by faith we can partake of that peace. (See Ro. 16:20.)

⌣· **Christlikeness**—To wear all of these military trappings is simply to become Christlike. As already stated, Jesus Himself wore this same defensive armor when He visited the realm of time. So to put on "the whole armor of God" is actually to "put on Christ." In Roman 13:12–14, Paul confirmed this truth, and also reminded us again of the danger of the hour, saying:

> *The night is far spent, the day is at hand. Therefore, let us cast off the works of darkness, and let us **put on the armor of light**.*
>
> *Let us walk properly, as in the day; not in revelry and drunkenness, not in lewdness and lust, not in strife and envy.*
>
> *But **put on the LORD Jesus Christ**, and make no provision for the flesh, to fulfill its lusts.*

This passage clearly asserts that living separated from the world and striving to be Christlike in all our attitudes is the only way to win the battles of life. *To put on Christ is to put on the armor of light.* Those who do this begin marching in the radiant ranks of those who are called **good soldiers of Jesus Christ.**

THE PRIMARY BATTLEGROUND

The following Bible passage noticeably singles out the mind as a primary arena of spiritual conflict:

> *For though we walk in the flesh, we do not war after the flesh:*
>
> *(For the weapons of our warfare are not carnal, but mighty through God to the pulling down of strongholds;)*

*Casting down imaginations, and every high thing that
exalteth itself against the knowledge of God, and bringing
into captivity every thought to the obedience of Christ.*
(2 Corinthians 10:3–5 KJV)

Exalted, deceived, and corrupt thoughts lodging in the "chambers of the imagery" have ever been a major downfall of the human race. (See Ezk. 8:12 KJV.) Since Eve reached out to partake of the tree of the knowledge of good and evil, the mind has been a war zone. The mind is the place where the carnality of the flesh and manipulative, demonic powers set up their near-impregnable strongholds. By doing so, men are set at variance with God, "because the carnal mind is enmity against God" (Ro. 8:7).

God deals in words constantly (directly and through His offspring). The devil deals in words (directly and through his offspring). God builds with words and fights with words. Evil spirits seek to tear down with words what God has built, fighting against Him by imitating His methods. Both God and evil spirits enter the minds and hearts of men by means of words.

When any worldly or demonic influence so deceives a person with wrong ideas that they become an established way of thinking, a stronghold has been reared. Many of those strongholds are thrown to the ground the very moment that we fulfill the command, *"Confess with your mouth the LORD Jesus and believe in your heart that God has raised Him from the dead...for with...the mouth confession is made unto salvation"* (Ro. 10:9–10). If quoting a simple salvation truth out of God's Word can deliver us from life-long bondage and instantly change our destiny from hell to heaven, then quoting and confessing other biblical truths can drastically alter our whole lives as well.

Not that words, in and of themselves, have some kind of mystical power, but God watches over His Word in us to bring it to pass. Generally speaking, this is the mystery of the matter:

- Words become ideas.
- Ideas grow into beliefs.
- Beliefs become habits.
- Habits produce character.
- Character generates lifestyle.
- Lifestyle determines destiny.

So it is easy to see how vitally important these intangible objects called *words* really are—and how they can be used effectively to win this war over our souls. Death and life truly are "in the power of the tongue" (Pr. 18:21).

No wonder Jesus rebuked Peter in the garden of Gethsemane and instructed him to put his sword into its sheath. He was trying to teach Peter that He was instituting a new way of fighting. (For the Savior had just spoken the words "I am He" and the hostile crowd in Gethesmane had fallen helplessly to the ground.) Peter learned the lesson well and on Pentecost he pulled out a new kind of weapon—"**the sword of the Spirit, which is the Word of God**"—and began to conquer amazingly (Eph. 6:17).

WIELDING THE SWORD OF THE WORD

At the onset, God set a cherub with a sword of fire at the east of Eden to keep the way of the tree of life. From that point forward, the Word of God has been likened in the Scripture to this very instrument of war. (Isn't it interesting that God invented this weapon of war before man did?)

Hebrews 4:12 declares that "the Word of God is living, and powerful, and sharper than any *two-edged sword*, piercing even to the division [the dividing asunder] of soul and spirit, and of joints and marrow, and is a discerner of the thoughts and intents of the heart" (NKJV, KJV). An ordinary sword may be able to slice a physical body into pieces, but it cannot penetrate the spiritual part of a man. Only God's Word can do that. When it does, it separates the soulish part of us (which is still contaminated with negative, human emotions and carnal thought patterns) from our regenerated spirit (which is "created...in righteousness and true holiness") (Eph. 4:24). By this process we are sanctified, separated unto God and changed into His image.

The two, sharp edges of this Word-sword surely represent the Old and New Testaments, forged together into one sword; or perhaps they represent God's commandments and promises. Jesus, the Captain of our Salvation, defeated the devil by wielding this Word-sword. During His wilderness temptation Jesus smote the tempter three times by firmly stating, *"It is written,"* then boldly quoting the written Word. If Jesus, the all-powerful LORD of glory, had to fight this way, we who are so inferior to Him dare not neglect such a spiritual maneuver.

Jesus, knew the power of the Word for He was the Word made flesh. He gloriously fulfilled the prophecy of Isaiah 49:2—"the LORD...has made My mouth like *a sharp sword.*"

By this weapon, He tore down Satan's strongholds everywhere He went.
He healed the sick with the spoken Word.
He cast out devils with His Word.
He attacked Satan, sin, deception and false religious traditions, cutting men free from such bonds, by piercing their hearts "to the dividing asunder."
He has since equipped every soldier in God's camp with this very same

slaughter weapon, commanding us to take up where He left off—fighting the same enemies and winning in the same fashion. Psalm 68:11 says, "The LORD gave the Word; great was **THE COMPANY** of those who proclaimed it."

The Hebrew word translated **company** is *tsaba* meaning *a mass of persons organized for war.* So this entire army fights with the same weapon. Because God's Word, "alive and full of power," still penetrates "to the deepest parts of our nature, exposing and sifting and analyzing and judging the very thoughts and purposes of the heart," it is "mighty through God" also when turned inward in self-examination (Heb. 4:12 Amp). Of course, we must dare to maintain a soldier-like attitude of submission if we are to benefit from its surgical, soul-probing influence.

Note that this Word-weapon is called "the sword of the Spirit." The Word is insufficient of itself; it must be wielded by the Spirit—for once the Word-sword lances the boil of sin, the Spirit brings the balm to heal. It also takes the anointing of the Spirit to reveal the true meaning of the Word, to make it powerful in fulfillment and full of manifested authority. So these two— the Word and the Spirit—must always work together.

OTHER WEAPONS OF WARFARE

There are many other God-given weapons that are "mighty through God" beside the sword of His Word. In a sense, every means of defeating sin or conquering satanic powers is a spiritual weapon imparted to God's warriors. Some of the primary ones in the church's stockpile are: the blood of Jesus, the name of Jesus, the gifts of the Spirit, the fruit of the Spirit and fasting. (See Lk. 10:17–20.) Even prophecies spoken over us can be utilized in spiritual warfare. Paul exhorted his pastor/protege:

> *This charge I commit to you, son Timothy, according to the **prophecies** previously made concerning you, that by them you may wage the **good warfare**.*
>
> (1 Timothy 1:18)

When we have a true prophecy, we can adamantly confess and claim what God has spoken in the face of all opposition, until it comes to pass.

Prayer, intercession, praise and worship are weapons of exceptional power and value. In Numbers 4:23 (KJV), Moses spoke of the duty of priests to *"perform the service...* in the tabernacle of the congregation." The Hebrew word translated *perform* and *service* has also been translated *war* and *warfare*. In Numbers 8:24 (KJV) it is also translated *"wait upon* the service of the tabernacle of the congregation." So as the priests *waited* on God, they were really *warring the warfare* of the tabernacle. This is a very appropriate rendering, for as long as the priests stood daily in the gap, ministering to God and interceding for God's people, Israel enjoyed victory on the battlefield.

So worship was the highest order of warfare, because through it, principalities were conquered in the spiritual sphere. Quite possibly, this rendered their demonically-controlled armies on earth far less effective. Moreover, even if the Israelites were not involved in a literal war, it still took the watchful prayers and atoning sacrifices offered up by faithful priests to keep God's holy nation under the fountain of His blessings. The warfare had to first be won in the spiritual realm, if victory, prosperity and blessings were to abound among the LORD'S people in the natural realm. Without a doubt, intercessors still *war the warfare* of the sanctuary now!

BECOMING GOD'S WEAPONS

Not only do believers wield the weapons of God in this 'War of the Ages'; according to certain unique passages of Scripture, **we actually become God's weapons.** In Romans 6:13, the Creator encourages His own to yield their members as **"instruments of righteousness to God."** The word translated **instruments** is the Greek word *hoplon*, the very word translated **weapons** in 2 Corinthians 10:4. In fact, two different versions of Romans 6:13 state that we are called to be **WEAPONS OF GOOD** or **WEAPONS OF RIGHTEOUSNESS** in the hands of God (PME, Mon).

Only those whose bodies are consecrated to God are useful to Him in this horrible conflict between the powers of darkness and the children of light. Those who claim allegiance to God's cause, yet walk in the darkness of sinful practices, are nothing more than traitors. But those who walk in the truth can be used of God to level an army of devils. No wonder Andrew Murray once asserted:

A holy minister is an awful weapon in the hands of God!

In Zechariah 10:4 we find the Messiah referred to as **"the battle bow."** The logical deduction is that anyone in covenant with the Messiah is an arrow loaded in His bow. Zechariah 9:14 agrees with this, calling God's covenant warriors **"HIS ARROW"** that goes forth like lightning. Also, Isaiah 49:2 depicts the Israel of God as **"A POLISHED SHAFT"** hidden in God's quiver (**"A POLISHED ARROW"**—NIV, **"A SELECT ARROW"**—NAS). Knowing this, and knowing the power of our calling, we can confess to the LORD, as David did in Psalm 45:5, "Your **arrows** are sharp in the heart of the king's enemies."

In Psalm 127 children are described as being "**arrows** in the hand of a mighty man." In other words, godly parents can influence their children in a positive way and, in a sense, shoot them toward the target of their destiny. Spiritually speaking, this is true as well. God shoots His offspring toward the mark of their destiny in Him. When we strike that mark, we strike terror in the heart of the adversary as well. It is also noteworthy that Judah is spoken of as God's "**BOW**" in Zechariah 9:13 loaded with the arrow-like people of God. The New Testament church now fills this Judah-role, 'shooting out' apostles, prophets, missionaries, pastors, teachers, evangelists and witnesses of the truth into this world of deception. *4

In Zechariah 9:13 God also said He would actually make the sons of Zion like "**THE SWORD OF A MIGHTY MAN**" (the NAS says "**A WARRIOR'S SWORD**," in the LB God calls His people "**MY SWORD**"). So not only do believers wield the sword of the Word; we actually become a Word-sword in the hands of the Almighty God. This calling speaks of yieldedness and bravery, for we must be totally yielded to the warrior-God who grips us in His hand, and we must be brave enough never to flinch when he thrusts us against the enemy. This calling also speaks of unity and selflessness, for we must be willing to be melted down—with others in the body of Christ—and be forged by God into one weapon fulfilling His purpose. When we learn to confess and decree God's Word and speak under the inspiration of the Holy Spirit, we can also claim the Isaiah 49:2 promise that God has made our mouths like "**a sharp sword**."

Bows, arrows and swords: by these weapons God has depicted the character His warring offspring should manifest. He is angry against the dark powers and principalities that rule this realm, and the corrupt, Babylon-like world system that rejects His sovereignty, to the harm of people in this world. God vents His righteous anger through His people by using them to deliver the oppressed. God is angry at the way people are destroyed by sin and oppression, but He has called His "mighty ones" for His anger (Is. 13:3). Through us, the truth sets men free. No wonder Isaiah 13:5, on the highest level of interpretation, speaks of God's saints as "**THE WEAPONS OF HIS INDIGNATION**," or as another translation puts it, "**THE WEAPONS OF HIS WRATH**." (KJV, NIV, See Is. 13:3.)*5

Zechariah 10:3 also explains that He has made us "**HIS ROYAL HORSE IN THE BATTLE**." (The NAS says "**HIS MAJESTIC HORSE IN THE BATTLE**." The KJV says "**HIS GOODLY HORSE IN THE BATTLE**.") This symbolizes the truth that He rides valiantly into the battle upon the hearts and lives of His offspring in order to fight the good fight of faith and reclaim this world for the will of God. Yes, we are His warriors. We are His weapons. We are His royal steed. He sees us as majestic when we fight in His name.

SEVEN IMPORTANT CHARACTER TRAITS

There are a number of soldier-like character qualities that God encourages His people to develop. These will enable God's 'volunteers' to emerge triumphant in all the battles of life. The following seven are some of the most important:

ᐁ **Selflessness**—The first soldier-like character trait is selflessness. The book of Revelation describes a time, in the last days, when Satan will come down to the earth having great wrath because he knows his time is short. Revelation 12:17 says his intentions are to "make war" with those who keep the commandments of God and have the testimony of Jesus. The angelic narrator of John's vision prophetically informs us: "they overcame him [Satan] by the blood of the Lamb, and by the word of their testimony and *they loved not their lives unto the death*" (Rev. 12:11 KJV). Such selflessness is required of anyone who rushes into a battlefield. This is even more true concerning the 'War of the Ages.' This attitude in any army makes it all the more formidable; and so it is with us.

ᐁ **Inspiration**—To successfully wage any kind of 'military campaign' against the forces of the enemy, we must walk under inspiration. We must be sensitive to the voice and the directions of the Commanding General. Israel's kings and prophets normally sought God's counsel concerning who should be fought, as well as when, where and how the battle should be executed. They knew success depended on God ordering the battle Himself. So they often consulted the high priest who utilized those curious objects called the "Urim and Thummim" to discern God's will. Furthermore, they never took a successful method (like shouting walls down) and used it repetitiously unless God said to do so. (How often we are guilty of getting stuck in repetitious, religious ruts.) The word **inspiration** means *to breathe into*. This is wonderful—that God would *breathe into us* His divine counsel. If we dare to inhale, in a spiritual sense, we must then exhale God-pleasing qualities such as spontaneity, boldness, trust and unquestioning obedience. (See examples: Jd. 6:14–40, 1 Sam. 30:8, 2 Sam. 5:19, 2 Chr. 20.)

ᐁ **Submission**—Good soldiers are known by their unquestioning submission and obedience to the authority of their chief commanders. Similarly, only those who are surrendered to the Lordship of Christ can effectively fight the good fight of faith. The maintaining of any other attitude is like walking into a battle without any armor or weaponry. For this cause James 4:7 (KJV) first exhorts, "*Submit* yourselves therefore to God" and then promises, "Resist the devil and he will flee from you."

❤· **Separation**—2 Timothy 2:4 declares, "No one engaged in warfare entangles himself with the affairs of this life; that he may please Him who enlisted him as a **soldier**." The NIV of this passage says, "No one serving as a **soldier** gets involved in civilian affairs [for] he wants to please his commanding officer." This speaks of much more than striving to live above sin. This speaks of a 'separated' life in which even the frivolous, unnecessary, temporal and mundane things that dominate most people's time are instead pushed aside to give God unrestricted command over our actions and choices. (See Pr. 18:1 KJV, Ro. 1:1, 2 Cor. 6:17, Gal. 1:15.)

❤· **Self-discipline**—Proverbs 16:32 says "he who rules his spirit" is mightier than "he who takes a city." Proverbs 25:28 adds, "whoever has no rule over his own spirit is like a city broken down, without walls." An undisciplined person cannot successfully conquer, and is very likely to be conquered. Lack of self-discipline leads to impotence and vulnerability. Surely for this reason Paul said, "I *discipline* my body and bring it into subjection…" (1 Cor. 9:27).

Every believer must fortify his soul with diligence and gird himself for the battle with zeal. Diligence and zeal give birth to self-discipline and nurture it to a state of maturity. So let us be consistent to pray, read God's Word, fast, witness and pursue our calling—not just when we feel like it, but rather, be "instant in season and out of season" (2 Tim. 4:2). Let us remember that "the LORD disciplines those He loves." Furthermore, "he who neglects discipline despises himself" and "whosoever loves discipline loves knowledge." (Heb. 12:6 NIV, Pr. 12:1 NAS, 15:32 NAS, See also Col. 2:5 NAS, 1 Tim. 4:7 NAS.)

❤· **Courage**—We can be selfless, inspired, submitted, separated and disciplined, yet still lack the courage to step out and do what God says to do. Prior to leading God's people into the Land of Promise, Joshua, that exemplary soldier, was commanded by God, "Be strong and of good courage" (Js. 1:6). It is not enough to merely recieve God's promises; we must courageously pursue their fulfillment.

Webster's dictionary defines courage as "mental or moral strength to venture, persevere, and withstand danger, fear or difficulty." These are contagious attitudes, just as their negative opposites. God certainly considered this when, under the Old Will, He told any "fearful and fainthearted" soldier to leave the battle and return home "lest his brethren's heart faint as well as his" (Dt. 20:8 KJV). The well-known saying is so true: "Courage is not the absence of fear, but the conquering of fear."

꙳ **Endurance**—Endurance is the ability to withstand hardship, adversity or stress. Simply put, it means standing up under the pressure. As Paul so aptly put it, "having done all...stand!" (Eph. 6:13). This is the very statement that directly precedes his directions concerning putting on the whole armor of God. In Scripture we are commanded to endure a number of things: afflictions (2 Tim. 4:5), the grief of false accusations (1 Pt. 2:19), sound doctrine (2 Tim. 4:3), temptations (Ja. 1:12), God's discipline (Heb. 12:7 NIV) and, of course, our crowning verse dictates that we each **"endure hardship as a good soldier of Jesus Christ"** (2 Tim. 2:3).

A **good soldier** is not a complainer or grumbler, but one who maintains silent resolution. Serious commitment to this calling is chiseled into the furrows of his brow. He always enters the battle ready to die, if necessary, for what he believes. In God's militia force the motive must be love—love for God, love for others and love for the truth—for love "endures all things" (1 Cor. 13:7). Possessing an attitude of endurance need not result in a posture of non-enjoyment of life. Quite the contrary, James 5:11 announces, "we count them happy who endure." So let us obey the Hebrews 12:1 injunction to "run with endurance the race that is set before us."

THE IMPORTANCE OF OUR STAND

A **good soldier** is unaffected by any Goliath-like opposition. Like David, in the face of any giant and in the face of scornful or fearful brethren, he or she will still cry out, *"Is there not a cause?"* So much hinged that day on David's courageous venture. So much depended on his willingness to sacrifice his own life, if need be, for the good of the whole. Had he failed to fight the good fight of faith and fulfill his God-given responsibility, all of Israel would have become slaves to the Philistines. In like manner, so much is hinging on whether or not we will accept our God-given charge to reach this last generation. Will we selfishly retreat into some 'safety zone' or will we lunge forward toward the front lines? So many will remain slaves to sin, so many will be swallowed up in everlasting darkness, if we do not fulfill our ordination.

We must approach every day with the utmost gravity, crying out, *"Is there not a cause!"* As John Knox prayed, *"God give me Scotland or I die!"* so we must plead, *"God, give us souls or we die! Give us revival in our land or we die!"*

Statistics reveal that over one hundred and twenty thousand people die every day. That means every two seconds, approximately three souls leave this planet to meet their Maker. Unfortunately, many are not ready to confront the Judge of all the ages and with great trembling they will stand before Him with no covering for their sin. The greatest tragedy of all is the fact that millions have never even heard the Gospel. A great portion of the world's population is, for the most part, unevangelized. Something is dreadfully wrong! We must repent and renew our commitment to winning the lost. We must make an all-out offensive thrust against enemy lines while there is yet time, if we are to see the last great harvest of souls promised in God's Word.

God, give us missionaries willing to be faithful unto death! God, give us soldiers of the cross! God, give us prayer warriors who will pray until breakthrough comes!

Transgression will soon come to the full, triggering judgments that will cause the earth to "reel to and fro like a drunkard" (Is. 24:20). God has already forewarned, "Wail, for the day of the LORD is near! It will come as destruction from the Almighty" (Is. 13:6). Yet He also announced in advance, "I have commanded **MY SANCTIFIED ONES**, I have called **MY MIGHTY ONES** for Mine anger, even them that rejoice in My highness." Two other translations of this same passage call those who are valiant for God's truth **"HIS WARRIORS"** and HIS **"MIGHTY WARRIORS"** (Is. 13:3, 6 NIV, NAS).

Sanctified ones are those who are set apart from this world, cleansed from sin and reserved unto God. Being sanctified, they seek not their own glory, but His. Being "strong in the LORD, and the power of His might," they are ready for any battle (Eph. 6:10). As **"HIS WARRIORS,"** their passion is to oppose all forces and penetrate all fronts by fearlessly declaring God's Word until the kingdom of God is fully established in this world. This is soldier-like commitment to a cause: exactly what God longs to see in His people.

GOD'S LATTER DAY ARMY

Anyone with a spiritual ear can hear the rumbling of the dry bones in Ezekiel's valley-vision. (See Ezk. 37:1–14.) This vision first applies to the physical seed of Abraham who, until 1948, were 'buried' in the Gentile nations. Ezekiel said there were "very many" bones in "the open valley" (a low place of great despair) and "they were very dry" (drained of hope and strength) (Ezk. 37:2).

From the burning of the temple and destruction of Jerusalem by Titus in 70 A.D., through all the ensuing centuries of oppression and persecution, culminating in that nightmare called 'the holocaust,' the anguish-filled soul of the nation of Israel was "dried up." Claiming the Land of Promise looked highly improbable. No wonder even God presented this prospect to Ezekiel in the form of a question:

Son of man, can these bones live?
(Ezekiel 37:3)

Because Ezekiel failed to respond affirmatively, God goaded the prophet with the words:

"...Prophesy to these bones, and say to them, 'O dry bones, hear the word of the LORD!'
Thus says the LORD God to these bones: "Surely...I will put sinews upon you and bring flesh upon you, cover you with skin and put breath in you; and you shall live. Then you shall know that I am the LORD."
(Ezekiel 37:4–6)

Ezekiel prophesied as he was commanded and "there was a noise... a rattling, and the bones came together" (Ezk. 37:7). Then the prophet prophesied to the wind:

Thus says the LORD God: "Come from the four winds, O breath, and breathe on these slain, that they may live."
(Ezekiel 37:9)

It happened! "Breath came into them, and they lived and stood upon their feet, **AN EXCEEDINGLY GREAT ARMY**" (Ezk. 37:10). Then God clearly identified the symbol: "Son of man, these bones are **the whole house of Israel**" (Ezk. 37:11). He then proceeded to explain that one day He would open the graves of His people and bring them back to their own land and in that day they would know that He is God. What do the details of this vision mean?

❀ The Flesh, Sinews and Skin

These represent the true and full revelation of the Word being restored and re-established as a covering for the seed of Abraham—life-giving promises (the flesh)—muscle-like, strength-imparting ordinances (the sinew)—and commandments that preserve (the skin). Jesus was, in a perfect and ultimate sense, "the Word made flesh," The Israel of God should be similarly clothed. God's people must have more than just the skeletal frame of traditionalism and ceremonialism; they need that revelation of truth which is "health to all their flesh." (Pr. 4:22, See Dt. 6:24.)

❀ The Wind

When the four winds of heaven breathed upon the resurrected multitude, it speaks of the very breath of the Almighty, the Spirit of the living God, filling His chosen ones with divine life. By this dual-revelation it becomes very clear that there will be, in our day, a great move of God among the Israelite people.

God is already doing this, revealing to them their New Covenant privileges and their blessed Messiah. When this fully happens, they will emerge "**AN EXCEEDINGLY GREAT ARMY**": not only a natural army empowered of God to defend the borders of Israel against their oppressors, but also an army of regenerated 'completed' Jews empowered of God to declare the truths of the New Covenant, uncontaminated by the mixture of heathen influence and Gentile misconceptions. (See Zec. 2:1–13; 12:1–9, 14:1–3.) Hallelujah! We are living in the hour in which this glorious vision is coming to pass! When it reaches fulfillment, it will mean, in an unprecedented way, "the riches of God" and "life from the dead" for the Gentile portion of the church. (See Ro. 11:12–15, Eph. 2:12.)

✤ This visionary symbol also applies to the restoration of the church to the original expression of New Testament Christianity ────────

For centuries this scenario has been progressively unfolding. From the days of Wycliffe, when the Bible was translated into the common language of the people, the true revelation of the Word has been increasingly unveiled. Now, with such depth of teaching going forth from so many anointed voices, it seems the Word is opening up in a new way to God's New Covenant offspring. In a sense, the flesh is coming back on the bones, and the church, instead of being entombed in lifeless traditionalism, is instead rising up and coming together in the unity "of the knowledge of the Son of God" (Eph. 4:13).

Furthermore, from the days of Francis of Assisi, Martin Luther, John Wesley and many of the early reformers, the power of the Holy Spirit has been progressively and increasingly poured out. Now, multiplied millions are receiving the born again experience and the infilling of the Spirit all over the world. Praise God! This is more than just a fortunate and timely blessing. This is a divinely-authored military uprising. This is God Almighty, the LORD of hosts, the LORD of Sabaoth, raising up **AN EXCEEDINGLY GREAT ARMY** of self-sacrificing, consecrated, Spirit-filled, Word-believing Jew and Gentile soldier-sons and soldier-daughters who will shake this world with revival one more time. They will march against the powers of darkness with grim determination and adamant, mountain-moving faith.

These last days will be tumultuous times, for Satan, as already mentioned, will "make war" with those who have "the testimony of Jesus Christ" and his pawn, the Antichrist, will also "make war with the saints" (Rev. 12:17; 13:7). So the battle will rage against God's elect, both naturally and spiritually. But "the people who know their God shall be strong and carry out great exploits. And those of the people who understand shall instruct many…" (Dan. 11:32–33).

Psalm 110:3 (NIV) speaks especially of God's spiritually militant ones under the New Will. Addressing the Creator in a prophetic utterance, Isaiah announced:

> Your **TROOPS** will be willing on Your day of battle.
> Arrayed in holy majesty, from the womb of the dawn...

Other versions render this verse, "Your people shall be **VOLUNTEERS** in the day of Your power," "Your people will offer themselves freely on the day You lead **YOUR HOST**," and "The people will proffer their assistance willingly on the day when You muster **YOUR ARMY** in holy array at early dawn" (NKJV, RSV, Har).

In essence, all these translations infer that with the New Covenant comes the dawning of a new day spiritually, a time of holiness and power. In this covenant, God's great host of **volunteers** (not draftees) will offer themselves willingly (literally rendered, they will be *freewill offerings* consecrated on an altar) to champion the cause of Christ in this world.

The NIV footnote explains they will offer themselves as **DEDICATED WARRIORS** to support God on the battlefield. (See Jd. 5:2.)

On the highest level, Micah 5:1 (NIV) speaks to heavenly Jerusalem and pleads, "Marshal, your troops O **CITY OF TROOPS** (**DAUGHTER OF TROOPS** in many versions)." In a similar meaning, Amos 9:6 (KJV) reveals He who builds "His stories in the heaven" has also "founded **HIS TROOP IN THE EARTH**."*[6] The Everlasting Architect that can construct the blue vault of an atmosphere surrounding the earth, and countless thousands of galaxies swirling through the natural universe, is also just as adept at raising up an invincible army of believers who will likewise encompass the globe. We are invincible, because nothing can separate us from the love of God. Whether we live or die, we still remain more than conquerors. We know in advance, the plan of the heavenly Bridegroom will propel His warrior-bride forward toward the ultimate conquest of this dark world.

Two times in the Song of Solomon this bride of Christ is spoken of as being "terrible as **AN ARMY WITH BANNERS**" (Song 6:4, 10 KJV). Though we are as tender as a bride in the arms of the heavenly Bridegroom, we are a terror to the enemy of our souls. As we march through every continent, we hold high the banners of victory that declare the everlasting kingdom and the unconquerable King in whose name we fight.

Yes, it is so! There is nothing in this world that creates chaos in Satan's camp and sends evil powers shrieking in horror like the advance of God's troops on the battlefield of the nations. We are commissioned to fearlessly tread on serpents and scorpions—in other words, to bruise satanic forces under our feet (a continuation and fulfillment of the prophecy given to Eve that was first fulfilled in Jesus). (See Gen. 3:15, Ro. 16:20.)

Only God knows the fullness of what awaits the church in this final era. We do know that when God's plan climaxes in this realm, His earthbound army will be joined by those who have gone on into the celestial sphere. Together, glorified and spectacularly arrayed, we will wrench this world free from the Antichrist's control.*7

John, the revelator, painted a picture full of graphic, prophetic detail, concerning the final battle and the glorious entrance of the heavenly Victor:

> *Now I saw heaven opened, and behold, a white horse. And He who sat on him was called Faithful and True, and in righteousness He judges and **makes war.***
>
> *His eyes were like a flame of fire, and on His head were many crowns...*
>
> *He was clothed with a robe dipped in blood: and His name is called The Word of God.*
>
> *And **THE ARMIES IN HEAVEN**, clothed in fine linen, white and clean, followed Him on white horses.*
>
> *Now out of His mouth goes a sharp sword, that with it He should strike the nations. And He Himself will rule them with a rod of iron. He Himself treads the winepress of the fierceness and wrath of Almighty God.*
>
> *And He has on His robe and on His thigh a name written, **KING OF KINGS, AND LORD OF LORDS.***
>
> (Revelation 19:11–16)

Yes, Jesus will descend with a shout and the voice of the archangel— joined by **THE HOST OF GOD**: a multitude of angels and redeemed celestial soldiers. The feet of our commanding General will "stand in that day upon the Mount of Olives...*and it shall be split in two, from east to west...*" (Zec. 14:4). "And the beast [will be] captured, and with him the false prophet that worked signs in his presence"...then these two will be "cast alive into a lake of fire burning with brimstone" (Rev. 19:20).

Satan will be bound securely in the bottomless pit.

The LORD of Sabaoth, the God of armies, will triumph in the end. And we, **THE LORD'S HOST, GOOD SOLDIERS OF JESUS CHRIST, FELLOW SOLDIERS** IN GOD'S ETERNAL ARMY, will celebrate the triumph with Him. As **THE GREAT** and **THE STRONG** we will share the spoil of war with the Captain of our salvation. (See Js. 5:15 KJV, 2 Tim. 2:3, Ph. 2:25, Is. 53:12.)

The battle will be over forever.

No longer will we be "**THE VIOLENT**," for the days of violence will vanish away. We will lay down our weapons and even beat our swords into plowshares. Good soldiers will then become godly gardeners as Adam was in the beginning.

We will inherit the earth. We will reign as kings and lords, the occupational force of a New World that will never know the horror of war again.

Two Powerful "Soldier" Quotes

General Booth (founder of the Salvation Army):

*Winning the lost is relatively easy, and not nearly as difficult...as converting the saved into saints, **soldiers** and saviors.*

C. T. Studd (founder of the Inland China Mission):

*Christ's call is to feed the hungry, not the full; to save the lost, not the stiff-necked; not to call the scoffers, but sinners to repentance; not to build and furnish comfortable chapels, churches, and cathedrals as homes in which to rock Christian professors to sleep by means of clever essays, stereotyped prayers and artistic musical performances, but to raise living churches of souls among the destitute, to capture men from the devil's clutches and snatch them from the very jaws of hell, to enlist and train them for Jesus, and make them into **an Almighty Army of God**. But this can only be accomplished by a red-hot, unconventional, unfettered Holy Ghost religion, where neither Church nor State, neither man nor traditions are worshiped or preached, but only Christ and Him crucified. Not to confess Christ by fancy collars, clothes, silver croziers or gold watch-chain crosses, church steeples or richly embroidered altar-cloths, **but by reckless sacrifice and heroism in the foremost trenches.***

Deep calls unto deep,
Hear the clarion call.
Fight the good fight of faith—
(Can you sacrifice all?)

For His cause is our banner;
His kingdom our goal.
We are part of His army—
(Have you accepted this role?)

Endnotes

*1 This term **host** is used in a variety of ways. Basically it means either *an army or a very large multitude.* In the King James Version, it is used in reference to Israel (Num. 2:4–30, Ex. 12:41), Canaanites (Jd. 7:1–22), all nations of the world (Jer. 3:19), all the heavenly bodies—stars, planets, etc. that make up this immense, natural universe (Jer. 33:22, 2 Kgs. 21:3–5), all fallen angels and satanic forces (Is. 24:21), all the elect angels of heaven (Lk. 2:13), and finally all the major divisions of creation at its start: the *host* of beasts, the *host* of birds, the *host* of fish, the *host* of mountains, etc... (Gen. 2:1). To refer to God as **the LORD of hosts** is, therefore, saying a little more than just the fact that He is **the God of armies**. It is a means of declaring the vastness of God by emphasizing the vastness of individual parts of His creation.

Variations of this title for God include: **the God of hosts** (Am. 3:13; 4:13) and **the LORD God of hosts** (Am. 5:15). Variations of this title for God's people, not used in the body of this chapter are: **the host** (Js. 3:2 KJV), **His hosts** (Ps. 103:21), **the hosts of the LORD** (Ex. 12:41 KJV), and **the host of the children of Israel** (Ob. 20).

*2 This statement does not negate the fact that God is very involved in the establishment and preservation of the state of Israel. Since 1948 no war against the Land of Promise has been able to succeed, neither will any war yet to transpire—even Armageddon. The LORD of hosts will see to that. However, such a truth does not mean God is anti-Arab; rather, He is pro-Word, honoring the promises made to the seed of Abraham, Isaac and Jacob. The Gospel is for Gentile (including Arab) and Jew alike. The land of Israel, though, is God's gift to the Israelite people.

*3 For more detailed explanations of this statement, see the chapter on *The Bride* in Volume Two and the chapter on *The Shulamite* in Volume Five of **Our Glorious Inheritance**.

*4 See the chapter containing *Judah* in Volume Two of **Our Glorious Inheritance**.

*5 On the first level, this prophecy speaks of the Medes and Persians as the "**weapons of God's indignation**" in conquering Babylon. On the highest level it most likely speaks of God's covenant people being used of God to war against the Babylon-like, world political and religious system that is basically Antichrist. (See Rev. 17–18.)

*6 The King James Version of Amos 9:6 may not be a correct rendering of this verse, so possibly, this application is not completely accurate.

*7 1 Corinthians 15:22–23 says, "For as in Adam all die, even so in Christ shall all be made alive. But every man in his own **order**: Christ the firstfruits; afterward they that are Christ's at His coming." The Greek word translated **order** is *tagma.* This can especially be a reference to *a military company.* In essence, there will be three such military companies glorified by God's power in the 'order' God has predetermined: first, those that arose simultaneous with Jesus (Mt. 27:51–53), second, those who died in Christ and third, those who are alive, translated at His return. (See 1 Cor. 15:51–52, 1 Th. 4:13–18.)

Good Trees

---

*Even so, every **GOOD TREE** bears good fruit,*
but a bad tree bears bad fruit.

(Matthew 7:17)

And even now the ax is laid to the root of the **TREES:** *Therefore every tree which does not bear good fruit is cut down, and thrown into the fire.*

(Matthew 3:10)

To console those who mourn in Zion, to give them beauty for ashes, the oil of joy for mourning, the garment of praise for the spirit of heaviness, that they may be called **TREES OF RIGHTEOUSNESS, THE PLANTING OF THE LORD**, *that He may be glorified.*

(Isaiah 61:3)

He shall be like **A TREE PLANTED BY THE RIVERS OF WATER**, *that brings forth its fruit in its season, whose leaf also shall not wither; and whatever he does shall prosper.*

(Psalm 1:3)

Blessed is the man who trusts in the LORD and whose hope is the LORD. For he shall be like **A TREE PLANTED BY THE WATERS...**

(Jeremiah 17:7–8)

TREES

TREES OF RIGHTEOUSNESS

THE PLANTING OF THE LORD

TREES PLANTED BY
THE RIVERS OF WATERS

TREES PLANTED BY
THE WATERS

THE TREES OF THE WOOD

THE TREES OF THE LORD

CEDARS OF LEBANON

BOUGHS

*As the apple tree among **THE TREES OF THE WOOD**, so is my beloved among the sons...*

(Song of Solomon 2:3 KJV)

THE TREES OF THE LORD *are full of sap,* **THE CEDARS OF LEBANON** *which He planted.*

(Psalm 104:16)

*On the mountain height of Israel I will plant it: and it will bring forth **BOUGHS**, and bear fruit, and be **A MAJESTIC CEDAR**. Under it will dwell birds of every sort; in the shadow of its branches they will dwell.*

(Ezekiel 17:23)

*Open your doors, O Lebanon, that fire may devour your **CEDARS**. Wail, O **CYPRESS**, for* **THE CEDAR** *has fallen, because* **THE MIGHTY TREES** *are ruined. Wail, O **OAKS OF BASHAN**, for* **THE THICK FOREST** *has come down.*

(Zechariah 11:1–2)

A MAJESTIC CEDAR

CEDARS

PALM TREES

THE OLIVE TREE

A CULTIVATED OLIVE TREE

A GOOD OLIVE TREE

A GREEN OLIVE TREE

OLIVE PLANTS

HIS FIG TREE

THE PINE TREES

THE FIR TREES

TREES OF LIFE

The righteous shall flourish like **THE PALM TREE...**

(Psalm 92:12 KJV)

And if some of the branches were broken off, and you, being a wild olive tree, were grafted in among them, and with them became a partaker of the root and fatness of **THE OLIVE TREE,** *do not boast against the branches. But if you do boast, remember that you do not support the root, but the root supports you.*

(Romans 11:17–18)

For if you were cut out of the olive tree which is wild by nature, and were grafted contrary to nature into **A CULTIVATED OLIVE TREE [A GOOD OLIVE TREE]** *how much more will these, who are natural branches, be grafted into their own olive tree?*

(Romans 11:24 NKJV, KJV)

Deep calls unto deep,
From the earth to the sky
This inward potential—
In mere seed doth lie.

As oak trees in acorns,
And pine trees in cones,
So an upward high-calling,
Resides in God's own.

"The Lord's planting" He calls us,
For His glory, we bear—
Good fruit from good trees,
His nature to share.

Other related titles contained in this chapter are: **Trees of Lign Aloes** - Num. 24:6 KJV, **Aloes Planted by the LORD** - Num. 24:6, **The High Cedar** - Ezk. 17:22, **A Stately Cedar** - Ezk. 17:23 NAS, **A Splendid Cedar** - Ezk. 17:23 NIV, **A Goodly Cedar** - Ezk. 17:23 KJV, **A Teil Tree** - Is. 6:13 KJV, **A Terebinth Tree** - Is. 6:13; **An Oak** - Is. 6:13, **Oaks of Righteousness** - Is. 61:3 NIV, **Oaks of Goodness** - Is. 61:3 Mof, **Oaks of Justice** - Is. 61:3 NAB, **Strong and Graceful Oaks** - Is. 61:3 LB, **The Cypress Trees** - Is. 14:8, **Cypress** - Zec. 11:2, **A Green Cypress Tree** - Ho. 14:8, **Pine Trees** - Zec. 11:2 NIV, **Oaks of Bashan** - Zec. 11:2, **The Thick Forest** - Zec. 11:2, **The Stately Trees** - Zec. 11:2 NIV, **The Forest of the Vintage** - Zec. 11:2 KJV, **The Dense Forest** - Zec. 11:2 NIV, **The Mighty Trees** - Zec. 11:2, **A Willow Tree** - Ezk. 17:5, **Olive Branches** - Zec. 4:12, **Green Trees** - Ezk. 20:47, **Good Figs** - Jer. 24:3–5.

The LORD called thy name, **A GREEN OLIVE TREE**, *fair, and of goodly fruit.*
(Jeremiah 11:16 KJV)

Your wife shall be like a fruitful vine in the very heart of your house, your children like **OLIVE PLANTS** *all around your table.*
(Psalm 128:3)

He has laid waste My vine, and ruined **MY FIG TREE**: *he has stripped it bare and thrown it away; its branches are made white.*
(Joel 1:7)

Even **THE PINE TREES [THE FIR TREES]** *and the* **CEDARS OF LEBANON** *exult over you and say, Now that you have been laid low, no woodsman comes to cut us down.*
(Isaiah 14:8 NIV, KJV)

The fruit of the righteous is a **TREE OF LIFE**, *and he who wins souls is wise.*
(Proverbs 11:30)

GOOD TREES

*Even so, every **GOOD TREE** bears good fruit, but a
bad tree bears bad fruit.*

(Matthew 7:17)

*T*his verse is taken from a parable that Jesus gave to help
His followers distinguish between true and false prophets. (See
Mt. 7:15–20.) In comparing the same to both good and bad trees, Jesus
pointed out, "by their fruits you will know them." In other words, He was
explaining that if certain persons claim to be leaders in the body of Christ,
their lifestyle, their character and the results of their ministry will either
validate or disprove their claim.

Good fruit indicates a good tree.
Bad fruit indicates a bad tree.
The analogy could not be any more simple or plain.
In another passage, Jesus warned concerning false teachers:

*Every plant which My heavenly Father has not planted
shall be rooted up.*
Let them alone: they are blind leaders of the blind...
(Matthew 15:13–14, See Mt. 12:33.)

This convicting tree-analogy was expanded in yet another passage to
embrace all those professing to be in a relationship with God. Jesus explained,
concerning all who claim to be His disciples:

*For a **good tree** does not bear bad fruit, nor does a
bad tree bear good fruit.*
For every tree is known by its own fruit...
(Luke 6:43–44)

Such symbolic language was nothing new to those Jews who heard the
Messiah's message. They could easily remember that God's judgment on the
Assyrians centuries before had been represented in Scripture as a forest of
trees set on fire. (See Is. 10:17–19.) They were well aware of proud
Nebuchadnezzar being represented in the book of Daniel as a great tree cut
down to a mere stump and humbled before the Most High God (Dan. 4). And
not long before, John the Baptist had rebuked certain hypocritical Scribes
and Pharisees, preaching that they should "bear fruits worthy of repentance"
(Mt. 3:8). This forerunner of Christ then gave the stern warning:

> *And even now the ax is laid to the root of* ***THE TREES.***
> *Therefore every tree which does not bear good fruit is cut*
> *down, and thrown into the fire.*
>
> (Matthew 3:10)

Jude 12 carries this symbol to an extreme. It describes ungodly men purporting to be Christian leaders as trees whose fruit withers, "without fruit, twice dead, pulled up by the roots."

If there are negative applications of this tree-symbol in the Word of God, there are certainly many positive ones as well. One of the most beautiful is a prophecy Isaiah gave to reveal the Messiah's purpose in coming:

> *To appoint unto them that mourn in Zion, to give unto*
> *them beauty for ashes, the oil of joy for mourning, the*
> *garment of praise for the spirit of heaviness; that they*
> *might be called* ***TREES OF RIGHTEOUSNESS, THE***
> ***PLANTING OF THE LORD****, that He might be glorified.*
>
> (Isaiah 61:3 KJV)

What valuable insight this verse provides into the great blessings available through the New Covenant! All of us can look back into the past and see the ashes of yesterday's defeats, mourning over our failures and walking under the heavy load of guilt. Then Jesus, the Anointed One, came into our lives to "proclaim the acceptable year of the LORD." (A term meaning **the year of Jubilee**—a year when debts were forgiven, possessions were restored and many Jewish slaves and prisoners were set free—See Lev. 25.)

He beautified our lives with the grace of salvation, filled us with the oil of the anointing and clothed us with a heaven-sent covering of Spirit-unctioned praise. And all of these benefits were bestowed on us that we might grow tall and strong spiritually: **TREES OF RIGHTEOUSNESS, THE PLANTING OF THE LORD.**

Other versions of this passage name God's people—"**Oaks of Goodness,**" "**Oaks of Justice,**" "**Oaks of Righteousness,**" and "**Strong and Graceful Oaks**" (Mof, NAB, NIV, LB). The Amplified Version of this passage is especially beautiful: "...that they may be called **OAKS OF RIGHTEOUSNESS** [lofty, strong and magnificent, distinguished for uprightness, justice and right standing with God]."

Such an awesome transformation is certainly not for our glory, but "that He may be glorified." Like stately trees that tower above passersby, we become **"LIVING MEMORIALS"** of the strength, the goodness and the graciousness of our God. (See Ps. 92:12–15 Amp.) As trees that grow straight toward heaven even when planted on a steep incline, so we should be heavenly-minded, upright in our attitudes, committed to moral standards, heralding the truth in the midst of a 'slanted,' treacherous and deceived world. New Covenant grace was not poured into our lives that we might get by with unrighteousness. Rather, grace was given that we might be rooted in the stability of divine life, consistent in living uprightly before the LORD.

THE CONTINUING REVELATION OF BLESSEDNESS

Another 'root' passage of this particular revelation is found in the first psalm. In the first two verses of this opening chapter of God's book of songs, David unveiled certain characteristics of **blessedness:**

> *Blessed is the man who walks not in the counsel of the ungodly, nor stands in the path of sinners, nor sits in the seat of the scornful.*
> *But his delight is in the law of the LORD, and in His law he meditates day and night.*
>
> (Psalm 1:1–2)

Then the Psalmist foretold the blessed benefits that would result for the person who meets this challenge:

> *He shall be like a **TREE PLANTED BY THE RIVERS OF WATER,** that brings forth its fruit in its season; whose leaf also shall not wither; and whatever he does shall prosper.*
>
> (Psalm 1:3)

This promise is very similar to the beatitude spoken through Jeremiah, the prophet:

> *Blessed is the man who trusts in the LORD, and whose hope is the LORD.*
> *For he shall be like a **TREE PLANTED BY THE WATERS,** which spreads out its roots by the river, and will not fear when heat comes; but its leaf will be green, and will not be anxious in the year of drought, nor will cease from yielding fruit.*
>
> (Jeremiah 17:7–8)

Such promises bring us to a firm conclusion. We who separate ourselves from ungodliness, delight ourselves in God's Word, and trust in the Almighty with all our hearts, are sure to enter the blessedness of stability in our relationship with Him. We are planted by the river of life and there we find an abundant water supply. Just as natural water is made up of two natural elements (hydrogen and oxygen) so spiritual water—the 'water of life'—is made up of two spiritual elements (the Word and the Spirit). Both are scripturally symbolized as being water—and both are constantly supplied to a yielded child of God. (See Jn. 7:37–39, Eph. 5:25–27.)

Even when the world around us seems to be withering away from drought-like conditions, we need not be "anxious"—for our water supply never diminishes. It is just as unending, inexhaustible and dependable as God Himself. Death may seem to creep close, like the cracked, parched ground of a desert inching its way into once fertile territory. But if our roots reach down into the infinite and unlimited resources in Christ, we can be ever green and fruitful, unaffected by changing seasons of life. We will be continually nourished by the life of God, flowing just as consistently through our spirits as the sap that flows through a well-watered, healthy tree.

As sap defies the downward pull of gravity to climb up into the highest branches of a tree, so also "the law of the spirit of life" in us defies the downward pull of "the law of sin and death." And though it is not always apparent, in a slow, consistent, tree-like manner, we are growing—day by day—little by little. As good trees, we are growing in God's strength. We are growing in His beauty. We are growing in His wisdom. We are growing in His abilities. We are growing in God's grace and His love. God could have performed the total work of salvation in us the very moment we were saved. But one of His curious character traits is that He loves to watch things grow over a period of time—especially that which reflects His likeness.

JESUS: THE APPLE TREE

If we, God's image-bearing offspring, are compared to trees in Scripture, it makes sense that God Himself be depicted this way, especially in the incarnation. This happens in a poetically beautiful way in the Song of Solomon. The young woman who represents the bride of Christ extols the virtues of her prospective groom by saying:

> As **THE APPLE TREE** among **THE TREES OF THE WOOD**, so is my beloved among the sons. I sat down under His shadow with great delight, and His fruit was sweet to my taste.
>
> (Song of Solomon 2:3 KJV)

When this passage is related to Jesus, it speaks of the contentment, security, serenity and sustenance that can be found in Him alone. Protected under His divine overshadowing, we have no fear. Breathing in the pleasant fragrance of His nearness, our spirits are infused with tranquility and hope. Partaking of the sweet fruit of His divine nature, we are nourished inwardly.

The bride pleads *"Comfort me—refresh me with apples: for I am lovesick— I am faint with love"* (Song 2:5 KJV, NAS, NIV). This is the longing of the espoused one to delightfully experience her Beloved. She must know Him in intimacy. She must eat of His succulent, *apple-like* character traits—His love, His joy, His gentleness, His mercy—digesting these into her inner being until a blending of hearts takes place.

Toward this goal *"deep calls unto deep"* every single day.

This passage reveals that none of the other **"trees of the wood"** can be compared to that person described by the bride as the one "whom my soul loveth" (Song 2:3, 3:2 KJV). So also, when we, as members of the bride of Christ, behold the excellent beauty of the heavenly Bridegroom, all other notable personalities in the body of Christ pale in comparison. Jesus, *"the apple tree among the trees of the wood,"* abides most excellent, chief among ten thousand—forever and ever.

JESUS: THE TENDER TWIG PRODUCING THE GOODLY CEDAR

In Ezekiel 17, we discover another important, Messianic tree-passage. In this chapter, the house of Judah is represented as a **high cedar tree.** This speaks of God's aspirations for His Old Covenant people: first, that they be upright, and second, that they grow like a cedar, spreading branches of God-given dominion throughout the world.

Other Scripture references uphold this cedar tree analogy. In Numbers 24:5–6 the tents of the children of Israel are likened to **"cedar trees** beside the waters," and in Psalm 92:12 we read that "the righteous...shall grow like **a cedar in Lebanon."** (See Zec. 11:1–2.)[*1–2]

Unfortunately, because of repeated transgressions, the Jews fell short of their 'cedar tree' calling. Instead, they were 'chopped down' at the hands of Nebuchadnezzar, King of Babylon. Defeated, humiliated, spoiled and enslaved, the towering cedar became "a spreading vine of low stature." But the Babylonians were not overly oppressive and Judah was allowed to continue as a vassal state. So it happened that the royal tribe of Israel was "planted in good soil by many waters, to bring forth branches, bear fruit, and become **a majestic vine"** (Ezekiel 17:6–8, **"a goodly vine"** in the KJV).

How God's mercy lingered still—until Zedekiah, the king of Judah, made the grave error of ignoring God's directions. He turned to Egypt for assistance in rebelling against Babylon. Brought under judgment as a result, the "majestic vine" was blasted by the east wind: it withered away and was plucked up by the roots. Then, thank God, the prophecy shifted to a message of future hope:

> *Thus says the LORD God: I will take also one of the highest branches of the high cedar and set it out. I will crop off from the topmost of its young twigs a tender one, and will plant it on a high and prominent mountain.*
>
> *On the mountain height of Israel will I plant it; and it will bring forth* **BOUGHS**, *and bear fruit, and be* **A MAJESTIC CEDAR**. *Under it will dwell birds of every sort; in the shadow of its branches they will dwell.*
>
> *And all the trees of the field shall know that I, the LORD, have brought down the high tree and exalted the low tree, dried up the green tree and made the dry tree to flourish; I, the LORD, have spoken and have done it.*
>
> (Ezekiel 17:22–24)

There are several major points in this 'majestic cedar' prophecy that need to be emphasized. First, historically these prophecies spoke of how the Jews were to be restored to their homeland under a governor named Zerubbabel. Second, on a higher level, this is a reference to the coming of the Messiah. He is "the tender plant and...root out of dry ground" whose appearance in this world Isaiah also foretold (Is. 53:2).

Third, this twig is described as growing into **A MAJESTIC CEDAR** or, as three other translations render this passage: **A STATELY CEDAR, A SPLENDID CEDAR** or **A GOODLY CEDAR** (NAS, NIV, KJV). This second cedar of Ezekiel 17 is clearly representative of the church, the body of Christ. It is pictured as bringing forth **BOUGHS** (individual churches and fellowships) and being filled with every kind of bird—for the Gospel has reached multitudes of every nation, race and tongue.

God's original desire for Old Testament Israel was to fulfill this cedar-calling herself and emerge in the beauty, holiness and worldwide dominion the cedar represents. Unfortunately, a great many of Abraham's seed were unable to fulfill this calling. Because "spiritual rebirth" was not available under the Old Will, God's people lacked the inward experience of the divine nature enabling them to grow tall and strong in God. Those who were strong in faith and committed to righteousness still found it impossible to fulfill every detailed facet of the law.

So God changed the covenant, to fill His people—whether they be Jews or Gentiles—with the 'sap' of His wondrous, life-giving grace.

In **The Parable of the Trees** (Judges 9:8–15), God's covenant people are again likened to stately cedars in Lebanon. However, in seeking to anoint a ruler, they foolishly chose to abide under the shadow of a mere bramble bush. This rough, prickly, thorn-covered shrub represented Abimelech, the wicked son of Gideon, who ruthlessly murdered all his half-brothers to secure his father's throne, certainly not a fit leader to follow. It also represents the heartbreaking truth that far too often people choose to be "ruled" by evil things which ultimately cause their ruin.

THE CEDAR SYMBOL

In order to fully appreciate why God represents His people as a cedar tree—both corporately and individually—let us inspect the various aspects of this beautiful biblical symbol.

⌣· **Nobility, Dominion and Greatness**—Of all trees, the cedar is considered a 'king' of the forest. Being sometimes up to forty feet or more in girth, this massive tree is one of the largest living things on earth. With its great height and perfect symmetry, it appears impressively majestic and is indicative of the royal calling, the God-given authority, the spiritual dominion and the exalted destiny given to all of God's elect.

⌣· **Endurance and Sanctity**—Cedar wood is a very durable wood, impervious to decay. This speaks of unchanging consecration, stedfast commitment and holiness of heart. It represents being kept safe from the putrefying influence of this 'rotting' world in which we live. It also speaks that, in a cedar- like way, sons of God are challenged in Scripture to be 'durable'—enduring hardship, discipline, chastening, temptation, grief, tribulations, persecutions and a great fight of afflictions. We can do it! For God always gives us sufficient grace—that we might "hold the beginning of our confidence stedfast unto the end" (Mk. 4:17, 2 Tim. 2:3; 4:5, Heb. 3:14; 12:7, Ja. 1:12, 1 Pt. 2:19).

⌣· **Incorruptness**—Cedar wood is noted for its repulsion of damaging insects. In a living state, it even kills certain worms that try to penetrate it. Because of this, it represents incorruptness: being strong enough and godly enough to repel the evil that ever seeks to lodge itself in the hearts of men. True cedar-tree sons and daughters of God are also those who exercise a purifying influence on the world around them. Possibly because of this characteristic, cedar wood was used in the purification rites for Jews who became unclean (Num. 19) and for the cleansing of lepers (Lev. 14:4–6, 49–52).

~• **Persistence, Peaceful Progress and Patience**—In a slow but steady way, the germinated seed from the cone of a cedar matures. From the tiny seedling and tender sapling stages it finally grows into an impressive, regal ruler of the plant kingdom. This is accomplished without anxiety, without strain and without grandiose displays of self-assertiveness. Such a natural growing process is peaceful, consistent and sure. So should we also grow in God, not straining or striving, but patiently progressing every day into the image of Christ.

~• **Beauty**—Cedars have a breathtaking grandeur about them, a striking beauty that captures both the eye and the heart of the beholder. This speaks of the way that God promises to "beautify the meek with salvation" in this life. On a higher level, it also speaks of the unutterable beauty of the future glorified state (Ps. 149:4 KJV).

~• **Permanence and Longevity**—God has spoken of old, "As the days of a tree, so shall be the days of My people, and My elect shall long enjoy the work of their hands" (Is. 65:22). Because the cedar is an evergreen, it represents the stability of a permanent covenant relationship with God. It symbolizes the everlasting life which sons of God have inherited from their Everlasting Father.

~• **Fragrance of Worship**—The rich aroma of cedar wood always permeates the forest area in which these celebrated trees grow. So also, the strong, fresh fragrance of pure-hearted adoration should permeate the 'atmosphere' around a true child of God. In the Song of Solomon, the bride possesses this trait. Her prospective groom extends the compliment, "O, My spouse...the fragrance of your garments is like *the fragrance of Lebanon*" (Song 4:11). Pleasant worship like this should be the 'clothing' of the soul. It should be constant, not spasmodic: the continual abode of the heart. To this also the Scripture testifies poetically when the bride of Solomon's song comments to her groom, "The beams of our house are *cedar*, and our rafters of *fir*" (Song 1:17).

~• **Spiritual Vitality**—Psalm 104:16 claims "**THE TREES OF THE LORD** are full of sap, **THE CEDARS OF LEBANON**, which He planted." This sap is the nourishing life of the Holy Spirit, the inward flow of the divine personality that keeps a believer spiritually prosperous, alive, healthy, vigorous and fruitful.

_____

Considering these points, it is plain to see that the cedar tree is highly descriptive of all that a son or daughter of God can be and should be! It is no wonder, therefore, that expensive cedar boards from Lebanon were the primary source of lumber used in the construction of the temple of Solomon. ("All was cedar; there was no stone to be seen" 1 Kgs. 6:18.) For it is only *cedar-like* offspring of the Most High who can be successfully 'built together' to provide a suitable dwelling place for God in this world.

For this to happen, though, "**THE TREES OF THE LORD**" must be sawn down, trimmed and shaped for a perfect fit. This speaks of the difficult, progressive process of dying to self. It speaks of being 'cut' free from our former, natural life and our ties to this earth. If we submissively yield to this process, as the boards in the temple were overlaid with gold, so our attempts at godliness will be luxuriantly 'overlaid' with the pure gold of His divine nature.

Of course, someone might ask, *"If the boards were to be overlaid with gold and hidden from view, why didn't the temple builders use a lesser grade of lumber?"* The answer is simple: *"Because God always demands the best. So it was only fitting that the cedar wood be used."* In like manner, another might ask, *"Why can't everyone in this world inherit eternal life?"* For those who understand this cedar-symbol, a similar response might easily be given: *"Only the cedar is worthy of the gold and only the gold is worthy of God's indwelling presence."*

THE PALM TREE SYMBOL

The palm tree is another predominant Scriptural symbol for the people of God. Countless images of palm trees were carved into the gold-overlaid cedar boards that lined the temple walls. Maybe this was God's way of communicating that He is quite involved in permanently carving certain *palm-like* character traits into those *cedar-like* sons and daughters who make up His temple. Psalm 92:12 (KJV) also ties these two trees together in biblical symbolism:

*"The righteous shall flourish like **THE PALM TREE**: he shall grow like a **CEDAR IN LEBANON**."*

The following beautiful, symbolic truths come to the surface as we study the particulars of this tree that is so common in the Middle East:

⌣˙ **Palm trees are especially fitted to grow in difficult and even desert-like conditions!** Almost all other trees require very fertile, well-watered areas in which to grow. In arid territory, they are stunted, fruitless and death-prone. On the contrary, the palm tree seems to enjoy defying the 'status quo' and choosing the impossible. In a similar way, if children of God are placed in relatively easy conditions of life, usually they will fall short of their full potential in God. O, how different it is when God's righteous ones are placed in some stark wilderness of tribulations, adversities and conflicts. Often, it is only then that the inward 'son of God nature' is challenged, stirred up and manifested in excellence. Therefore, if reacted to correctly, desert-like circumstances should always work together for our good. God did promise, "Behold, I will do a new thing...I will even make a way in the wilderness, and rivers in the desert" (Is. 43:19 KJV).

⌣· **Because the life of palm trees is in the "heart," they are especially able to recover from damaging treatment!** In most trees the sap runs just underneath the bark, leaving the inner trunk hard. Such trees are always vulnerable, for if their bark is stripped, they could possibly die. Not so with the palm, for the life-giving sap flows through its heart. Strip its bark, scar its trunk, and it will keep living right on! In a parallel way, men and women who are of the world usually depend on external things such as natural possessions, human relationships and career achievements to supply their feeling of self-worth. Strip them of these things and emotionally they 'die'—for their life is 'on the surface.' On the contrary, if true sons of God are stripped down to nothing, they often exhibit an extraordinary ability to 'live right on'—bearing fruit regardless. This is possible because their source of fulfillment is in "the hidden man of the heart"—and the God who lives there. Scarred, weather-beaten, or torn by the circumstances of life, 'palm tree believers' still rejoice to say, "In all these things we are more than conquerors through Him who loved us." Their source is the Almighty God and by Him, they are inwardly "renewed day by day" (1 Pt. 3:4, Ro. 8:37, 2 Cor. 4:16).

⌣· **Palm trees are especially fitted to survive storms!** In severe storms, forceful winds will often break the limbs off ordinary trees. There are two reasons for this: first, the shape of the leaves, which serve to 'catch' the wind; and second, the rigidity of the limbs. The palm tree is much different. Its leaves are long and slender and its limbs easily bend. In fact, the entire trunk of a palm tree can yield so fully to the force of the wind that sometimes its trunk and crown will almost bend parallel to the ground. Such is the ability given to God's righteous offspring. The infusion of His love enables us to endure "all things." This life with all its stormy blasts will end up destroying those who are unregenerated, but we will recover with no damage done. The storm-winds only serve to 'bend us over' with humility as we cast all our cares toward the One who gathers up "the wind in the hollow of His hands." (See 1 Cor. 13:7, Pr. 30:4 NIV.)

⌣· **A palm tree sheds the growth from former years, so that its crown of evergreen foliage always stays as far from earth and as close to heaven as possible.** An ordinary tree will keep the limbs that grow on its trunk from the very start. The older the limb, the larger it grows. On the other hand, the palm tree sheds its former limbs. This relates to the privilege that palm tree Christians have of "forgetting those things which are behind" (Ph. 3:13). Not only do we forget the former failures; we forget the former successes. We refuse to live in the past, for we have been given a perpetual new beginning "in Christ"—a future full of heaven-authored opportunities and challenges.

꘎ **Palm tree roots grow deep, strong and thick.** So it is with a child of God who loves righteousness. Our devotion causes us to become so deeply embedded "in Christ" that it is nearly impossible for us to be uprooted. Our roots do not run along the surface of the ground as those who are 'of the world'; in palm tree fashion, they have penetrated downward into the deep, flowing, eternal waters where *"deep calls unto deep."* The Scripture challenges followers of Jesus to be "rooted and grounded in love" and "rooted...in Him" (Eph. 3:17, Col. 2:7).

꘎ **A palm tree can continue to be productive up to a century.** Some sources say that the older a palm tree is, the more luscious the fruit that it yields. No wonder the psalmist went on to say in Psalm 92:13–14, "Those who are planted in the house of the LORD shall flourish in the courts of our God. They shall still bear fruit in old age; they shall be fresh and flourishing."

꘎ **The graceful and tall palm tree provides an excellent symbol of worshipful fellowship with the LORD and of believers who are grace-filled and upright.** This is indicated by a statement made by the bridegroom in the Song of Solomon to his prospective bride, "This stature of yours is like a palm tree...I said, I will go up to the palm tree, I will take hold of its branches" (Song 7:7–8).

꘎ **Groupings of palm trees in wilderness areas show where the water source is located.** So wherever God's 'palm trees' gather to worship, an oasis of the 'water of life' can always be found.

꘎ **Palm branches are used in scripture to symbolize great victory, great prosperity and great joy!** They represent the ultimate triumph of God's people over death and over all of earth's misery. When Jews celebrate the Feast of Tabernacles, to this day, they make their temporary booths partially out of palm branches to memorialize their passage through the wilderness. During this celebration in Jesus' day, the Jews carried palm fronds with them to the temple to worship. These Bible-based traditions reveal certain blessed truths.

First, the temporary booths are a message that our sojourn in this flesh is just temporary; second, that God will preserve us as we journey through this wilderness of sin; and third, that one day, just as the palm tree defies and conquers the desert wasteland, so we will emerge totally victorious over this desert-like world at the resurrection of the dead. Surely it was for this cause that the ecstatic worshippers used palm branches (called "Hosannas") to herald Jesus' first triumphant entry into Jerusalem. This must also be the reason that in the book of the Revelation, the innumerable bloodwashed throng is shown coming out of great tribulation, "clothed with white robes, with **palm branches in their hands,** and crying...Salvation belongs to our God" (Rev. 7:9–10).

The Amplified Version of Psalm 92:12–15 (quoted in the KJV at the beginning of this section) sums up this "palm tree" and "cedar tree" revelation beautifully:

> The [uncompromisingly] righteous shall flourish like **THE PALM TREE** [be long-lived, stately, upright, useful and fruitful]; he shall grow like a **CEDAR IN LEBANON** [majestic, stable, durable and incorruptible].
>
> Planted in the house of the LORD, they shall flourish in the courts of our God.
>
> [Growing in grace] they shall still bring forth fruit in old age; they shall be full of sap [of spiritual vitality] and rich in the verdure [of trust, love and contentment];
>
> They are **LIVING MEMORIALS** to show that the LORD is upright and faithful to His promises; He is my rock, and there is no unrighteousness in Him.

THE OLIVE TREE

The olive tree is used many times in the Old Testament as an emblem of prosperity, beauty, peace, strength, abundance, fruitfulness and wealth, both naturally and spiritually. In the highest metaphorical sense, those who are truly 'of Israel' qualify as "**the olive tree.**" They will surely be found prospering in God, beautified with salvation, at peace with heaven, strong in faith, spiritually wealthy and bearing the fruit of the divine nature in the midst of a fruitless world. Jeremiah revealed God's original hope for the seed of Abraham when he prophesied:

> The LORD called thy name, **A GREEN OLIVE TREE,** fair, and of goodly fruit…

> (Jeremiah 11:16 KJV)

Also, Hosea foretold the condition of restored Israel, saying:

> His branches shall spread, and his beauty shall be as **THE OLIVE TREE**…

> (Hosea 14:6 KJV)

Because the olive tree is quite stout, thriving in rocky soil, perhaps this was first God's way of saying that His people Israel would be spiritually 'stout': able to endure all the hardships and persecutions that would come their way. Second, this was also God's way of complementing the spiritual beauty of His covenant nation as opposed to this fallen world, so ugly because of carnality. One commentator writes of the olive tree, "Though its bark is gnarled and its contour unsymmetrical, its shimmering veil of misty blue-green lanceolate leaves, whose under surface is scurfy white, contributed an ethereal beauty to many a poor man's garden." In like manner, the Israel of God has been and will ever be beautiful in God's sight.*3

This "olive tree" symbol becomes even more meaningful when we realize that olives, and the oil produced from them, were two of the main staples of life for the Israelite people. In a similar way, oil is representative of the anointing, the richness of God's personal presence, which is even more a necessary 'staple of life' for all who are in covenant with God.

Moreover, we who are called **a green olive tree** are 'oil-producers'; we are part of an anointed body of believers who are perpetuating the work of the Messiah, the Anointed One, in this world. As He was anointed to heal the brokenhearted and set the captive free, so are we. (See Is. 61:1–3, Ac. 10:38, 2 Cor. 1:21, 1 Jn. 2:27.)

It is also symbolically significant that the fruit of the olive tree contains only one seed! We are not of many seeds—many doctrines, religious ideas and theological concepts. We are of one seed: the everlasting Word of God that was in the beginning with God and was God. (See Jn. 1:1–2.) From this singular seed, God's entire plan has evolved from generation to generation. Without controversy, life is hidden in the seed and as Jesus verified, "The seed is the Word of God" (Lk. 8:11). This is the original seed out of which **the olive tree** has grown.

THE NEW TESTAMENT PERSPECTIVE

In the epistle to the Romans, Paul also employed the use of this 'olive tree symbol.' He compared New Covenant Gentile believers to branches of a wild olive tree (a fruitless variety called the oleaster tree). Then he described some of these branches being grafted by God into the true Israel of God which He depicted as **A CULTIVATED OLIVE TREE** (rendered **A GOOD OLIVE TREE** in the KJV) (Ro. 11:24).*4

A **graft** takes place when a severed branch or shoot from one plant is joined to the living body of another plant—to eventually grow together inseparably as one. Both plants must be cut for this to be effected. Though many Israelites reverently received Jesus as the Messiah, unfortunately many did not. Tragically, like fruitless limbs, they were 'broken off' **the olive tree** as a result.

In a sense, this left an exposed place on **the olive tree** so that those Gentiles, who proved themselves willing to be *cut off* from the world, might be grafted in, included among the people of God. In developing this line of thought,

Paul warned the Gentile converts against any haughty treatment of those Israelites still abiding in unbelief. He rather urged them to deeply respect the special calling placed on the seed of Abraham. He explained:

> *And if some of the branches were broken off, and you being a wild olive tree, were grafted in among them, and with them became a partaker of the root and fatness [the nourishing sap] of THE OLIVE TREE;*
>
> *Do not boast against the branches. But if you do boast, remember that you do not support the root, but the root supports you.*
>
> (Romans 11:17–18 NKJV, NIV)

✤ The Root of the Olive Tree

This passage describes believers as being *"partakers of the root...of the olive tree."* This *"root"* is most likely a reference to the patriarchs—Abraham, Isaac and Jacob—who were all ordained of God to be heirs of the righteousness which comes by faith. And the promise is this: that "if the root is holy" [sanctified and made acceptable to God] "so are *the branches*" (Ro. 11:16). We must always remember that even though we are of the New Will, we will ever be partakers of what took place under the Old. The God who made them righteous has now made us righteous as well. And if we are commanded to honor our fathers and mothers naturally, how much more should we honor our spiritual forefathers who ushered in the correct revelation of God.

The Israel of God is an eternal entity that spans the covenants. It is made up of all who abide in a covenant relationship with the God of Israel. In the New Covenant era, not all who claim to be part of Christendom are truly Christian. So also, "they are not all Israel which are of Israel." (Ro. 9:6, See 7–8.)

There have been many natural born Israelites who were ungodly and, therefore, cut off from "the olive tree." Even in the Old Will, there were proselyted Gentiles, like Ruth, who were grafted into "the olive tree." So there is only one "olive tree"—and only those who have known the true God and are known of Him can claim being a part.

✤ The Fatness of the Olive Tree

The *fatness of the olive tree* (or *the nourishing sap* as the NIV puts it) is expressive of the blessing of Abraham that was passed on to his offspring. There are at least sixteen different facets of this "blessing," all of which God's Covenant offspring have inherited. Galatians 3:13–14 reveals that Christ became a "curse" for us that "the blessing of Abraham might come on the

Gentiles in Christ Jesus."*5 So whether they are Jews or Gentiles, New Covenant believers can trace their heritage back to Abraham and back to the true and living God that Abraham loved and served. How appropriate it is that even modern-day Jews often call Christians *netzer* meaning *a shoot off the root of the olive tree!* And how wonderful it is that we are living in the hour in which the following prophecy is in the process of being gloriously fulfilled in the Israelite people:

> *And they also, if they do not continue in unbelief, will be grafted in, for God is able to graft them in again.*
>
> *For if you were cut out of the olive tree which is wild by nature, and were grafted contrary to nature into A* **CULTIVATED OLIVE TREE,** *how much more will these, who are natural branches, be grafted into their own* **OLIVE TREE.**
>
> (Romans 11:23–24)

THE FULL "BLOSSOMING" OF THE OLIVE TREE REVELATION

There are several other related thoughts that help this revelation of the olive tree to fully 'blossom.'

⌣· **The Noah/Dove Symbol**—When the dove brought back to Noah "a freshly plucked olive leaf" it indicated the flood waters had abated from off the earth. The dove was then sent forth again, never to return. (Gen. 8:8–12) Much more was being communicated symbolically, spiritually and prophetically than that which was apparent. Noah, whose name means *rest*, represented the Everlasting Father, who grants us *rest* in the midst of every storm, in an ark of safety called the truth. The dove symbolizes the Holy Spirit who was sent forth upon the Son of God when He was baptized in Jordan. Three-and-a-half years later 'the dove' carried Jesus back to the Father in heaven as "a freshly plucked olive leaf" from the olive tree of Israel. Then, all because of the Messiah's death, burial and resurrection, the "flood waters" of the curse of death abated and the dove of the Spirit could be sent forth permanently into the world.

⌣· **The Temple Door Symbol**—It is no coincidence that the doors leading to the holy place and the holy of holies in Solomon's temple were made of *olive wood* (also called *oil wood*) overlaid with gold. This speaks of Jesus, the One who said, "I am the door" (Jn. 10:7). As olive wood, He was cut out from the olive tree of Israel, overlaid with the gold of the divine nature. Through His incarnation, He became a door to intimate fellowship and communion with God for all who are privileged to enter.

⌣· **Zechariah's 'Olive Tree' Vision**—In Zechariah 4:1–14 Joshua, the high priest, and Zerubbabel, the governor of Judah, were depicted by Zechariah as "**two olive trees**" standing on either side of a golden lampstand! The lampstand (after the pattern of the temple menorah) was symbolic of Israel, restored out of Babylonian bondage. (Incidentally, the menorah flanked by two olive branches is the emblem of Israel today.) The "**two olive trees**" were these two prominent leaders used of God to supply the 'oil' of the anointing in order to keep the light of truth burning in Israel. Zechariah also called them "**the two olive branches** which through the golden pipes empty the golden oil out of themselves" and "the two anointed ones, who stand beside the LORD of the whole earth" (Zec. 4:3, 12 KJV, 14).

We are told by John, the Revelator, that there will yet be two witnesses, two anointed individuals, who will fulfill this "olive tree" calling again. In the last days they will also empty the golden oil out of themselves prophesying in Jerusalem for "a thousand two hundred and sixty days, clothed in sackcloth" (Rev. 11:3). By these scriptures especially, we can assume that God's anointed representatives are not only called to be individual olive branches on God's corporate olive tree; they are also called to be individual olive trees.[*6]

⌣· **David's Confession**—When Doeg betrayed David to King Saul, the former shepherd boy wrote Psalm 52. In that song, David decrees divine judgment falling on Doeg, then declares:

> But I am like **A GREEN OLIVE TREE** in the house
> of God; I trust in the mercy of God for ever and ever.
> (Psalm 52:8)

So should our confession be in times of persecution. As we arise in boldness to declare our olive tree status, God will protect us and cause us to flourish in the secret of His tabernacle.

⌣· **Olive Tree Offspring**—Another beatitude out of the book of Psalms states, "Blessed is everyone who fears the LORD, who walks in His ways." Then it goes on to promise, "Your wife shall be like a fruitful vine in the very heart of your house, your children like **OLIVE PLANTS** all around your table" (Ps. 128:1–3). As we raise children in the nurture and admonition of the LORD, we stir up the 'olive tree' potential within them. This makes any of us truly blessed: supremely happy and spiritually prosperous, for seeing the blessing of God on our offspring is of all blessings most excellent.

⌣· **The Mount of Olives**—How significant it is that Jesus will actually come back to the Mount of Olives. For as He descends to the place where He once travailed in blood-sweating agony, surely the many olive trees with limbs outstretched will represent the many thousands of spiritual 'olive trees' that will lift their hands all over the world to welcome and praise Him at His return. Hosanna in the highest!!!

THE TREE-SYMBOL COMPLETED

There are several other tree-symbol Scripture passages that bring this unique title-revelation to completion.

The Fig Tree—In Hosea 9:10 God described the Israelites who came out of Egypt as "the firstfruits on **THE FIG TREE** in its first season." The many seeds in a fig could be representative of the multitude of offspring, under both the Old and New Covenants, that can trace their roots to Abraham. In Joel's writings, God again refers to Israel as **HIS FIG TREE**, stripped of its bark by the Chaldeans, then graciously restored (Jl. 1:7, 12, 2:25). Those responding to God's grace at that time were even described as "**good figs**," as opposed to those wicked persons, called "bad figs," who refused to respond. (See Jer. 24:3–10.)

Because many in Israel were found to be fruitless at Jesus' first coming, He literally cursed a fig tree. This fig tree then withered away, drying up from the roots. This happened right after the cleansing of the temple and Jesus' triumphant entry into Jerusalem. It was the only 'dark' miracle Jesus ever performed—and it symbolically spoke of a very dark era awaiting the Jewish people. (See Mt. 21:1–22; Mk. 11:12–23.) The promise was given, though, of a much brighter era yet to come. Jesus prophesied that in the last days, the fig tree's branch, yet tender, will put forth its leaves and that this will be a sign of the soon coming of the LORD (Mt. 24:32–33). This most likely speaks first of Israel being restored as a nation in 1948, and second, of a national revival of Jews recognizing Jesus (Yeshua) as their Messiah in the end time. Then the Kingdom Age will come when:

> ...lo, the winter is past, the rain is over and
> gone...and...**THE FIG TREE** puts forth her green figs.
> (Song of Solomon 2:11, 13)

This is a beautiful, figurative statement revealing that the Israel of God, ultimately consisting of the redeemed of all ages, will bring forth sweeter fruit than ever during the Millennial Era to come. She will rule this world in righteousness, peace and the fear of the LORD.

The Fir or Cypress Trees—In the King James Version of Isaiah 14:8 the people of God are referred to as **FIR TREES** (**CYPRESS TREES** in the NKJV, **PINE TREES** in the NIV). Also, in Hosea 14:8, we find God declaring the importance of His own watchfulness over restored Ephraim, saying, "I am like

A GREEN FIR TREE; [**A GREEN PINE TREE**; your fruitfulness comes from Me"] (KJV, NIV). In other words, God was explaining to Israel the benefit of abiding in the 'shade' of His care and authority. If they did, they would bear fruit. If we abide under His influence, we also take on His image and become evergreen **FIR TREES** or **PINE TREES** in this world (alive and flourishing even in the dead of winter and providing watchful care over others).

⌣ˑ **The Tree of Life**—Proverbs 11:30 says, "The fruit of the righteous is *a tree of life*, and he who wins souls is wise." This is probably one of the most powerful tree symbol passages in the Bible. Notice it is not the unrighteous, but the righteous that possess this potential of imparting the life of God to others. How is this done? Many ways, but primarily through the words we speak. Proverbs 3:18 speaks of wisdom as *"a tree of life"* and Proverbs 15:4 reveals that *"a wholesome tongue is a tree of life."* If our words are full of faith in God, consecration to God and wisdom from God, they can revive the most weary and famished soul. By cultivating a righteous character, full of the fruit of the Spirit, and by speaking divinely inspired words of wisdom, each son of God, in a sense, becomes **A TREE OF LIFE**. Furthermore, when we take on this role, we are simply emerging in the image of the firstborn Son. (See also Pr. 3:18; 13:12.)

There was most likely a literal "tree of life" in the garden of Eden. And there will most likely be a similar literal "plant of renown" in New Jerusalem. This life-giving tree will forever sustain God's offspring. In the highest sense, the *"tree of life* in the midst of the paradise of God" may be Jesus Himself (Gen. 2:9–17, Rev. 2:7). He is the "Righteous LORD" and the "Eternal Word" whose righteousness, wisdom, and wholesome tongue have become, for all time and eternity, *a tree of life* to all who believe. How thrilling it is also that those who truly partake of Jesus, eventually become like Him! If He is *a tree of life* to His people, we in turn should become *trees of life* to each other.

In one sense, the tree of the knowledge of good and evil is comparable to the law, (that brought a curse and death) while the tree of life is comparable to the message of grace (that brings God's blessing and life, now and forevermore). If we are agents of the message of grace, we are *trees of life* bringing restoration to the fallen seed of Adam.

THE ULTIMATE OUTCOME

Isaiah described the grand day of Satan's overthrow by symbolically relating it to the overthrow of the king of Babylon. This profound prophecy begins with the exclamatory statement, "How the oppressor has come to an end!"—then it continues with the prophecy:

> *The LORD has broken the rod of the wicked…All the lands*
> *are at rest and at peace; they break into singing. Even **THE***
> ***PINE TREES [THE FIR TREES]** and **THE CEDARS OF***
> ***LEBANON** exult over you and say, Now that you have been*
> *laid low, no woodsman comes to cut us down.*
>
> (Isaiah 14:4–8, NIV, KJV)

This passage of Scripture communicates, in parabolic language, that once Lucifer is fully 'cut down to the ground' there will be no satanic powers seeking to cut us down. There will be no evil 'woodsmen' hacking at our minds with a daily attack of sharp-edged, axe-like temptations.

Thank God! That will all be over! We will be free from all pain and free from all fear. We will enjoy undisturbed bliss in the presence of the LORD. We will be 'evergreen trees,' like the pine, the fir and the cedar, planted forever in the land of our inheritance. (See Amos 9:15.)

No wonder Isaiah foretold that in the day of restoration, the mountains and hills will break forth into singing and "all the trees of the field shall clap their hands" (Is. 55:12). Also, the Psalmist declared:

> *Let the field be joyful, and all that is in it. Then all **THE***
> ***TREES OF THE WOOD** will rejoice before the LORD.*
>
> *For He is coming, He is coming, to judge the earth. He*
> *shall judge the world with righteousness, and the peoples*
> *with His truth.*
>
> (Psalm 96:12–13)

In that day, we will be, in an absolute sense, **TREES OF RIGHTEOUSNESS, THE PLANTING OF THE LORD**. We will be made perfect in every way, rooted in our ordination forever.

As the poetic language of Scripture testifies, we will ever be **CEDAR TREES BESIDE THE WATERS** of eternal life. We will finally arrive at full fruition (in the same way as all plants do) by our reactions to, and our interactions with, the external elements and influences we encounter in this world.

In the most glorious sense, we will be **THE TREES OF EDEN** flourishing evermore in the garden of our God. (See Ezk. 31:8–9.)

We will be **LIVING MEMORIALS** of the goodness of our God.
Our leaves will not wither.
Our fruit will never fall to the ground.
Our limbs will ever be uplifted in worship of the Gracious Gardener and Orchard Overseer who first planted the seed of this tree-potential in our

hearts—and then, with patient perseverance, nurtured it to fruitfulness, maturity and eternal glory.

Will we then be fully grown? Probably not! For living trees never stop growing—and neither do we. For "of the increase of His...peace, there will be NO END" (Is. 9:7). We will ever be growing in the peace of God as we eternally pass from glory to glory.

Endnotes

*1 In Numbers 24:5–6 Balaam also prophesied that the tabernacles of the Israelites bore the resemblance of "**trees of lign aloes**" (KJV) or "**aloes** planted by the LORD." These are large, luxuriant trees containing a resin and an essential oil necessary in the production of a perfume highly prized in ancient times. This perfume-producing tree is included in the orchard that represents the garden-bride of the Song of Solomon (Song 4:14). Also, the "smell of myrrh, and aloes, and cassia" is said to be resident (prophetically and symbolically) in the very garments of the Son of God (Ps. 45:8). We assume, therefore, that this precious ointment represents the sweet fragrance of eternal life that was poured out on Jesus, and is excellently bestowed on every one of those redeemed ones who make up His bride. Although the "**trees of lign aloes**" were used to describe the tabernacles of the Israelites, the analogy is applicable to the homes of all those who are serving the truth.

*2 Other examples of the seed of Abraham being represented as trees include: (1). The nation of Israel after the invasion of the Assyrian army being reduced to a remnant, like **A Teil Tree** (KJV) (also called **A Terebinth Tree** in the NKJV) or an **Oak Tree** being cut down to a stump, but sprouting again. (See Is. 6:13 KJV, NKJV, Jb. 14:7–9.) Isaiah 1:30 describes Zion as a "**terebinth** whose leaf fades." (2). Israel is also described as a forest devoured by fire and destroyed in Zechariah 11:1–2. In this passage, God's holy nation is described as the **Forest of the Vintage** in the KJV, the **Thick Forest** in the NKJV, and the **Dense Forest** in the NIV, made up of **Cedars, Cypress Trees, Fir Trees, Pine Trees, Mighty Trees, Stately Trees** and Oaks of Bashan (KJV, NKJV, NIV). (3). Judah's destruction during the Babylonian invasion is described in Ezekiel 20:45–49 as the **Forest Land, the South.** (NKJV), **the Forest of the South Field** (KJV), or the **Forest of the Southland** (NIV), consumed with a raging fire destroying both **green trees and dry trees** (the good and the evil). (4). The Jews in Babylon are described as **A Willow Tree** (Ezk. 17:5). (5). The Assyrian empire is described in Ezekiel 31 as a very majestic **cedar** envied by the other "**trees in the garden of God.**" The other nations of the world are also spoken of as "**the trees of Eden**" and "**the cedars in the garden of God,**" fir trees and chestnut trees. (6). Hypocritical leaders are described as being "**fig trees** without figs" in Jeremiah 8:13 and wicked leaders are compared to "**a green bay tree**" (KJV) or "**a green tree** in its native soil" (NIV) spreading itself over a wide area in Psalm 37:35. (7). In Jeremiah 11:19 the prophet's enemies say concerning him, "Let us destroy **the tree** with its fruit."

*3 Miller, *Harper's Bible Dictionary*, (NavPress Inc., Colorado Springs, Colorado) p. 504, under **Olive**.

*4 Dake, Finis Jennings, *Dake's Annotated Bible*, (Dakes Bible Sales, Inc., Lawrenceburg, Georgia) New Testament, p. 169, col. 4, note p.

*5 To fully grasp this term "the blessing of Abraham," read the chapter on *The Children of Abraham* in Volume One of **Our Glorious Inheritance**.

*6 It is possible that these two olive trees also represent Israel and the church, who will both be used in these last days as 'witnesses' in the earth of the reality and power of the God of Abraham.

THE JUST

---

*...as it is written, **THE JUST** shall live by faith.*

(Romans 1:17)

Other related titles included in this chapter are: **Just Persons**—Lk. 15:7, **Just Men**— Heb. 12:23, **Instruments of Justice**—Ro. 6:13 DouRh.

THE JUST

*...as it written, **THE JUST** shall live by faith.*

(Romans 1:17)

$\mathcal{T}$his very title-scripture kindled the first spark in Martin Luther's heart that eventually ignited a blaze of fiery reformation sweeping across the European continent. This fire has never gone out. It is still burning today (even in my heart as I write this chapter).

Martin Luther was a soul-searching Catholic monk who was desperate to secure a right relationship with God. He was impassioned for truth. He was an extremist in His attempts at capturing God's attention and favor. In the monastery, he studied the Word in depth, pursued many means of self-abasement and zealously involved himself in all the established rituals and ceremonies—but to no avail. Regardless of what he did, how much he prayed, or how deeply he sacrificed, he still felt totally unacceptable in the sight of heaven. He made the statement that for two years he went through *"such anguish as no pen can describe."*[*1]

The veil fell from his eyes in 1508 A.D. when Romans 1:17, like an arrow, penetrated his heart (the title-scripture given above). Describing the experience, Luther explained:

> *Night and day I pondered until I saw the connection between the justice of God and the statement that '**the just shall live by his faith.**' Then I grasped that the justice of God is that righteousness by which through grace and sheer mercy God justifies us through faith. **Thereupon I felt myself to be reborn and to have gone through open doors into paradise.** The whole of Scripture took on new meaning and whereas before the justice of God' had filled me with hate, now it became to me inexpressibly sweet in greater love. **This passage of Paul became to me a gate of heaven...**[*2]*

In a moment, what had been a confusing, religious maze instead became a straight and plain path. Martin Luther finally understood the depth of what the apostle Paul meant when he quoted Habakkuk 2:4 in his epistle. Man is never justified before God by works of righteousness alone. Man is never justified by participating in mere religious rituals. Man is never justified by becoming a member of a certain church or denomination. MAN IS JUSTIFIED

BY SIMPLE FAITH IN THE FINISHED WORK OF CALVARY AND SINCERE, FAITH-FILLED SUBMISSION TO THE AUTHORITY OF GOD'S WORD.

This is the true Gospel of Christ of which Paul said he was not ashamed, for "in it the righteousness of God is revealed from faith to faith..." (Ro. 1:17).

Another translation says this is **"God's plan for making men right in His sight, a process begun and continued by their faith"** (PME).

Martin Luther must have realized more than ever on that day (and we should echo his sentiments now) that no earthly organization possesses the exclusive authority of imparting to its adherents a right standing with God. Only heaven can grant this salvation-gift. And without a doubt, any humble and believing person can obtain this life-transforming touch on an individual basis. Ephesians 2:8–9 communicates this truth well:

> *For by grace you have been saved through faith, and*
> *that not of yourselves; it is the gift of God,*
> *Not of works, lest anyone should boast.*

As we gaze upward to fully comprehend this towering truth of the reformation, it is a moving thing to see as well that the name **Habakkuk** means *love's embrace* (YC). This is significant, because it was through Habakkuk's prophecy—*"The just shall live by his faith"*—that the true revelation of the love of God *embraced* Paul's heart and life. Through Paul, the same effect was then transferred to Martin Luther.

Now, we who believe in justification by faith have all received *love's embrace,* for our faith has brought us into intimate contact with the God who is no longer afar off. We have learned, quite the contrary, that He is ever-present and ever-ready to fill our lives with His personal, compassionate touch.

RIGHTLY DIVIDING THE TRUTH

Rightly dividing the doctrine of **justification**, and rightly identifying those who are truly **just** in God's sight, is an essential spiritual activity. The biblical information on this subject is often carried to two erroneous extremes. Liberal theology tends to **include** some who do not measure up to God's standard, while a legalistic approach to God's Word tends to **exclude** some of the very ones God has accepted and included. Concerning this dilemma, Proverbs 17:15 warns, "He who **justifies** the wicked, and he who condemns **the just,** both of them alike are an abomination to the LORD." (See Is. 29:21.) So let us carefully and prayerfully proceed.

Those definitions of the word **just,** relevant to this study, are:

(1) That which conforms to a standard of correctness: PROPER
(2) Acting or being in conformity to what is moral, ethical, upright or good: RIGHTEOUS
(3) That which is legally correct: PROMOTING JUSTICE

Reduced to simplicity, "just persons" are righteous persons—those whose lifestyle and attitudes are in conformity with the laws of God. (Lk. 15:7, See Ezk. 18:5, 9, Pr. 20:7 KJV, NKJV.)

This simple definition is doubly confirmed when we see that, quite often, the same Hebrew and Greek words translated **just** (Heb. *tsaddiq, tsedeq, yashar;* Gr. *dikaios*) are also rendered **righteous.**

Though many more have surely qualified for such a status, God has used this descriptive term specifically in reference to only seven individuals in the King James Version of the Bible (Noah–Gen. 6:9, Joseph–Mt. 1:19, John the Baptist–Mk. 6:20, Simeon–Luke 2:25, Joseph of Arimathea–Luke 23:50, Cornelius–Acts 10:22, and Lot–2 Pt. 2:7).[*3]

To cite one particular instance, Genesis 6:9 says that "Noah was a **just** man, perfect in his generations. Noah walked with God." By this Scripture, it is clear that Noah was a very moral, righteous, God-fearing man. But even though this Old Testament patriarch was honorably described this way, it is also apparent that his own righteousness was insufficient to fully justify him before God. According to Genesis 6:8, Noah received "**grace** in the eyes of the LORD" (which is *the unmerited favor of God*). Also Hebrews 11:7 (KJV) reveals that by obeying his particular revelation of God's Word, Noah became "an heir of the righteousness which is *by faith.*" So by grace and faith he was justified and by grace and faith he was saved: not by works of righteousness alone.

We can conclude, therefore, if it was compulsory for righteous Noah to obtain imparted righteousness from God, then we, too, must have more than the righteousness achieved by mere works. Ecclesiastes 7:20 confirms the dilemma of our fallen state:

> There is not a **just** man on earth who does good and does not sin.

Though this passage may sound contradictory to the information already offered, it is not. Speaking relatively (compared to the rest of the world) there have been many just men and women. Speaking in an absolute sense (compared to God) there are no just men and women, for all have erred in His sight.

Moreover, if the Creator failed to intervene for us, we would all be hopelessly given over to the unjust status we inherited from Adam. No wonder in the book of Job, Bildad, the Shuhite, posed the following question:

> *"How then can man be **justified** with God? or how can he be clean that is born of a woman?*
>
> *Behold even...the stars are not pure in His sight. How much less man, that is a worm? And the son of man, which is a worm?"*
>
> (Job 25:4–6 KJV, See Ps. 143:2 KJV)*⁴

This is the distressing issue, the recurring inquiry, that has weighed heavily on the minds of God-fearing men and women for centuries. The Bible is not only a choice, unique and ideal revelation of the answer; it is the only legitimate answer!

THE OLD WILL DILEMMA
THE NEW WILL ANSWER

The Old Testament revealed God's great power and love toward His chosen, but also—through the law—it exposed the impassable gulf between God and the human race. The New Testament built a Word-bridge to the other side. The Spirit now woos all of humanity—both Jews and Gentiles—to cross over and be saved. Paul explained the purpose and the effect of the law in his epistle to the Romans:

> *Therefore by the deeds of the law no flesh will be **justified** in His sight, for by the law is the knowledge of sin.*
>
> (Romans 3:20, See Gal. 2:16.)

And again...

> *For sin, taking occasion by the commandment, deceived me, and by it killed me.*
>
> *Therefore the law is holy, and the commandment holy and just and good.*
>
> *Has then what is good become death to me? Certainly not! But sin, that it might appear sin, was producing death in me through what is good, so that sin through the commandment might become exceedingly sinful.*
>
> (Romans 7:11–13)

In other words, Paul was explaining that the law proved, beyond the shadow of a doubt, the utter depravity of the flesh. Technically and legally, it labeled us all among **"the unjust"** by exalting the holiness of God. The law not only put a restraint on the flesh, it convinced fallen men and women (who could not attain to the law) of their absolute need for a Savior and a Justifier. (See also Gal. 2:16; 3:10–13; 5:1–4.)

There is only one Man in all of history who can fill up the measure of this great demand of the human race. His name is Jesus and it is certain that He alone can save.

JESUS—OUR DAYSMAN AND MEDIATOR

In the days of three of the most righteous, anointed prophets who ever lived (Jeremiah, Ezekiel and Daniel) God spoke the following words:

> *I sought for a man among them, that should make up*
> *the hedge, and stand in the gap before Me for the land,*
> *that I should not destroy it: but I found none.*
> (Ezekiel 22:30 KJV)

How terribly disturbing this is—that there was no mediator, even among God's most elite representatives, who could successfully reconcile Israel back to the Almighty God! How distressing it is to realize that on a certain level this scripture refers, not only to Israel, but also, to the sum of humanity! For there has never been a man good enough to "stand in the gap" (the awful gap created by the fall of Adam) and "make up the hedge" (the hedge of protection and grace around all humanity, broken down by the entrance of satanic powers).

Since lust and uncleanness invaded this realm, there has never been a human being holy enough to stop the progress of sin, nor repair the severed relationship between God and man. No patriarch, no prophet, no priest, no king, no earthly prince, no ascetic or person of great religious fervor. No, not one. That is, until the incarnation, when Jesus became the **"Daysman"** (the arbitrator) "that might lay His hand upon us both," or as Paul put it, the **"Mediator** between God and man" (Jb. 9:33 KJV, 1 Tim. 2:5).

Now, through Jesus' intervention and mediation we can obtain and maintain a right standing in the presence of the Father. Through Him we can legally claim the wonderful status of being **justified**, a beautiful biblical term that means:

(1) To be judged, or treated as righteous and worthy of salvation.
(2) To be formally acquitted of guilt by God Himself (just as if we never sinned).

Sanctification is the *act* of being cleansed, made righteous, and separated unto God. Justification is the status that results: being reckoned clean and righteous by God Himself. Logically speaking, believers must be first *sanctified* before they can be *justified*. Believers must first be *made holy* before they are recognized as *being holy* in heaven's sight—and this happens the very moment the blood of Jesus touches our wayward hearts.

OUR SUPREME AND PERFECT EXAMPLE

It is only right that Jesus be the sole source of this redemption-miracle taking place in our lives. He ran the course first and then paved the road with mercy and hope for those who would follow. He graciously made a way for sin-filled, **unjust** men and women to be washed, cleansed, transformed and included among that blessed group entitled **the just.**

Jesus, our Forerunner, bore this title Himself. In Acts 3:14 He is called "the Holy One and **the Just.**" Then in 1 Peter 3:18, the apostle explained that Jesus " suffered once for sins, **the just** for **the unjust**, that He might bring us to God." Yet even though the firstborn Son of God was referred to as "**the just,**" 1 Timothy 3:16 brings out a unique aspect of this revelation:

> *And without controversy great is the mystery of godliness:*
> *God was manifested in the flesh, **justified in the Spirit**,*
> *seen by angels, preached among the Gentiles, believed on*
> *in the world, received up in glory.*

This is such a thought provoking passage of Scripture!

First (and admittedly, this is the most logical interpretation) it could mean that although Jesus appeared to be only a man in the flesh, He was *justified* before the people by the miraculous manifestation of the power of the Holy Spirit and His claim to deity was confirmed.

But second, it could also be a revelation that Jesus Christ Himself, the spotless, sinless Lamb of God, was, in a certain sense, not even *justified in the flesh!* How could this be? Because His flesh became sin on Calvary's hill. It was then that He became one with us in our state of separation from the Father. (See 1 Pt. 2:24.)

The Spirit that came to Him in Jordan may have lifted temporarily from Him as he writhed in anguish on the cross. He cried, "Eloi, Eloi, lama sabachthani?" which is interpreted as meaning "My God, My God, why have You forsaken Me?" (Mk. 15:34).

As heaven's sent-forth scapegoat, the judgment that we should have received was instead transferred to Him. He became "a worm, and no man; a reproach of men, and despised of the people" (Ps. 22:6).[*5]

Immediately after His natural demise, though, 1 Timothy 3:16 reveals He was *"justified in the Spirit."* Several other major translations of the same passage say that He was *"vindicated in the Spirit."* (To be **vindicated** means *to be delivered, avenged, exonerated, confirmed, or defended and protected from attack.*)

Whatever this fully involved with respect to the Son of God, only God knows, but one thing is sure: though "the chastisement of our peace was upon Him" in the flesh, He was delivered from that terrible, substitutionary judgment "in the Spirit." Though Jesus, as the Son of Man, bore all of our sin and shame, He was *exonerated* and *confirmed* as the Son of God when He was resurrected from the dead. (See Ro. 1:4.) The Father *defended* and *avenged* Him, purposing to neither leave His soul in sheol (Abraham's bosom), nor suffer His Holy One to see corruption (Ps. 16:10). Jesus was *protected from attack* and restored to His former glory and position of righteousness (for the wicked one came and found nothing in Him).

1 Peter 3:18 (KJV) adds that He was "put to death in the flesh, *but quickened by the Spirit."* (The NKJV says *"made alive."*) When He was *quickened* (*made alive* again) He was judged utterly pure and reckoned the absolute of holiness. He was made perfect (whole and complete) (Heb. 5:9).

Sin could not penetrate Him.
The world could not contaminate Him.
Death could not hold Him.
Satan could not conquer Him.

He arose victorious, completely and supremely *justified* in the sight of heaven. Now all those who believe are *quickened* together with Him and *justified* by Him. (See Gal. 2:17, Col. 2:13 KJV.)

This possible interpretation of 1 Timothy 3:16 should automatically birth a question in our minds. **If the Son of God Himself could not be justified 'in the flesh' at the dawn of the New Covenant (though He was absolutely flawless) how can we expect to be justified 'in the flesh' now (for admittedly, we have been full of flaws)?**

Logic and reason demand the following logical and reasonable conclusion: our justification is also "in the Spirit." Through faith, humility and sincere repentance, we are resurrected in Jesus Christ, inheriting the right to share in His supreme triumph. We obtain entrance into His procured position of blamelessness and holiness. We are made alive with the very life of God. We are birthed into righteousness, for the Holy One of Israel, "that Just One," has come to live in our hearts (Ac. 22:14). He was "delivered for our offences, and was raised again for our *justification*" (Ro. 4:25 KJV).

Our heavenly Father now sees us "in Christ." By His indwelling Spirit we are considered as perfect and as righteous as He. (See 2 Cor. 5:21, Col. 1:28.) In the flesh we would all surely stand condemned before the throne of the Almighty, "for all have sinned and come short of the glory of God." In the Spirit, though, we are "holy and without blame before Him in love" (Ro. 3:23 KJV, Eph. 1:4). We are "unreproveable in His sight" [holy, and blameless, and above reproach] for if Christ be in us, "the body is dead because of sin; but the spirit is life [your spirit is alive] because of righteousness" (Col. 1:22 KJV, NKJV, Ro. 8:10 KJV, NIV).

This is not that righteousness which is supposedly attained by religious or moral works (upon which almost all the religions of this world are based).

This is the righteousness which is "from God, by faith" (Ph. 3:9).

This righteousness, like a brilliant light, has permeated our spirits, dispelling the darkness of sin. His Spirit and our spirits have blended together and become one. Because of this sacred union, now we can shout aloud—"Not only are we forgiven; we are righteous; we are clean!"*6

The God who proved Himself quite capable of making *something out of nothing* in the beginning has now proved Himself to be just as adept at making *nothing out of something.*

Our sins were surely *something.*

Though unseen by man and hidden behind the veil of the past, still, there was no way that we could deny their existence. Neither could we escape the resulting condemnation and guilt. But the precious blood of Jesus has worked a wondrous work—actually blotting out our sins as well as "the hand-writing of ordinances [requirements] that was against us" (Col. 2:14 KJV, NKJV).

THE "BLOTTING OUT" OF SIN

If our iniquities have been 'blotted out,' then they have been obliterated, wiped out of existence. (See Ac. 3:19.) Let's explore this terminology. A *blotter* (used for *'blotting out'*) can be some kind of spongy material used to absorb ink, or it can be a mark that covers or hides something from view. Either way, the idea of *'blotting out'* speaks especially of this status of justification (the status of being righteous in God's sight, just as if we never sinned). As far as God is concerned, these former sins no longer exist. This all-knowing, omniscient Creator, who never suffers lapses of memory, has given the gracious and generous promise to His people:

> *I will forgive their iniquity, and their sin I will remember no more.*

> (Jeremiah 31:34)

Think of the awesomeness of such a statement.

Because we have sincerely repented, the God who cannot forget has forced Himself to forget the awful stains of our past. This is simply marvelous and nothing less than miraculous. (And if God has been so compassionate as to bury the grievous memories of our former failures, how dare we be so foolish, unbelieving and guilt-ridden as to unearth them again!) As King Hezekiah prayed, so should we rejoicingly declare to our heavenly Father, "You have lovingly delivered my soul from the pit of corruption, for You have cast all my sins behind Your back" (Is. 38:17).

Though we may have faltered along the way, we can still say, "Because He delights in unchanging love...He will again have compassion on us; He will tread our iniquities underfoot"...He will "cast all our sins into *the depths of the sea*" (Mi. 7:18–19 NAS, NKJV). How beautiful this statement is—especially when we realize that in the New Creation to come, there will be *"no more sea"*! (Rev. 21:1).

If our sins have been thrown behind God's back and hurled into the depths of the sea (and the sea will one day be non-existent) surely this is God's beautiful way of confirming again and again that our sins, once forgiven, are also non-existent—never to be remembered again!

No wonder Paul made the bold assertion:

> *Who shall bring a charge against God's elect?* **It is God who justifies.**
> *Who is he who condemns? It is Christ who died, and furthermore is also risen, who is even at the right hand of God, who also makes intercession for us.*
>
> (Romans 8:33–34)

Because of this truth, "there is therefore now no condemnation to those who are in Christ Jesus, who do not walk according to the flesh, but according to the Spirit" (Romans 8:1). To walk "according to the flesh" is to seek carnal, sinful things with no thought of repentance and no intention of change. There definitely is condemnation upon those who maintain such a rebellious attitude, even if they happen to claim salvation.

To walk "according to the Spirit" is altogether different. If we truly fit in this category, we have set before ourselves the high goal of perfection. Such a supreme challenge is normal for children of the covenant for *"the way of* **the just** *is uprightness"* and *"the just* man walketh in his integrity" (Is. 26:7, Pr. 20:7 KJV).

Uprightness is simply the *way* we should think, the *way* we should feel, the *way* we should act. We are the just offspring of a just God—and being just is simply a manifestation of who we are. It is part of the divine nature we have inherited.

JESUS—OUR ADVOCATE

1 John 2:1–2 declares, *"...If anyone sins, we have an Advocate with the Father, Jesus Christ the righteous: and He Himself is the propitiation for our sins..."* Note that John said *"if* anyone sins," not *"when* anyone sins." This scripture was never given as a loophole for unbridled, sinful activity. But it is a sure source of strength for that person who is unfortunately overwhelmed by temptation or overtaken in a fault. In times of weakness or failure, the promise is that Jesus Christ, the *righteous* (Gr. *dikaios*, pr. *dik'-ah-yos*, the *Just* One) will be our **Advocate** (our Defense Attorney).

He is not a prosecuting attorney seeking to prove our guiltiness. He is not "the accuser of the brethren"—for such is the nature of Satan (Rev. 12:10).

Jesus' passion and longing is to justify.

Now this same Defender of the weak and the repentant has ascended into heaven. He has assumed, not only the role of the Judge of all the earth, but also the position of being our Advocate, our defense attorney. He is delighted to supply the very evidence that proves the innocence of those in covenant with Him. Because of Calvary, in the celestial courtroom, we already stand acquitted of all guilt, if we dare to boldly appropriate that which is rightfully ours.

This is the miracle of salvation—that Jesus was, and is and always will be *"the propitiation for our sins."* This means that He was the *appeasement.* He *propitiated* or *appeased* the Father by satisfying the demands of justice. And now, because of Jesus' substitutionary, sacrificial death, any person can rightfully and legally enter the presence of God expecting to obtain mercy.

We are free from fear and can recover from the worst of circumstances. Proverbs 24:16 explains that a *just* man (a righteous man) may fall seven times, but he rises up again. If this rebounding from failure was true under the Old Testament order, how much more true it is under grace. None of us should intentionally err, but if, unfortunately, this is the case, neither should we expect to be rejected by God. Jesus went through the horror of rejection in our stead.

On the contrary, we are accepted now—and restoration grace is a grand part of our spiritual heritage. No wonder the Bible claims that "blessings are upon the head of **the just**" (Pr. 10:6 KJV).

Our sins prior to salvation no longer have any power over us. Our errors since that time will not reverse God's decision (if we maintain faith, humility, sincerity and repentance before His throne). Any mistakes yet to come in our future have already been provided for through the cross.

This is exactly why the Bible asserts that **"the just shall live by his faith..."** for we keep ourselves spiritually alive and we perpetuate our communion and harmonious relationship with the Father by **constantly maintaining faith** in the wonderful promises of God.

So we see, in this era especially, faith is the beginning and the end of the quest for a right standing with God.

ELEVEN MEANS OF JUSTIFICATION

The following are eleven different means by which justification is effected toward believers. All are witnessed clearly in the Scripture. Some are the result of God's action toward us (1–6), while others are the result of our actions toward Him (7–11). Of course, these last five are not possible without His inner influence. So all the glory, in the end, belongs to God. All of these means of justification must blend together harmoniously if the song of justification is to be sung over our lives.

(1) Our Position "in Christ"—The NIV of Galatians 2:17 speaks of believers being "justified *in Christ*." When we submit to His headship and surrender to His authority, we are placed in His body ("in Christ"). Automatically, we become heirs to His flawless character, just as accepted in the presence of the Father as He. (See 2 Cor. 5:21, Eph. 1:6, 1 Jn. 4:17.)

(2) Grace—Titus 3:7 declares that *"being justified by His grace,* we should be made heirs according to the hope of eternal life." We must never lose sight of this source of justification. Galatians 5:4 warns, "Christ is become of no effect unto you"—"you who attempt to be *justified* by the law; you have fallen from grace" (KJV, NKJV). Grace is unearned divine favor and God's ability imparted to us. Grace is never earned; it is God's gift to those who believe. (See Eph. 2:8.)

(3-4) The Name of Jesus and the Spirit of God—1 Corinthians 6:11, like a clarion call of victory, trumpets out the message that we are *"justified in the name of the LORD Jesus and by the Spirit of our God."* This is true because normally it is only when we call on *the name* of the LORD that He enables us to appropriate His life-giving promises—and these blessings and benefits always come to us "through *the Spirit.*"

(5) The Blood of Jesus—Romans 5:8–9 reveals how we are initiated and kept in a justified state:

> *But God demonstrates His own love toward us, in that
> while we were still sinners, Christ died for us.*
> *Much more then, having now been **justified by His
> blood**, we shall be saved from wrath through Him.*

By the continual flow of the precious blood of Jesus through our regenerated spirits, we are kept clean and pure before the LORD. By this we maintain a status of sanctification and justification, if we maintain an attitude of repentance and submission in His sight.

Natural blood serves a twofold purpose: purging the body of poison and replenishing the body with life-giving oxygen from the lungs and nutrients from the digestive system. In like manner, the blood of Jesus serves a twofold purpose: constantly purging our hearts of the poison of sin and replenishing our spirits, moment-by-moment, with the life-giving, righteousness-imparting presence of the Spirit of God. By this miraculous process we are "saved from wrath through Him." That Scripture could be referring to the wrath that will manifest at the final judgment or simply the wrath that we deserve now because of our failures. The justifying blood of the Lamb liberates us from both. (See Heb. 9:22.)

(6) The Knowledge of God—Only those who actually know the LORD partake of these justification promises. Isaiah prophesied long ago of the horribleness of the crucifixion, then he climaxed his fifty-third chapter declaring "by *His knowledge* My righteous servant shall *justify* many" (Is. 53:11). The "knowledge of the LORD" speaks of more than head knowledge. It is personal contact with the LORD of glory. We draw near to Him and He draws near to us—and in 'knowing' Him we are justified. (See Ho. 6:6, 1 Cor. 15:34, 2 Cor. 4:6, 1 Pt. 1:2–6.)

(7) Faith—Romans 5:1 says, "Therefore, having been *justified by faith*, we have peace with God through our LORD Jesus Christ." Other verses verify the requirement of faith, such as: Galatians 2:16; 3:8, 24 and Acts 13:39. This last verse announces concerning the Son of God, "by Him everyone who believes is justified FROM ALL THINGS from which you could not be justified by the law of Moses."

(8) A Correct Confession—Justification also comes by properly confessing God's Word. Jesus said "by your *words* you will be *justified*, and by your words you will be condemned" (Mt. 12:37). Romans 10:10 further reveals, "For with the heart one believes unto righteousness, and with the mouth confession is made unto salvation." If we speak doubt and self-condemnation, we push ourselves away from God's justifying power, but if we speak faith-filled words concerning God's provisions for us, then, as a general rule, what we say is what we get. Therefore, except in rare cases, vocally claiming the Word is also an absolute necessity if we are to be reckoned among **the just**.

(9-10) Contrition and Humility—A proper faith-confession is not sufficient, of itself, to justify us in the sight of God. Confessing God's Word must be balanced with *humility* before Him. It was not the proud, self-assured Pharisee, but rather the contrite, breast-beating publican that "went down to His house *justified*" (Lk. 18:14). In that same passage of Scripture, Jesus went on to assure us that everyone who "humbles himself will be exalted." And one of the grandest ways God exalts us is to reckon us righteous in His sight.

(11) Works—Finally, it must also be mentioned that if we truly manifest *justifying faith* and receive *justifying grace*, automatically, *justifying works* will result. For this cause, James exhorted that "faith without works is dead" and *"by works a man is justified, and not by faith only"* (Ja. 2:24, 26).

This is not a contradiction of the scriptures we have studied up to this point. The "works" referred to are not the dead, ceremonial works that resulted from certain ordinances of the law. THEY ARE LIVING, SPIRITUAL, WORSHIPFUL WORKS THAT ARE BIRTHED INTO BEING THROUGH FAITH AND ARE, THEREFORE, THE VERIFICATION AND EVIDENCE OF FAITH.

Abraham demonstrated that he possessed faith by offering up Isaac. Rahab proved that she had faith by hiding the Jewish spies. Joshua proved the existence of his faith by marching, along with the armies of Israel, around the walls of Jericho and shouting the seventh time around. Elijah confirmed his faith by rebuilding the altar and covering the sacrifice with water before calling fire down from heaven. We also reveal and substantiate our claim to faith when spiritually effected works manifest.

It must be reemphasized that it is by faith that we are justified. But again, these kinds of faith-effected works are the very proof of faith's existence and proof that we can legally claim the status of being *reckoned right with God!*

PROMOTING JUSTICE

If we have been granted this grand status of being **the just**, automatically we should become God's means of establishing divine **justice** in the earth. Proverbs 21:15 even announces, "It is joy for **the just** to do **justice**." These two related qualities are inseparable. Once repentant sinners are justified in the sight of God, our passion should be to infiltrate society as a whole with God's righteous judgments: the moral standards that proceed from Him. **Justice** could be defined as **just-ness**: being ruled by just and right attitudes in our relationships with God and others. We are commanded to meditate on "whatever things are…just," but this should be followed by doing—or the seed is unsown, stored in the seed-bag of our own minds (Ph. 4:8).

Weary of mere formalism and empty religiosity, the Most High complained to Israel of old, "Take away from Me the noise of your songs—*but let justice run down like water and righteousness like a mighty stream*" (Am. 5:23–24). His feelings are still the same. When we, the church of the living God, become self-centered, blessings-oriented and primarily focused on our own needs being met, quite often spiritual slackness sets in, robbing us of our calling to be standard-bearers. However, when we boldly lift up the standard of justice in the world, automatically increased blessings should follow.

Doing justice means setting things right or maintaining what is right. It means pursuing, establishing and maintaining honorable relationships with fellow human beings. God refused to withhold from Abraham the revelation of judgments soon to fall on Sodom, for He knew this great patriarch would command his offspring to "keep the way of the LORD to do righteousness and *justice*" (Gen. 18:19). In like manner, God will surely reveal to the body of Christ in these last days the unfolding of His mysterious plan if we maintain a passion for treating others justly in the name of the LORD.

Proverbs 21:3 convincingly asserts that doing "righteousness and *justice* is more acceptable to the LORD than sacrifice." As we do this, yielding our "members as...**INSTRUMENTS OF JUSTICE** unto God" (Ro. 6:13 DouRh) we will rejoice to fulfill the following mandate:

> *Will the LORD be pleased with thousands of rams, ten thousand rivers of oil? Shall I give my firstborn for my transgression, the fruit of my body for the sin of my soul.*
>
> *He has shown you, O man, what is good; and what does the LORD require of you but to **DO JUSTLY**, to love mercy and to walk humbly with your God.*
>
> (Micah 6:7–8)

This is still God's feeling on the matter and His longing and expectation toward His people. He is called "the habitation of justice" in Jeremiah 50:7. When God's people abide in Him, they tend to become like Him. When they become like Him, they will also be a habitation of justice in the earth. Martin Luther King once said that *"Injustice anywhere is a threat to justice everywhere."* May this truth ring in our inner conscience daily.

GRAND RESULTS

Understanding this mystery of justification is an immeasurable blessing, for once we grasp it with our hearts, we become forever rich! We also possess the supreme privilege of transferring such spiritual wealth to others. No wonder Proverbs 10:20 (KJV) explains that "THE TONGUE OF **THE JUST**

IS AS CHOICE SILVER." Choice silver is refined silver: that which has been purged of impurities and foreign alloys. So our speech must also be 'refined': purged of the impurity of carnality and of religious ideas that are foreign to the truth.

This happens by the very experience of life itself.

As we go through fiery trials and temptations, we learn the faithfulness of God, the availability of grace and the constancy of His justification promises. Going through the fire this way 'refines the silver,' causing a testimony to be written in our hearts.

This **justification testimony** is created with Spirit-inspired words that are choice, valuable, full of life and rich with authority. This is a precious gift from God, freely given to His righteous offspring. We are constrained to freely give it away to others as well. We must let the multitudes know that they, too, can be free from the awful bondage of depression and guilt, and be "accepted in the beloved" (Eph. 1:6). We must let them know that the salvation, sanctification and justification we have received, they can receive as well—for God is "just, and the justifier" of all those who believe in Jesus (Ro. 3:26).*7

Though many in this world may consider our hope to be foolishness, still, we hold fast our profession of faith, awaiting the day when we will finally be *"recompensed at the resurrection of the just"* (Lk. 14:14 KJV). Such a grand climax has certainly been God's expectation from the start. This is wonderfully revealed by the peculiar wording of Romans 8:30; speaking of God's predestined and called people, it declares, *"whom He justified, these He also glorified."* Though the day of glorification is a future event, notice in this verse God puts it in the past tense. Maybe this is His way of revealing that He fully intends to do a total work in His own. From the beginning of His intervention in our lives, He fully anticipates its completion. His divine design from the foundation is to carry us ultimately from justification to glorification.

On that wonderful day, not only will the children of God be fully justified; as Jesus pointed out in Luke 7:35, wisdom shall also be *"justified by all her children."* In other words, the depth of God's wisdom, unveiled in His plan of salvation, will be unquestionably, irrevocably and eternally proven right and good—by the glorious manifestation of the sons of God.

Though many deceived individuals have mocked the crucifixion and denied its validity, the resurrection will utterly dissolve their ridicule, proving them rather to be fools—and proving God's chosen ones to be wise. This is our blessed hope, for we have been begotten of the wisdom of God. **We are wisdom's children, therefore, we are the very source of wisdom's justification.**[*8]

When we receive the gift of ultimate glorification, through our final triumph, the Word of God, so often blasphemed, will be proven utterly true, and the wisdom of God, so often defamed, will be exonerated and confirmed forevermore. This will also be the proof of God's infinite and unlimited power, for the results of His salvation plan are infinite and unlimited in scope.

Such a destiny of utter perfection will most assuredly come to those honorably referred to as **THE JUST** WHO LIVE BY FAITH. For the highest fulfillment of this calling is the fact that, through faith, **WE WILL LIVE FOREVER!** We will be those just men and just women whose spirits are "made perfect" according to Hebrews 12:23. No wonder Proverbs 4:18 declares:

> *The path of **the just** is as the shining sun that shines*
> *ever brighter unto the perfect day.*

Though our sojourn in this world has been a constant assault of imperfection, we who are called the just will eventually experience a "day"—an eternal era—of utter perfection. As the Proverb writer promised, in an absolute sense, "**the just** shall come out of trouble" into a New Creation that will never know pain or trouble again (Pr. 12:13 KJV).

Considering all of these wonderful truths, we must admit (like Martin Luther of old)—Romans 1:17 has become for us *a gate to heaven and an open door into paradise.*

We thank God with every passing moment that He has so graciously included us!

> *O LORD my God...let the wickedness of the wicked*
> *come to an end; but establish **the just**...*

(Psalm 7:1, 9)

Deep calls unto deep,
*To be **righteous** I cry.*
Yet how can this be,
For one such as I?

Conceived in iniquity,
(Innocent with first breath?)
No, a sinner by birth,
And guilty of death.

Then the mystery of faith
Arose in my spirit,
Canceling sin's curse,
So I no longer fear it.

By His Word and His name
And the death Jesus died,
I'm acquitted of guilt,
Yes, I stand justified!

Endnotes

*1 Halley, *Halley's Bible Handbook*, *"The Reformation"* (Grand Rapids, Michigan: Zondervan Publishing House, 1967) page 787.

*2 Roland H. Bainton, *Here I Stand, A Life of Martin Luther* (Nashville Tennessee: Abington Press, 1978) page 49.

*3 Jesus was also described as being "just," but this list only references natural human beings.

*4 Some scriptures dealing with the nature and destiny of *the unjust* are: Ps. 43:1; Pr. 11:7, 29:27; Zeph. 3:5; Mt. 5:45; Lk. 16:10, 18:11; 2 Pt. 2:9 and Rev. 22:11.

*5 We are reminded of Bildad's statement—"How then can man be justified—that is a *worm?* And the son of man which is a *worm?*" Then we see how that the Son of man in identifying with us in our low estate—*"became a worm and no man"*—feeling our separation from the Father and our degradation. Of course, He did this so that we could identify with Him in His glory! It is noteworthy that the word translated *worm* in Psalm 22:6 is the Hebrew *tola* meaning *maggot, the crimson-grub, a coccus worm.* The eggs of this worm were crushed to make a scarlet colored dye. Because of this, the same word is translated *crimson* one time (Is. 1:18) *scarlet* thirty-one times (Ex. 25:4, 26:1, Lev. 14:4, Num. 19:6 etc.) and *worm* eight times. How appropriate a word-choice this was! For in becoming a *worm*, Jesus, crushed by death, supplied the *"crimson-scarlet* dye" that would wash our sins away and change us within, giving us the Calvary nature of self denial (DARB, page 557 of OT, col. 1, note 1...UBD, page 213, under *red*).

*6 For a thorough study of righteousness and cleanness in God's sight, refer to the following two chapters: *The Righteous* in Volume Five and *The Clean* in Volume Eight of **Our Glorious Inheritance.**

*7 In Ezekiel 18:5–9 God lists fifteen things that a just person will or will not do. A number of these include compassionate treatment of those who are financially destitute. Maybe it is this 'sowing' that brings forth the 'reaping' promise of provision in Proverbs 13:22 KJV—"the wealth of the sinner is laid up for **the just.**"

*8 For more insight on this title-calling, refer to *Children of Wisdom* in Volume Five of **Our Glorious Inheritance.**

PEACEMAKERS

---

*Blessed are the **PEACEMAKERS**: for they shall be called the children of God.*
(Matthew 5:9 KJV)

*And if a **SON OF PEACE** is there, your peace will rest on it; if not, it will return to you.*
(Luke 10:6)

*Consider the blameless, observe the upright; there is a future for the **MAN OF PEACE**.*
(Psalm 37:37 NIV)

*Deceit is in the heart of those who devise evil, but **COUNSELORS OF PEACE** have joy.*
(Proverbs 12:20)

SONS OF PEACE

MEN OF PEACE

COUNSELORS OF PEACE

Deep calls unto deep,
"To be like You," we pray,
As peacemakers spreading
Your peace every day.

Reconciling lost sinners
To You is our goal
'Till the Prince of Peace reigns,
In every man's soul.

Sowing harmony in dissension,
And love where there's hate,
Planting hope in despair
No, it's never too late.

For this is the calling
Of the counselors of peace,
Spreading heaven on earth,
And His Kingdom—increase.

PEACEMAKERS

*Blessed are the **PEACEMAKERS:** for they shall be
called the children of God.*

(Matthew 5:9 KJV)

*T*he most noted award presently given for peacemaking in this
world is something called *the Nobel Peace Prize*. How ironic it
is that the originator of this prize was Alfred Bernhard Nobel, the Swedish
scientist who invented *dynamite*!

Guilt-ridden over the fact that his invention, intended for the benefit
of mankind, had caused many deaths and injuries, and could potentially be
used for war, Nobel apparently sought to make amends. He set up a fund of
about nine million dollars, purposing that the interest be used to award
annual prizes in six different categories to individuals making notable and
valuable contributions to the 'good of humanity.' One of those categories is
described as "the most effective work in the interest of international peace."

How fitting it was that the first peace prize was presented in 1901 to
Jean Henri Dunant, founder of the Red Cross! Dunant was a young
businessman who "during the War of 1859 between Italy, Austria, and
France—visited the battlefields and was shocked to see men dying because
there was no way to take care of their wounds."[*1]

While others never got beyond the stage of feeling sorrow over such a
tragedy, this Swiss citizen purposed to do something about the problem. So
he formed the international relief organization that still identifies itself with
that sign quite similar to the emblem of Calvary. Though Dunant was destitute
financially himself when he received the Nobel prize, still, he immediately
gave the sum of it away to charity. This was to be expected, for selflessness
evidently was a character trait that often ruled his choices in life.

All of these things speak a beautiful message to our hearts.

In the beginning, God made man and created him with authority and a
free will, intending such a bestowal to be only beneficial. But men rebelled.
They began warring against God and against each other—misusing and
perverting the gifts that the Almighty had given. The Creator, grieving over
the resulting curse of death that filled the earth, purposed to 'mend' the
situation. He came to this world in the form of a man and successfully
conquered every foe. He then ascended into heaven and, in a sense, put all
of the power He procured in a 'celestial trust fund.'

Now, from that 'fund', He promises to grant an eternal 'peace award' to anyone who will take the emblem of the cross and go forth to care for hurting humanity. Those who truly receive this challenge go beyond the stage of just feeling sorrow over the world's condition. They dare to do something about it. On a day-to-day and often one-by-one basis, they minister the peace-producing, red-cross message of reconciliation to an estranged and fallen human race. The God-given 'prize' for such service is the recognition of truly being included in the divine family. Because those who go forth producing peace in a war-torn world are successfully carrying on the family tradition. Jesus, the Firstborn Son of God, said it in such a choice way:

> *Blessed are the **peacemakers**: for they shall be called the children of God.*
>
> (Matthew 5:9 KJV)

THE DEFINITION OF THE CALLING

The definition of peace is threefold.

First, it can be a state of tranquillity, rest or security.

Second, it can be a state of harmony in personal relations.

Third, it can be freedom from any kind of civil disturbance, such as criminal violence, rioting, anarchy or war.

Peacemakers are simply those who impart peace to others. Peacemakers are especially capable of reconciling parties that are at variance with one another. Of course, if we are to successfully impart peace, we must first be at peace. If we have yielded to the authority of the Prince of peace and He rules over our hearts, we automatically inherit peace three different ways.

We receive peace *with* God.

We receive peace *from* God.

We receive the peace *of* God.

And without controversy—what we receive, we can also give away.

❧ Peace with God ———————————————————

Romans 5:1–2 says, "Therefore, having been justified by faith, we have *peace with God* through our LORD Jesus Christ, through whom also we have access by faith into this grace in which we stand…" Having *peace with God* hinges on the fact that we have been justified (acquitted of all guilt, reckoned righteous and blameless in the sight of God). Because we have legally obtained this status, God now rejoices to open the door of divine fellowship to us. Miraculously, we are just as accepted in the presence of the Father as the firstborn Son, because we are "in Christ."

Ephesians 1:6 explains that we are now "accepted in the Beloved." In other words, because Jesus is accepted and perfectly loved, and because He is at peace with the Father, we are at peace with the Father. Though we were at "enmity with God" ("enemies in your minds by wicked works") now our hearts have been reunited with the Creator (Ja. 4:4, Col. 1:21).

We can always enter the Father's presence expecting to be received. If we maintain repentance, humility and faith before His throne, the life-giving, righteousness-imparting blood of Jesus flows through us constantly. Because of this consistent source of sanctification we are kept in harmony with the Almighty. And there is probably no better way of expressing this wondrous truth than to say, *"We have peace with God."*

⚜ Peace from God

In the beginning of his epistle to the Romans, Paul gave the salutation, "Grace to you and *peace from God* our Father and the LORD Jesus Christ" (Ro. 1:7). Apparently, this was a normal way of greeting others in the early church, appearing in similar wording fifteen times. At least thirteen times this prayer for peace is combined with *grace* because the grace of God overflowing our lives always brings great peace. (See 1 Cor. 1:3, 2 Cor. 1:2, Gal. 1:3, Eph. 1:2, etc.)

In fact, everything that comes *from God,* toward those who are receptive, ultimately ends in peace. For instance, James 3:17 says, "the *wisdom* that is *from* above is first pure, then *peaceable...*"

Another passage describing God-breathed wisdom says, "all her paths are *peace*" (Pr. 3:17). Even discipline or chastisement coming *from God,* though difficult to endure, afterward yields *"peaceable* fruit" (Heb. 12:11).

No wonder the Bible writer declared "our sufficiency (our adequacy, our competence) comes *from God*" (2 Cor. 3:5 NKJV, NAS, NIV). When we realize that we are "complete in Him"—that we have no lack, that He is our sufficiency—we are no longer searching, straining, striving (Col. 2:10). We are at rest. As Romans 1:7 explains, we have *"peace* from God."

⚜ The Peace of God

The glory of our inheritance brightens when we read one of the final promises Jesus gave His followers:

> ***Peace** I leave with you, **My peace** I give to you...*
>
> (John 14:27)

Building on this truth Paul exhorted, "Be anxious for nothing, but in everything by prayer and supplication, with thanksgiving, let your requests be made known to God." Then he pledged, "and *the peace of God* which surpasses all understanding, will guard your hearts and minds through Christ Jesus" (Ph. 4:6–7). If we have *the peace of God*, we have the same peace that God Himself experiences. We possess the same inner tranquillity, the same sense of confidence that His plan will surely evolve to perfection.

This is a seal on our minds and a seal on our hearts.

This *peace of God* is far more than just an emotional sensation of serenity or a calmness of mind. This peace is supernatural. Being "peace in the Holy Spirit," it "surpasses all understanding" (Ro. 14:17, Ph. 4:7).

When Jesus gave us this depth of divine peace He simply gave us Himself, pouring His very essence into our hearts. For the peace of God is not a virtue; it is a person. If we know this person and know how to sincerely pray to Him, we can have undisturbed peace in the worst of circumstances. The Scripture celebrates the fact that true peace is "in Christ Jesus" and "by Jesus Christ" (1 Pt. 5:14, Ac. 10:36 KJV).

He is the Vine and we are the branches: the sap that flows through all His 'offshoots' contains life-giving peace. Transferring this divine attribute to His followers was certainly the passionate purpose of the risen Christ. So it is no wonder that having conquered sin, and having stripped Satan of his authority, Jesus appeared to His disciples, saying:

> *Peace be to you! As the Father has sent Me, I also send you.*
>
> (John 20:21)[*2]

THE GOD OF PEACE

A number of names and titles are given to God in both the Old and New Testaments that reveal this wonderful divine personality trait.

The patriarch Jacob prophesied of the coming of the Messiah and called Him **Shiloh**—which most likely means *rest, tranquillity* or *the peaceable and prosperous One* (Gen. 49:10).

Gideon revealed the Almighty as **Yahweh-Shalom** (or Jehovah-Shalom if the traditional rendering is used), meaning *the LORD our peace or the LORD send peace*. In a time of great national crisis and oppression for Israel, Gideon received a plan from God that would enable the Israelites to crush their enemies, the Midianites. This hero of Bible history tore down his father's idols, built an altar and by faith called it **Yahweh-Shalom**. Though war and strife were still raging in Israel, Gideon's act was his way of decreeing that God's peace would rule in the land. (See Jd. 6:24.)

Many years later, this same God of peace compassionately chose to take upon Himself a body and visit this war-ravaged planet. How appropriately the angels announced the birth of the heaven-sent child, singing:

> *"Glory to God in the highest, and on earth **peace**,*
> *goodwill toward men!"*

(Luke 2:14)

Because the establishment of peace was one of His primary purposes in coming, it was only fitting that Jesus be called: *the LORD of peace, the Prince of peace, the God of peace, the Author of peace and the Son of peace* (2 Th. 3:16, Is. 9:6, Ph. 4:9, 1 Cor. 14:33, Lk. 10:6 KJV).[*3]

The mystery deepens as we read Isaiah's prophetic declaration that *"the chastisement for our peace was upon Him."* In other words, through the severe punishment He suffered (taking our place in death, receiving the chastisement we should have received) boundless peace was procured for all those who submit to His Lordship (Is. 53:5).

Like those animals offered as *peace offerings* under the Old Will, so Jesus was consumed with the fire of judgment on that altar of sacrifice called Calvary—and all to bring us back to God. Even as the priests heaved the shoulder and waved the breast of the *peace offering* in a dual motion resembling a "T," so Jesus offered all His strength and all His heart on the cross so that we could have the availability of divine fellowship. (See Lev. 3:1–17; 7:11–36.)[*4]

Ephesians 2:14 declares that "HE...IS OUR **PEACE**"—for He broke down the middle wall of partition between Jews and Gentiles, and He rent the temple veil that stood between man and God.

He purposefully came to bring reconciliation in this twofold way. **He was the original Peacemaker sent from above.**

He built a bridge of compassion from heaven to earth in order to mend the horrible rift caused by Adam. When He accomplished this goal, thank God, not only did He reach out to the Jews of the Old Will; He extended nail-scarred hands to 'whosoever will': preaching "peace" to those who were "afar off" [the Gentiles] and "to those who were near" [the Jews] (Eph. 2:17).

He came with *"words of peace"* and *"terms of peace"* (Dt. 2:26, 20:10 NAS). He came to establish with His own *"a covenant of peace"* (stability, calmness and rest of soul even in tumultuous times—See Is. 54:10, Mal. 2:5). He came to "guide our feet into the *way of* peace," (Luke 1:79). He still lifts His voice against the storms of our lives, saying, *"Peace,* be still" (Mk. 4:39). Understandably, therefore, His message has been hailed as *"the gospel of peace"* (the 'good news' that men and women, through the help of God, can be at peace with God, at peace with each other, and at peace with themselves) (Ro. 10:15, Eph. 6:15). No wonder our God is titled *"the God of peace"* who sanctifies us completely and bruises Satan under our feet. (See Ro. 15:33; 16:20, Ph. 4:9, 1 Th. 5:23, Heb. 13:20.)

A FAMILY OF PEACEMAKERS

Again, let it be emphasized—reconciling us was the fulfillment of only part of the Savior's plan. *The God of peace* also came to birth His nature within us. Since peace is one of His most predominant characteristics, the firstborn Peacemaker came to raise up a family of peacemakers! To every one of His offspring, He has given "the word of reconciliation" and "the ministry of reconciliation" to accomplish this end (2 Cor. 5:18–19).

We have been filled with the sweet Holy Spirit, heaven's gentle dove, that we might become channels of His tranquil, healing and soothing nature. Like the Messiah who came before us, we are called to be *peace offerings,* crucified with Christ, offering all of our heart and all of our strength in order to promote His *peace* in this strife-filled world. Though we are soldiers sent forth into a global, spiritual war, part of our military regalia includes having "our feet shod with *the preparation of the gospel of peace"* (Eph. 6:15). This is part of the mystery: that we succeed in the spiritual war by establishing peace in the hearts of men.

We are commanded to "seek peace," "pursue peace," "live in peace," and "keep the unity of the Spirit in the bond of peace." We are even exhorted to "follow peace with all men" (not by sacrificing righteous principles, but by building and developing godly relationships). (Ps. 34:14, 2 Cor. 13:11, Eph. 4:3, Heb. 12:14 KJV, See also Ro. 12:18.)

Because believers are anointed of God to fulfill this charge, it makes sense that our anointing is also called our *"peace."* In Matthew 10:12–13 Jesus commissioned His representatives, saying:

> *...when you go into a household, greet it. If the household is worthy, let your **peace** come upon it. But if it is not worthy, let **your peace** return to you."*

In the Gospel of Luke, we find a little different wording:

> *But whatever house you enter, first say, 'Peace to this house.' And if a **son of peace** is there, your **peace** will rest on it: if not, it will return to you.*

(Luke 10:5–6)

If those households to whom we present the Gospel react with sincerity, humility and faith—if the head of the household is a *peace-loving* person— then God will witness to our hearts that a *son of peace* is there (bringing God's favor on the family as a whole). If we do not receive this 'Spirit-witness' and if we meet with rejection, we certainly cannot minister the life of God. It is then that our *peace* returns to us. (See also Lk. 10:5–6 TEV.)[*5]

Something similar to this happened on a much larger scale—with the incarnation of the Son of God. When Jesus visited the earth, had He been rejected by all who heard Him, *His peace* would have returned to Him. The world would have then begun a swift descent into utter destruction. There would have been no healings, no miracles, no outpouring of the Holy Spirit on Pentecost, no multiplied millions of souls saved throughout the New Covenant Age. All these things have been effected by Jesus' *peace*—by the anointing that rested upon Him—something that always brings great *peace* to those who receive heaven's Prince.

Thank God, Jesus was not totally rejected in His day. He found many men and women of peace in this world, who appreciated that unique peace evidenced in the Messiah. And they desired that same peace to be evidenced in their own lives.

This, too, is *"the deep calling to the deep"*: from God's heart to ours and from our hearts to the hearts of others.

PERFECT PEACE, GREAT PEACE, SALTY PEACE

There are many means of experiencing *the peace of God*—but three especially beg for our attention:

- **Staying Focused on God**—Isaiah 26:3 announces to the LORD, "You will keep him in *perfect peace* whose mind is stayed on You."
- **Loving God's Word**—Psalm 119:165 claims *"Great peace* have those who love Your law and nothing causes them to stumble." The King James Version says, "nothing shall offend them."
- **Maintaining Covenant Relationships with Other Believers**—In Mark 9:50 Jesus urged, "Have salt in yourselves and have *peace* with one another."

Because of its longlasting quality, salt is a symbol of a permanent covenant bonding. (See Num. 18:19, 2 Chr. 13:5.) When we honor right relationships by faithful commitment through all the ups and downs of life, peace is the inevitable result. This kind of loyal love often results from the two previous attitudes mentioned: staying focused on God and loving His Word. When we are constant toward Him, automatically we will tend to be constant toward others. And constancy usually produces peace.

THE BLESSEDNESS OF THE CALLING

Our title-scripture says, *"**Blessed** are the **peacemakers**, for they shall be called the children of God."* In other words, peacemakers are recognized as being God's children primarily because they reflect the nature of their Father. God boasted of His power in Isaiah 45:7 by saying, *"I make peace."* All who represent Him should be able to make a similar boast. (See Ps. 147:14, Col. 1:20.)

This impartation of the divine nature is termed "the fruit of the Spirit" (the normal outgrowth of the indwelling presence of God). How significant it is that the third in this list of nine is *peace!* (See Gal. 5:22–23.) Fruit is developed by any plant, not to nourish itself, but to nourish something or someone else. In like manner, we are called to develop the fruit of peace, not that we might be peaceful ourselves, but that we might produce peace in others: calming those who are worried, distraught, anxious and at war with themselves.

> *Therefore let us pursue the things which **make for peace**
> and the things by which one may edify another.*
>
> (Romans 14:19)

Let us also believe in the value of our task.

For "the fruit of righteousness is sown in peace by those who *make peace*." The NIV puts it beautifully, "**peacemakers** who sow in peace raise a harvest of righteousness" (Ja. 3:18). Unfortunately, those who are carnal minded usually neglect this opportunity. On the contrary, Romans 8:6 says "to be spiritually minded is life and *peace*." So evidently, the more spiritual minded we become, the more peace will abound in our lives and the lives of those we affect. The harsh, the divisive, those who are quick to react with hostility, only succeed in making hearts unsettled, but "the meek [those who are humble toward God and man]...shall delight themselves in *the abundance of peace*." (Ps. 37:11, See 72:7.)

No wonder Jesus said peacemakers are "**blessed**" (a word meaning *supremely happy, spiritually prosperous, enriched with benefits, well-spoken-*

of, highly favored or having attained qualities of character God considers to be the highest good). This definition fits so well. For *supremely happy* are those who learn how to be repairers and restorers. *Enriched with benefits* are those who learn to tear down the walls of prejudice, hate and bitterness that men erect between themselves. *Well spoken of* in heaven are those who take the love, wisdom, righteousness and spiritual-mindedness they receive from above and then transfer these peace-producing gifts to others. By learning how to bring unity in the midst of division and harmony in the presence of discord, we really do succeed in *attaining one of those qualities that God considers to be the highest good.*

THE PEACEFUL ENDING

Jesus' *peacemakers*, heaven's blessed ones, and the *peace* they have to share will never be fully accepted by this world. Jesus even warned that we will be hated of all nations for His name's sake. In this men will greatly err, for to reject *the Prince of peace* is to reject peace itself. He is the only source. Men may experience a semblance of peace for a season, but in the end it will prove shallow and short-lived (for "there is no *peace,* says my God, for the wicked") (Is. 57:21).

This world will even accept a false peacemaker, a counterfeit Messiah, who for a season will seem to bring harmony to the nations and peace to the earth. Daniel forewarned that this devil-inspired, political genius "by *peace* shall destroy many" (Dan. 8:25 KJV).

Paul also prophesied of the Antichrist era. He foretold that "while they are saying, *Peace* and safety: then destruction will come upon them suddenly like birth pangs upon a woman with child; and they shall not escape" (1 Th. 5:3 NAS). Those who give their allegiance to this coming "man of sin" will be overtaken and overwhelmed by a time of great tribulation like the world has never seen. But we who know *the call of the deep* can look beyond all of the imminent turmoil and danger, and gaze in the future with eyes full of hope. Our Father has assured us:

> *...I know the thoughts that I think toward you, says*
> *the LORD, thoughts of **peace** and not of evil, to give you*
> *a future and a hope.*
>
> (Jeremiah 29:11)

The King James says, "to give you an expected end." So nothing unexpected will ever come the way of God's offspring. Maybe we do not expect certain things that happen, but God anticipates it all and He prepares for it by granting us more than enough grace. Yes, we can have the calm assurance that our future really is in the hands of God.

We know that when Jesus descends from above, more than ever before, righteousness and peace will kiss each other. (See Ps. 85:10.) This will give birth to a holy solemnity and tranquility that will fill the earth. All reconcilable things will be reconciled as God's people are "led forth with *peace*" ...and the mountains and hills break forth into singing. (See Is. 55:12 KJV, Col. 1:20.) Yes, as Psalm 37:37 (NIV) foretells, "there is a future for **THE MAN OF PEACE**": the men and women who know the rest of God.

Isaiah also gave the following prophecies concerning the future of war-ravaged **Jerusalem** (a city historically embroiled in conflicts and wars, yet whose name curiously means *possession of peace*):

> *Your eyes will see Jerusalem, a **peaceful** abode, a tent that will not be moved; its stakes will never be pulled up, nor any of its ropes broken.*
>
> (Isaiah 33:20 NIV)
>
> *...Behold, I will extend **peace** to her like a river, and the glory of the Gentiles like a flowing stream...*
>
> (Isaiah 66:12)
>
> *...I will also make your officers **peace**, and your magistrates righteousness.*
>
> (Isaiah 60:17)

This last scripture speaks a soul-calming truth. It conveys that the glorified saints abiding in the "city of the great King" will be in such perfect and permanent harmony with God that there will be no need of any type of law enforcement agencies. The priceless peace of paradise will rule all hearts, so deep and full that none would dare even think of departing from its influence. All who dwell in this "peaceful abode" will be filled with such righteousness that they will automatically give God their all. (See Col. 3:15.) Yes, a "time of peace" will finally come to "the land of peace" (Ec. 3:8, Jer. 12:5).

Furthermore, God has promised to "make a COVENANT OF PEACE with them, and cause wild beasts to cease from the land." He also pledged, "I will abolish the bow, the sword and war from the land, and will make them lie down in safety." (Ezk. 34:25, Ho. 2:18 NAS, See also Ps. 46.) "The wolf and the lamb shall feed together, the lion shall eat straw like the ox...They shall not hurt nor destroy in all My holy mountain." "They shall beat their swords into plowshares, and their spears into pruning hooks: nation shall not lift up sword against nation, neither shall they learn war anymore" (Is. 2:4, 65:25).

> *My people shall dwell in a **peaceable** habitation, in secure dwellings, and in quiet resting places.*
>
> (Isaiah 32:18)

> *For the earth shall be full of the knowledge of the LORD as the waters cover the sea.*
>
> (Isaiah 11:9)

The Scripture testifies again and again of the undisturbed serenity that will be one of the predominant characteristics of this coming kingdom of God. Isaiah takes us one step higher, revealing concerning the Messiah:

> *Of the increase of His government and **peace** there will be no end.*
>
> (Isaiah 9:7)

So throughout eternity to come, God will ever be enlarging the borders of His creation (that over which He governs) and He will ever be increasing and deepening His peace within our grateful hearts.

In anticipation of such an infinite gift let us do all we can to be His **PEACEMAKERS** even now.

Let us "pray for the peace of Jerusalem" (Ps. 122:6).

Let us lead others in "the way of peace" and fulfill the calling to be **"COUNSELORS OF PEACE"** (Ro. 3:17, Pr. 12:20).

And let us proclaim that the Prince of peace will soon come and rule this earth. When He does, each one of God's glorified saints will surely rejoice, more than ever before, to fulfill Isaiah 52:7 (NIV):

> *How beautiful on the mountains are the feet of those who bring good news, who proclaim **peace**, who bring good tidings, who proclaim salvation, who say to Zion, Your God reigns!*

TWO 'PEACE PROCLAMATIONS' FOR YOU

I pray the following 'peace proclamations' for all who are studying this "peacemakers" revelation:

The Levitical Blessing — Old Testament

The LORD bless you and keep you; the LORD make His face shine upon you, and be gracious to you; the LORD lift up His countenance upon you, and give you peace.

(Numbers 6:24–26)

A Pauline Blessing — New Testament

Now may the LORD of peace Himself give you peace always in every way. The LORD be with you all.

(2 Thessalonians 3:16)

Endnotes

*1 *Illustrated World Encyclopedia* (Bobley Publishing Corp., Woodbury, New York) p. 530, under *Dunant*.

*2 Actually during all three of His initial visitations described in John 20, the resurrected Messiah appeared, saying, *"Peace unto you."* Most likely the Hebrew word *Shalom* was the word He spoke. This traditional Hebrew greeting has multiple meanings beyond just the idea of peace or tranquillity. *Shalom* figuratively speaks of being well, happy, friendly, healthy and prosperous. It also implies safety and wholeness. So when Jesus said *"Shalom"* to His disciples, He was saying, "I pray happiness, wellness, peace, health, prosperity, safety and wholeness into your lives…and the peace that results from all of these things."

*3 This is only a possible interpretation of the title **"Son of Peace"** found in Luke 10:6. That verse may not be referring to Jesus. It may rather be speaking of the householder being a **"man of peace"**: something that fits in with the calling to be **peacemakers.** (See the section under the subtitle A FAMILY OF PEACEMAKERS and also footnote #5.)

*4 A **peace offering** was the last of five kinds of offerings presented to God under the Mosaic order. It was the only offering eaten, not only by the priests, but the offerers as well. Because previous offerings had already dealt with the sin problem and consecration to God, the peace offering was especially a celebration of restored fellowship with the Creator. It was as if the celebrants were invited to God's table to feast with Him, indulge in His goodness and enjoy His outpoured benefits. This is the symbol and the message conveyed.

It is also noteworthy that there were three different categories of peace offerings: 1. **Thank offerings,** 2. **Votive offerings** (offerings presented with a vow) and 3. **Free will offerings** (offerings presented willingly as an act of worship). All three of these speak prophetically of three means by which consecrated New Covenant believers maintain a harmonious and peaceful relationship with the Creator: by continued expressions of thankfulness over what He has done, renewed expressions of commitment to Him and spontaneous outbursts of heartfelt worship. When thankfulness, commitment or worshipfulness are absent from believers' lives, peace is lacking as well. But when present, these things keep our lives overflowing with the peace that passes understanding. (For more information on sacrificial offerings and the symbolic message they convey, see the chapter entitled *A Sweet Savour of Christ* in Volume Eight of **Our Glorious Inheritance.**)

*5 The King James Version of Luke 10:6 says "if **the son of peace** is there," implying that Jesus, the Son of peace, is invisibly present in the home, accepting the people because of God-fearing, truth-seeking attitudes and their humility toward Him. He comes in response to their sincerity to impart the benefits of the Gospel of peace. He pours out His peace to draw them into a harmonious relationship with Himself. This could be a correct wording and a correct interpretation of this passage.

THE POOR IN SPIRIT

Blessed are **THE POOR IN SPIRIT**: *for theirs
is the kingdom of heaven*

(Matthew 5:3)

When **THE POOR AND NEEDY** seek water, and there is none, and their tongue faileth for thirst, I the LORD will hear them, I the God of Israel will not forsake them.

(Isaiah 41:17 KJV)

For He will deliver **THE NEEDY** when he cries, **THE POOR** also, and him who has no helper.

He will spare **THE POOR AND NEEDY**, and will save the souls of **THE NEEDY**.

(Psalm 72:12–13)

He will bring justice to **THE POOR OF THE PEOPLE**; He will save **THE CHILDREN OF THE NEEDY**, and will break in pieces the oppressor.

(Psalm 72:4)

For He stands at the right hand of **THE NEEDY ONE**, to save his life from those who condemn him."

(Psalm 109:31 NIV)

THE POOR AND NEEDY

THE POOR

THE NEEDY

THE POOR
OF THE PEOPLE

THE CHILDREN
OF THE NEEDY

NEEDY ONES

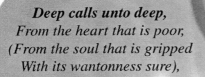

Deep calls unto deep,
From the heart that is poor,
(From the soul that is gripped
With its wantonness sure),

Yet casting its trust
Toward the King on His throne:
(Inexhaustible wealth
Does He grant to His own).

When we give Him the credit
And the praise that is due,
What is His becomes ours
(And our status, brand new).

No longer mere beggars
In the dunghill of sin
But princes in glory
(How we tremble within!).

For the kingdom of heaven
Belongs even now
To God's offspring redeemed,
(From sweat-curse on our brow).

THE POOR IN SPIRIT

Blessed are **THE POOR IN SPIRIT**: *for theirs is the kingdom of heaven.*

(Matthew 5:3)

*I*n the third chapter of this volume, we studied the revelation of what it is to be **the Blessed of the Father.** This chapter, like **Peacemakers** and **the Pure in Heart**, is an outgrowth of chapter three, for it defines another specific category of 'blessedness.'

In His famed "Sermon on the Mount" Jesus presented this first beatitude that is possibly the most mysterious of all. Two other translations express this passage differently and beautifully:

> *How blest are those who know their need of God; the kingdom of heaven is theirs.*

(NEB)

> *Happy are those who know they are spiritually poor: the kingdom of heaven belongs to them!*

(TEV)

These renderings help bring the correct interpretation into full focus. In essence, they reveal that all who come to Jesus for salvation or restoration must first realize their neediness in the sight of heaven. They must realize their state of want spiritually, their utter destitution without God. Such an admission is not a destructive thing spiritually, what some might call a warped self-image or a negative confession. It is rather an honest and realistic way of viewing our present status. In the doctrine of the Son of God, it is something described as *poverty of spirit.*

The blessedness of the matter is this: that such an attitude is pleasing to God and ends up becoming a gateway to happiness, abundance and glory. Why? Because only that person who humbly admits his spiritual bankruptcy "in Adam" can ever go on to be endowed with "the unsearchable riches of Christ." Only that person who concedes, "Without Him I can do nothing" can progress to the statement, "I can do all things through Christ who strengthens me." (See Jn. 15:5, Ph. 4:13.)

Maybe, just maybe, this beatitude was placed first in Jesus' list of eight to reveal that *poor-spiritedness* will ordinarily precede all the other *blessed* qualities of character mentioned. The Jamieson, Fausset and Brown commentary on this passage explains, "this self-emptying conviction that 'before God we are void of everything' lies at the foundation of all spiritual excellence."*[1] So this first main statement of Jesus' first main sermon was the door opener for all the revelation yet to flow from His lips.

Negatively defined, the opposite of "poverty of spirit" is pride, self-sufficiency, arrogance, rebellion and vanity. The Bible clearly states that the wicked walk in a vain show, vainly puffed up by their fleshly minds, deceiving one another with vain words. But *the poor in spirit* own up to what they are in the flesh, knowing that God first desires truth in the inward parts, then in the hidden part He will make us to know wisdom. (See Ps. 51:6.)

Paul was rich in spiritual gifts, but he simultaneously and meekly assessed himself to be "less than the least of all the saints" (Eph. 3:8). In an exemplary and consistent way, the apostle maintained *poverty of spirit*. He even described himself as being "*poor*, yet making many rich; as having nothing, and yet possessing all things." (2 Cor. 6:10, See 12:10.)

The Greek word translated *poor* in Matthew 5:3, is *ptochos*. According to Thayer's definition, this word can mean many things, including: *reduced to beggary, destitute of wealth, influence, position, honor and virtue, or powerless to accomplish an end.* Strong's Concordance promotes the idea that *ptochos* is akin to the word *pipto* meaning *to fall*. According to Young's Concordance *ptochos* can mean *trembling*. This latter reference relates to the command of Psalm 2:11 that we "serve the LORD with fear, and rejoice with *trembling*." The person who walks in poverty of spirit realizes his *fallen* status, that he is *powerless* to save himself, and he often *trembles* with gratitude and submission toward the God of all grace who made salvation possible.

Such temper of spirit constrains a believer to confess just as the sweet psalmist of Israel, "I am *poor and needy*," but then to add as well, "yet the LORD thinks upon me." (Ps. 40:17, See 1 Chr. 29:3–5 KJV, NIV.) Having this attitude is the key to abundant living. Isaiah 41:17 (KJV) says it beautifully:

> *When* **THE POOR AND NEEDY** *seek water, and there is none, and their tongue faileth for thirst, I the LORD will hear them, I the God of Israel will not forsake them.*

God did not preface this promise with the statement, "When the proud and self-sufficient seek water." He rather said, "When *the poor and needy* seek water…I will open rivers in high places and fountains in the midst of the valleys: I will make the wilderness a pool of water, and the dry land springs of water" (Is. 41:17–18 KJV). In this passage, the Almighty pledges more than enough living water to sustain us in this arid wilderness world: not a cup, a bucket or even a well, but rivers, fountains, pools and springs—much more than we could use up in an entire lifetime. Jesus is the source of this abundant grace. Isaiah prophesied of His coming that the Messiah would be "as rivers of water in a dry place" (Is. 32:2). The driest place is often the human heart, but Jesus promised that if we believe, out of our innermost being will flow "rivers of living water" (Jn. 7:38).

The LORD knows how to feel our infirmities and is passionate to move in our behalf. We know He can relate to us because He has walked the same road. Psalm 40:17 describes Him as being *"poor and needy."* Psalm 109:16 even prophetically names Him, *"the poor and needy man."* And Ecclesiastes 9:15–16 symbolically speaks of Him as the *"poor wise man"* who delivered the 'city' because of His wisdom, but was forgotten. Because Jesus possessed *poverty of spirit*, because He understood His own utter dependency on the Father, He also understands our utter dependency on Him.

THE LAODICEAN ATTITUDE

All the valuable truth revealed so far is quite noticeably in direct opposition to the spirit of the Laodicean church, the seventh church receiving a direct message from the risen Christ in the book of the Revelation. This message was first, a specific and prophetic word to the Laodiceans, and second, a relevant message to any portion of the church in any era.

The original Laodicean church was a lukewarm, self-satisfied church, somewhat devoid of the fear of God and true conviction. *Poverty of spirit* was not to be found in her list of attributes. She boasted, "I am rich, and increased with goods, and have need of nothing." The risen LORD reacted to this attitude with a strong rebuke, "You…do not know that you are wretched, miserable, poor, blind, and naked" (Rev. 3:17).

Possibly, the greatest tragedy was not their terrible, spiritual condition, but the fact that they 'knew it not.' How often this is the case! Worldly segments of the professing church, guilty of compromise, doctrinal error and spiritual negligence, often do not even realize they have missed the mark. But God graciously supplied the Laodicean church (and all who trust in His Word) with the following proposition:

> *I counsel you to buy from Me gold refined in the fire, that you may be rich; and white garments, that you may be clothed, that the shame of your nakedness may not be revealed; and anoint your eyes with eye salve, that you may see.*
>
> *As many as I love, I rebuke and chasten. Therefore be zealous and repent.*
>
> (Revelation 3:18–19)

God may have been revealing to this erring church that they were not as rich spiritually as they thought. Or He could have been making a literal reference, that the acquisition of riches or material possessions was not a correct indicator of how wealthy they were in the things of God. Whichever wrong attitude it was that corrupted the Laodiceans, "it was this most deceitful conviction that cut the nerves of their spiritual diligence."*2

We must not be like them. We must never allow ourselves to become lax, careless, insensitive or spiritually slothful. Rather, we must always view ourselves as a needy people in the sight of God, always hungering for more—more of His love, more of His power, more of His presence and more of His promises manifested in our lives. Those who are self-satisfied, who assess themselves to be sufficiently rich in God, may all the while be paving the road to spiritual bankruptcy. On the contrary, those who daily acknowledge their indigence and neediness in God's sight are the very ones who can then proceed by faith into the limitless wealth available in Him.

⬛ The Gold of the Divine Nature

God brought the Laodicean church through the 'fire' of a divine rebuke and chastening for a purpose: to motivate them towards 'purchasing' the thing that enriches men the most: the 'gold' of the divine nature, a God-like character refined of carnal impurities. And how is this 'gold' bought?

First, **by self-denial**—by giving up those things that so nauseate God that He must spew out the lukewarm; and second, **by faith**—by believing God to bring good out of all the pressure we face—and by believing God to birth in us a humble, loving, submissive and obedient nature as a result of the fiery trials through which we pass. This is 'gold' and this is the kind of possession that matters most: characteristics that definitely qualify us to be included among *the poor in spirit.* (See Jb. 23:8–10, 1 Pt. 1:6–7.)

Such an acquisition is so necessary; for if believers act on all of God's promises concerning prosperity and see them fulfilled in their lives—yet if they fail to develop true Christlikeness—all their attainments are relatively vain. Such deceived persons may boast of their effective faith by confessing, "I am rich and increased with goods and have need of nothing," but God will pierce all the religious facade with the pointed observation—*"You are poor."*

Therefore, it must be reemphasized: the path that leads to becoming truly rich in God first involves recognizing how poor we really are without His full favor and fellowship. Only then can the Word of Christ dwell in us "richly" and only then can we lay up treasure in heaven and be "rich toward God" (Col. 3:16, Lk. 12:21).*3

The White Raiment of Imparted Righteousness

The Laodiceans were also commanded to buy white raiment that they might be clothed, that they might not be shamed because of spiritual nakedness. This covering—for the shame we inherited from Adam—can never be just the 'fig leaves' of the creeds, philosophies and religions that fill this world. Neither can righteousness be attained through self-effort, through mere religious works or attempts at moral reformation. Ours must be robes washed in the blood of the Lamb—the blood that imparts to believers a right standing with God, the blood that makes us just as pure in the sight of heaven as the firstborn Son Himself. (See Rev. 7:9, 14–15; 19:7–14, 2 Cor. 5:21.)

This possession alone is worth far more than all the riches of the world combined. Yet how peculiar and true it is that such imparted righteousness can only be procured by those who are described as being *poor in spirit*—those who recognize all their own attempts at righteousness are as "filthy rags." (Is. 64:6, See Pr. 30:12.)

The Precious Eye Salve

The statement made to the Laodiceans—"anoint your eyes with eye salve, that you may see"—is a reference to spiritual sight. This is that potential inner ability, resident in every child of God, to discern and comprehend God's feelings and will. It enables us to view life and our choices in life from His perspective. The blind Laodiceans had a distorted view of truth and self, even as many who profess Christianity in this hour.

So they were exhorted to apply to their 'eyes' some type of spiritual balm that they might recover. This 'medicinal ointment' could well be "the spirit of wisdom and revelation": that ministry of the Holy Spirit which unveils to us both the true nature of God and our true nature. (Eph. 1:17, See Jn. 16:7–11.)

One commentary states, "The Holy Spirit's unction, like the ancient eye salve's first smarts with conviction of sin, then heals. He opens our eyes first to ourselves in our wretchedness, then to the Savior in His preciousness."*4

THE SEEMING CONTRADICTION RECONCILED

God wants his people blessed materially and financially. This is irrefutable truth. 3 John 2 says, "Beloved, I pray that you may prosper in all things and be in health, just as your soul prospers." And Deuteronomy 8:18 announces it is "the LORD your God...who gives you power to get wealth, that He may establish His covenant which He swore to your fathers."

Yet God also warned of serious repercussions if "your heart is lifted up, and you forget the LORD your God...Then you say in your heart, My power and the might of my hand have gained me this wealth" (Dt. 8:14, 17). So there is a delicate balance between two extremes that every covenant believer must seek in order to be pleasing to the Most High.

God certainly does not want us poor, but simultaneously He certainly does not want us to make the grave error of becoming excessively enamored with money and things. Proverbs 28:6 strongly affirms, "Better is the poor who walks in his integrity than one perverse in his ways, though he be rich."[*5]

We are to first seek the kingdom of God and His righteousness, setting our affection on things above. (See Mt. 6:33, Col. 3:2.) This is God's mandate for us and must be our first priority. Maintaining such an attitude keeps us *poor in spirit* whether we are rich or poor.

We are commanded "not to be haughty, nor to trust in uncertain riches but in the living God, who gives us richly all things to enjoy" (1 Tim. 6:17). We must count Him our only source of true happiness. In cultivating such a contented heart, we succeed in toppling any 'idol of covetousness' and we get much closer to embracing all the spiritual abundance available in the kingdom of heaven. (See Col. 3:5.)

We become truly steadfast and happy regardless of the changing conditions of life. Therefore, as strange as it may seem, being *poor in spirit* often involves a contentedness to be poor, a willingness to be empty of worldly gain, if God so orders our steps. Paul said it so well:

Not that I speak in regard to need, for I have learned,
in whatever state I am, to be content.
I know both how to be abased, and I know how to abound.
Everywhere and in all things I have learned both to be full
and to be hungry, both to abound and suffer need.

(Philippians 4:11–12)

These verses are not a confession of unbelief, opening the door to financial or spiritual disaster. They are a declaration of satisfaction, fulfillment and contentedness in the LORD alone, opening the door to steadiness of heart and constancy of worship. It was such an attitude that kept Job from charging God foolishly in the midst of all of his tragedy and compelled him to instead confess:

Naked I came from my mother's womb, and naked shall
I return there. The LORD gave, and the LORD has taken
away; BLESSED BE THE NAME OF THE LORD.

(Job 1:21)[*6]

Nothing encountered in life can shatter the faith, steal the joy, or undermine the stability of the person who has reached such a high peak of confidence in God. So it is no wonder that Jesus also preached, *"Blessed are you poor, for yours is the kingdom of God"* (Lk. 6:20).

The One who had no place to lay His head was definitely not putting his stamp of approval on poverty itself, but rather on the positive effect that poverty, at times, can produce. How often the poor, already unattached to that which is material and worldly, show themselves most receptive to the things of God. ("Has God not chosen the poor of this world to be rich in faith and heirs of the kingdom which He promised to those who love Him?" Ja. 2:5.)

Of course, this need NOT be the case, for a person certainly does not have to be poor naturally to be blessed spiritually! It is NOT wrong for us to possess possessions, but it IS wrong when possessions possess us. When this happens, we lose *poverty of spirit* and the blessing becomes an idol, like the spoiled gold of Egypt becoming the golden calf on the plains of Mt. Sinai.

MAINTAINING THE RIGHT SPIRIT

King David evidently had a huge, personal treasury, as well as the riches of the kingdom of Israel at his disposal, yet he still looked beyond all of his affluence and influence and prayed:

> *Bow down Your ear, O LORD, hear me; for I am **poor** and **needy**...Save your servant who trusts in You!*
> (Psalm 86:1–2)

Never one to become heady or overconfident because of his possessions, his position of leadership, or his many former victories supernaturally won, David kept himself utterly dependent on God. He indicated this admirable attitude by making statements like the following:

> *...I am **poor** and sorrowful: let Your salvation, O God, set me up on high.*
> *For the LORD hears **the poor**, and does not despise His prisoners.*
> (Psalm 69:29, 33)

So again, let it be repeated—even if God's people become rich or influential, they must always be *poor* in their own estimation if they are to continually increase in the wealth and authority of God's kingdom. They must look past all of their pride-producing possessions and attainments, and consistently declare their great need before God. This is the secret to capturing God's heart and the means of procuring all of the abundance He delights to supply, both now and forevermore.

*For he will deliver **THE NEEDY** when he cries, **THE POOR** also, and him who has no helper.*
*He will spare **THE POOR AND THE NEEDY**, and will save the souls of **THE NEEDY**.*

(Psalm 72:12–13)

*He will bring justice to **THE POOR OF THE PEOPLE**; He will save **THE CHILDREN OF THE NEEDY**, and will break in pieces the oppressor.*

(Psalm 72:4)

These are glorious promises—especially for those who love giving all the glory to God. (See also Ps. 9:18; 35:10; 72:2; 109:31 NIV; 140:12, Is. 25:4.)*7

THE WONDERFUL END RESULT

2 Corinthians 8:9 states, "For you know the grace of our LORD Jesus Christ, that though He was *rich,* yet for your sakes He became *poor,* that you through His *poverty* might become rich." The reference to Jesus being *rich* is a reference to the glory of the celestial state He enjoyed prior to the incarnation. He was *rich* in the full fellowship that He shared with the Father above. Never beset by temptations or satanic opposition in heaven, He was *rich* in joy unhindered, peace undisturbed and splendor unsurpassed.

Then Jesus "became *poor*"—taking upon Himself the form of a servant, humbly assuming the limitations of human flesh. He even submitted to the misery of the cross, that He might fully identify with us in our low estate. He pledged that if we identify with Him in His poverty—humbling ourselves, taking the form of servants and sharing the cross—He will also make us "rich" with all the abundance of the kingdom of heaven.

Meditate for a moment on the promise of our foundational passage:

*Blessed are **the poor in spirit**, for theirs is the kingdom of heaven.*

(Matthew 5:3)

Notice Jesus said "is," not "will be." He evidently did this because inheriting the kingdom of heaven is more than just a future hope. It is a present tense happening in the lives of all true believers. Inheriting the "kingdom of heaven" can mean experiencing the glory of heaven yet to come, but it can also mean experiencing heaven's influence in our lives, right here, right now. It means natural human beings experiencing and enjoying supernatural realities.

Heaven is a place of perfect love, excellent power, fullness of wisdom and inexhaustible grace. Simply put, it is God. The character of the kingdom of heaven is the character of the King who rules it—for it is permeated with His royal and glorious personality. 1 Corinthians 4:20 teaches that the "kingdom of God is not in word but in power." Romans 14:17 reveals that God's kingdom is not "eating and drinking" (dietary laws from the Old Testament) but "righteousness and peace and joy in the Holy Spirit." In other words, inheriting the kingdom of heaven involves the manifest presence and rich reality of God overflowing into our lives.[*8]

Again, what is most amazing—this promise is only given to those who admit their bankruptcy in Adam. In humbling ourselves, we are exalted: lifted into a heavenly sphere and made to "sit together in heavenly places" (Eph. 2:6). And the best is yet to come! We will yet proceed from glory to glory!

As it was prophesied that the Jews would come out of Egypt with "great possessions," so we who are freed from the bondage of sin will depart from this world far richer as a result (Gen. 15:14). Because of our sojourn in the realm of time we will 'possess' great insight into the hidden nature of the God: the glorious One, who is rich in mercy and rich in grace. This enriching revelation will reach its zenith at the resurrection when we fully emerge in the image of the firstborn Son and inherit "all things" (Rev. 21:7).

According to Revelation 5:12, even the *poor-spirited* Lamb of God will ultimately inherit great "riches" as a result of all that He suffered during His earthly sojourn. Quite possibly, the formation of the bride of Christ and the eternal communion He will share with her is the thing that He will consider His greatest treasure. We, in like manner, should consider this eternal fellowship with the Most High God a far more enriching possession than the streets of gold or the walls of jasper.

How we thank God for the promise—"Blessed are THE POOR IN SPIRIT; for theirs is the kingdom of heaven" (Mt. 5:3). But, how much more grateful we should be concerning the blessed expectation of walking forever in intimacy with the King of the kingdom Himself. A reward as *rich* as this could never be suitably described in mere, earthly words.

OUR BLESSED HOPE

The world system is primarily based on self-will, self-gratification and self-promotion. All of these are quite opposite to *poverty of spirit*. On the highest level of interpretation, Isaiah 26:4–6 symbolizes this corrupt world system as a singular city and foretells its ultimate collapse.

Trust in the LORD forever, for in JAH, the LORD, is everlasting strength.

For He brings down those who dwell on high, the lofty
city, He lays it low, He lays it low to the ground, He brings
it down to the dust.

The next verse identifies those who will emerge as final victors:

*The foot shall tread it down - the feet of **the poor** and*
*the steps of **the needy**.*

We know our Advocate and Savior will defend us before all the accusations of those demonic powers who continually accuse the brethren:

*For He shall stand at the right hand of **the poor**, to*
save him from those that condemn his soul.

(Psalm 109:31 KJV, See Psalm 82:4.)

Hannah, the mother of Samuel, also prophesied of the unique people who will emerge from this earthly exile totally triumphant through the God who:

*...raises **the poor** from the dust and lifts the beggar*
from the ash heap, to set them among princes and make
them inherit the throne of glory."

(1 Samuel 2:8, See also Psalm 113:7–8.)

How ironic it is that only those who are 'poor' in their own estimation will ever obtain this royal inheritance that defies description: the very throne of God! Yet this is one of the mysteries of the kingdom of God. We should *tremble* with gratitude at the very mention of this truth.

Endnotes

*1 *Bethany Commentary of the New Testament* (Bethany House Publishers, Minneapolis, Minnesota 1983) p. 30, Jamieson, Fausset, Brown, under verse 3.

*2 *Bethany Commentary of the New Testament* (Bethany House Publishers, Minneapolis, Minnesota 1983) p. 1447, Adam Clarke, under verse 17.

*3 See the Chapter on *Fine Gold* and the chapter on *The Rich of the Earth*, both in Volume Seven of **Our Glorious Inheritance**.

*4 *Bethany Commentary of the New Testament* (Bethany House Publishers, Minneapolis, Minnesota 1983) p. 1447, Jamieson, Fausset, Brown, under verse 18.

*5 See the chapters on *The Prosperous of the Earth* and *The Rich of the Earth*, both in Volume Seven of **Our Glorious Inheritance**.

*6 Job misinterpreted the source of his dilemmas. The LORD did not 'take away,' Satan did.

*7 Though these scriptures may be referring primarily to those who are "poor and needy" naturally, they are certainly applicable as well to those who are "poor and needy" spiritually.

*8 For an in-depth study of the kingdom of heaven, see the chapter on *Good Seed, the Children of the Kingdom* in this volume of **Our Glorious Inheritance**.

THE PURE IN HEART

A PURE PEOPLE

THE PURE

Blessed are **THE PURE IN HEART**: *for they shall see God.*

(Matthew 5:8)

*He gave Himself for us, to rescue us from all wickedness and make us **A PURE PEOPLE** who belong to Him alone and are eager to do good.*

(Titus 2:14 TEV)

*The way of a guilty man is perverse; but as for **THE PURE,** his work is right.*

(Proverbs 21:8)

THE PURE IN HEART

Blessed are **THE PURE IN HEART***: for they shall see God.*

(Matthew 5:8)

*T*o be **pure** is to be clean, chaste, virtuous, moral and ethical. In some cases, it describes those who have been delivered from that which is base, carnal or wickedly sensual. It can also mean containing nothing inappropriate or unnecessary—or freedom from any foreign or contaminating influence.

Perfect purity is a major facet of the personality of God. The Most High is so utterly pure that He "cannot be tempted with evil, nor does He...tempt anyone." Habakkuk even states that He is "of purer eyes than to behold evil, and cannot look on wickedness" (Ja. 1:13, Hab. 1:13).

This does not mean it is impossible for God to observe the sinful activity that is so rampant in this world. It rather means that He cannot gaze on any evil or wrongdoing with the slightest bit of consent. The above passage in the New American Standard Bible affirms this, explaining that God's eyes are too pure to "approve evil" and He cannot look on iniquity with "favor." Though this pure-eyed Savior is longsuffering, gentle, merciful and always forgiving, still, He never has and He never will continually tolerate impurity and rebellion, especially among His people.

Everything about God is pure—His Spirit, His nature, His mind, His attitudes, His motives, His goals and His plans for us.

In Psalm 119:140, the writer declared to God, "Your Word is very *pure,* therefore Your servant loves it." Enhancing this passage is Psalm 19:8, "The commandment of the LORD is *pure,* enlightening the eyes."

Consider also James 3:17, "the wisdom that is from above is first *pure.*" In other words, as soon as a person comes under the influence of heavenly wisdom, one of the first main results is the purification of the heart. What a change this is, for "the way of man is froward and strange" (meaning *perverse, unclean, crooked, devious and habitually inclined toward rebellion)* "but as for **the pure,** his work is right" (Pr. 21:8 KJV, NKJV). The fallen nature, full of carnal character traits, definitely is strange compared to God. It is completely alien to the utterly pure atmosphere of heaven. Yet unfortunately, these evil traits are common in the earth. Considering this, and considering that Job 25:5 claims the stars are not even *pure* in God's sight, how can man ever hope to rise above his dilemma?

We were all conceived in iniquity. We were all born in sin. Therefore, how can we possibly change? Can the leopard change his spots? (See Jer. 13:23.) How then can we who are so prone to impurity ever attain the status of being truly pure?

GOD'S PURIFICATION PROCESS
THE OLD WILL UNVEILS THE NEW

The answer to the disturbing and penetrating questions just presented is quite evident to most believers now, but it was veiled in symbolic language under the Old Will.

A good example is Numbers, chapter 19. In this passage of Scripture we find a curious set of rules dealing with some of the things that rendered an Israelite unclean or impure. It also explains the purification process that God provided and demanded. **Notice that the following twelve reasons for an unclean, impure status all deal, either directly or indirectly, with death.**[*1]

(1)   Touching a dead body (vs. 11–16).
(2)   Going into a place where a person was dying (v.14).
(3)   Being present when someone died (everyone and everything in the room was declared to be unclean) (v.14).
(4)   Touching someone slain (v.16).
(5)   Touching a bone of a dead person (v.16).
(6)   Touching a grave (v.16).
(7)   Touching an unclean person (v.22).
(8)   Touching anything an unclean person touched (v.22).
(9)   Preparation of the red heifer (vs. 9–10).
(10) Burning the red heifer (v.8).
(11) Gathering the ashes of the red heifer (vs. 9–10).
(12) Sprinkling water of separation on an unclean person (vs.18–21).

This twelvefold ordinance of the law primarily emphasizes how unclean and abhorrent death is in the sight of God. It also reveals, in its spiritual application, how disgustingly impure and contagiously unclean we all became in the sight of heaven because of the original sin of Adam. Because of that horrible event the curse of death was brought on the human race in all its forms: spiritual death, mental death, emotional death and ultimately, physical death. **Thankfully, God has always made a way for His covenant people to be restored to purity and cleanness in His sight.**

Statutes such as those just mentioned were probably given to the Jews for three main reasons: first, to impress their minds with the need for purity; second, to give them confidence that God longs to provide a means of purification; and **third**, to provide rich typology—a symbolic and prophetic view—of the purification yet to manifest in the future, through the coming of the Messiah and the New Covenant Age.

In Numbers 19 God gave the answer for a state of uncleanness or impurity. It involved being sprinkled with "**the water of separation**" (also called "**the water of purifiying**" and "**a purification for sin**" Num. 8:7; 19:9 KJV). This solution was called "the water of separation" because it was sprinkled on those persons who were temporarily separated from God and His sanctuary because of uncleanness. It was called "the water of purifying" because it purified them from their uncleanness and restored them to God's favor and fellowship.

All contributing details concerning this "water of purifying" are highly important and greatly symbolic. Let us inspect them now:

⌐· **In making "the water of purifying" the presiding priest would utilize a red heifer, without spot or blemish, which had never worn a yoke.** This red heifer, being a beast of burden, was a type of Christ, who was also a burden bearer. He was never under the yoke of the sin nature, but was without spot or blemish ("in all points tempted as we are, yet without sin.") (Heb. 4:15, See Is. 53.)

⌐· **The unique demand for the animal to be red was the only color requirement given in any Old Will sacrifice.** It doubly emphasized the concept of our redemption and purification from death only being achievable through the shedding of blood. Also it reemphasizes, though our sins be "as scarlet, they shall be as white as snow" (Is. 1:18).

⌐· **The heifer was to be slaughtered without the camp.** This relates to how the Messiah would go outside the camp of Judaism to reach the Gentiles. The exact location for this slaughter of the heifer during the Temple Era was the Mount of Olives (also called the Mount of Anointment) just across the valley from the Temple Mount. How fitting it is that this is where Jesus sweat blood in agony of prayer to fulfill the symbol of the "red heifer," not only for the Jews, but for all nations. (See Luke 22:39–44.)

⌐· **The officiating priest then dipped his finger in the blood and sprinkled it seven times toward the sanctuary.** This signified that the sacrifice was accepted by God (meeting the demands of justice) and that there was a complete removal of sin (something Jesus accomplished later to the fullest). The number seven speaks of completeness and perfection.

⌐· **The entire heifer was then burned in the sight of the priest: her skin, flesh, blood and dung.** This speaks of Jesus, on the cross, being totally consumed with the fire of that divine judgment which should have fallen on us.

⌣˙ **Cedar wood, hyssop and scarlet were then cast into the midst of the burning heifer by the officiating priest.** Because the **cedar** is normally a very tall, stately, long-lived tree, its wood speaks of majesty, endurance and permanence. (Refer to the chapter on *Good Trees* in this volume.) The **hyssop** was a small, bushy plant that was used in several Jewish rituals. It always denoted some kind of transfer (usually the beneficial effects of a sacrifice). (Compare Ex. 12:22, Lev. 14:4–6, 49–52, 1 Kgs. 4:33, Ps. 51:7, Jn. 19:29, Heb. 9:19.) **Scarlet** was made from a dye produced by crushing the eggs of the coccus worm. This process speaks of how Jesus became "a worm" and was "crushed" by judgment on the cross in order to yield the "crimson/scarlet flow" that washes us from our sin and grants us an inheritance among those who are sanctified. (See Ps. 22:6.) This threefold symbol speaks collectively of the divine nature (cedar) being transferred (hyssop) by the substitutionary sacrifice (scarlet).

⌣˙ **The ashes of the heifer were gathered up and preserved without the camp in a clean place.** These ashes represent the remembrance of Jesus' agony and atoning death, which has similarly been preserved outside the camp of established Judaism.

⌣˙ **Before being applied, the ashes of the heifer were mixed with running water in a vessel.** They were then sprinkled, by means of a bunch of hyssop, on whatever needed to be made clean. The running water is a symbol of the Word and the Spirit blended together (Jn. 7:37–39, Eph. 5:26)—which are certainly never stagnant, but ever flowing and alive with the life of God. Being mixed with ashes, this water speaks of how the Word and the Spirit bring "all things to our remembrance" concerning the beneficial effects of the death of Jesus. The water being sprinkled represents the impartation and subsequent absorption of the Gospel, through the Spirit, in those who hear, believe and receive.

⌣˙ **This sprinkling was to take place the third and seventh days.** This typified two purifying experiences granted to God's people: the initial salvation experience that enables us to overcome spiritual death, and the ultimate glorification experience that will enable us to overcome physical death. First we receive inward purity; then, at the end, we will receive absolute purity. Three is the number of divine intervention and seven, the number of perfection.

Having accomplished these prescribed rituals, Jewish worshippers could then boldly claim freedom from the defilement of death. They could boldly claim the status of being separated, purified and clean. Little did they realize the detailed, prophetic picture they were painting for us—a picture we desperately needed to see—for we too have been defiled. We have touched death and known its horror.

We were born into this world spiritually dead—and contrasted to the initial perfection of Eden, emotionally and mentally dead as well. We are progressively journeying toward ultimate physical death when our souls will depart from these physical bodies. In that climax of physical existence, eternal death awaits those who have refused to serve God. This will culminate in "the second death": the death of both body and soul in the lake of fire. (See Rev. 20:12–15.)

If we have been born again, we are new creatures in Christ and none of these things move us. Why? Because we have been filled with the very life of God. We have been made pure.

Now our challenge is to abide in purity by abiding in the life of God. We enter into death if we lie, hate, covet, lust, judge unrighteously, or rebel against God even in the smallest, most insignificant ways ("For to be carnally minded is *death*" Ro. 8:6). 1 John 3:14–15 even declares, "He who does not love his brother abides in *death*" and that "whoever hates his brother is a *murderer*."

In other words, not only do we *touch death* when we yield to that which is carnal—we *administer death* to others as well. O, what a terrible dilemma! How can we possibly escape? Only by truly repenting, as David of old. He touched death when he backslid, but cried, "Have mercy upon me, O God...*Purge me with hyssop,* and I shall be clean: wash me, and I shall be whiter than snow" (Ps. 51:1, 7). In other words, this erring king was pleading, not for a priest, but for God to sprinkle him.

He apparently had insight into the true source of purification. He understood that it was not the various rituals of the law, but the God that instituted those rituals who truly purifies. How much more is such splendid truth evident now— for we are partakers, not of Old Covenant symbolic ceremonies, but of New Covenant living realities!

Hebrews 9:13–14 says it so well:

> For if the blood of bulls and goats, **and the ashes of a heifer, sprinkling the unclean, sanctifies for the purifying of the flesh:**
> How much more shall the blood of Christ, who through the eternal Spirit offered Himself without spot to God, cleanse your conscience from dead works to serve the living God.

How our hearts should melt when we see the awesome price that our Savior paid for the purification of His people! He did not give mountains of gold and valleys filled with precious jewels. He did not sacrifice swirling galaxies or myriads of angels. Titus 2:14 (TEV) asserts that "He gave **Himself** for us, to rescue us from all wickedness and make us **A PURE PEOPLE** who belong to Him alone and are eager to do good." Just realizing Jesus' commitment to this process should make us all the more full-of-faith that God will grant such grace to even the most sin-sick soul. It should birth in us a passion as well to be fully committed to the One who made this process possible.

THE BIRTH OF PURITY
THE COMMAND OF PURITY

When we made our entrance into this world we became sinners three ways: by birth, by nature and later, by choice. When we were born again the opposite took place. We were spiritually conceived in purity and born again into the very righteousness of God. At that precise moment, we became heirs of the utterly pure nature of the firstborn Son.

But even though sons of God are automatically pure by birth and pure by nature, still, we receive this inheritance in vain unless we become 'pure by choice'—striving daily to manifest this purity in every area of our being. God expects us to purify the attitudes, actions and reactions that fill our lives.

- **The Soul**—1 Peter 1:22 urges, "Since you have *purified your souls* [the seat of the mind, the will and the emotions] in obeying the truth through the Spirit in sincere love of the brethren, love one another fervently with a *pure heart*."

- **The Heart**—James 4:8–10 follows a similar vein saying, "*purify your hearts,* you double-minded. Lament and mourn and weep…Humble yourselves in the sight of the LORD…"

- **The Conscience**—1 Timothy 3:9–10 commands that we hold "the mystery of the faith with a *pure conscience.*"

- **The Mind**—2 Peter 3:1 (KJV) tells how the Word stirs up our "*pure minds* by way of remembrance.*" (This is a reference to the spiritual mind, the mind of Christ). Philippians 4:8 adds, "whatever things are *pure*…meditate on these things." And Philippians 1:17 (NAS) encourages those in ministry to have "*pure motives.*"

Pure actions, pure thoughts, pure minds, pure consciences, pure motives, pure hearts, pure emotions, pure souls and pure bodies: to all of these we are called. We are even warned against knowledgeably or even unwittingly being partakers of other men's sins. Concerning this, Paul urged

Timothy (and each one of us), "Keep yourself *pure*" and also, "be an example of the believers…in *purity*" (1 Tim. 4:12, 5:22).

We should even be careful that our prayers and doctrine are both *pure*, just as Job of old (Jb. 11:4, 16:17). 1 Peter 2:2 exhorts us to "desire *the pure milk of the Word*" that we might grow in God.

Also, we are told that *"pure and undefiled religion* before God and the Father is this: to visit orphans and widows in their trouble, and to keep oneself unspotted from the world" (Ja. 1:27). This is the true Gospel in simple terms. Far from the flamboyant attempts at 'puffed up' religiosity that have become so common, this verse takes us back to the basics. It challenges us to be loving, humble servants and clean vessels before the LORD. This is *pure and undefiled religion:* not contaminated with the prideful, self-seeking, self-exalting motives to which we are so prone.

So let us "cleanse ourselves from all filthiness of the flesh and spirit, perfecting holiness in the fear of God" (2 Cor. 7:1). Let us be diligent and disciplined, ever guarding our hearts and minds against the slightest entrance of that which is unchaste, immoral, or unethical. For the maxim spoken years ago by Benjamin Franklin still rings true:

> It is easier to suppress the first desire than to satisfy all that follow it.[*2]

THE REWARD OF PURITY

The Bible reveals certain promises that are lovingly bestowed on those who qualify to be numbered among **the pure.** The most significant are:

✤ 2 Samuel 22:27, **"With the pure You will show Yourself pure; and with the devious You will show Yourself shrewd"** ─────────────

In other words, God cannot open the door of His heart to those who are deceitful and prone to selfish rebellion. But to **the pure** He can. He allows Himself to be accessed by those whose hearts are transparent in love toward Him. He shrewdly withdraws Himself from the devious and becomes distant and unapproachable. Because if they had a relationship with God they would not value it, nor treat Him with the reverence He deserves. The King James Version translates the last part of this verse with a somewhat different flavor: "with the froward Thou wilt shew Thyself unsavoury." The word **froward** means habitually inclined toward rebellion. God's righteous reaction to such behavior definitely is "unsavoury"—bitter to the soul eternally. But, O how sweetly he manifests Himself to those He calls **the pure.**

❧ Proverbs 22:11, 15:26, **"He who loves purity of heart, and has grace on his lips, the king will be his friend"** ————————————————————————

This is true because "the thoughts of the wicked are an abomination to the LORD: but the words of the pure are pleasant words." These two scriptures reveal once again that if we are truly pure in our attitudes, the King of kings will bring us into an intimate relationship with Himself. He is attracted to us because our words are pleasantly pure and sweet to His ears, especially when we commune with Him in prayer.

❧ Matthew 5:8, **"Blessed are the pure in heart: for they shall see God"** —

Evidently, this main title scripture means more than just *seeing* the LORD in the spectacular display of His Shekinah glory in the heavenly sphere. It also means *seeing* God move in our lives right now—in divine visitations, revealed wisdom, manifested gifts, fruits of the Spirit and miraculous answers to prayer.

THE "REFINER" AND "LAUNDERER"

As we strive to attain the high goal of purity, let us remember that all self-effort will eventually prove insufficient. Only God can make us pure. The One who said "their righteousness is from Me" could just as easily say "their purity is from Me" (Is. 54:17). We owe it all to Jesus and we can quickly trace any purity we acquire back to Him.

The prophet Malachi described the coming and the purpose of this "Purifying One" when he prophesied the following:

> *...the LORD, whom you seek, will suddenly come to His temple, even the Messenger of the covenant in whom you delight. Behold, He is coming, says the LORD of hosts.*
>
> *But who can endure the day of His coming? And who can stand when He appears? **For He is like a refiner's fire and like launderer's soap.**"*
>
> *He will set as a **refiner** and a **purifier** of silver, He will **purify** the sons of Levi, and purge them as gold and silver, that they may offer to the LORD an offering in righteousness."*
>
> (Malachi 3:1–3)

❧ **Jesus: the Refiner** ————————————————————————————————

A refiner is one who purifies metals, freeing them from dross or alloys. The refiner's fire is used to melt the metal down in order to effect this process. In the passage just mentioned we find Jesus spoken of as a "refiner's fire."

Hebrews 12:29 names Him **a consuming fire**—for His passion and purpose is to consume every part of our being with the holy fire of His Word and His Spirit. (See Jer. 23:29, Mt. 3:11.) The end result is that our wills melt in submission and we come forth as silver and gold—purified of carnal 'dross.' Our God, the refiner, will ultimately devour the earth with fire as well. Every trace of carnality and uncleanness will be gone, not only from us, but from this entire rotating orb.

❈ Jesus: the Launderer (the Fuller KJV)

In Bible times especially, a **launderer** (or **fuller**) was one who "fulled" or thickened, laundered, bleached and sometimes dyed cloth in the process of its manufacture and upkeep.[*3] Ordinarily, cloth to be whitened was washed in lye, rubbed, beaten and dried in the sun. A special field was often used for this purpose (Is. 7:3, 2 Kg. 18:17). The root of the Hebrew word *kabac*, translated *fuller's* in the KJV, actually means *to trample, hence to wash by stamping with the feet* (SC).

All of this speaks of the spiritual process to which true sons of God are often subjected. A fuller did not trample the cloth being cleansed with an attitude of enmity or destructiveness, but rather with expertise and loving concern over the future usefulness, beauty and value of the cloth.

Parallel to this, God knows that if we were left to our own devices, we would never progress. The 'dirt' would never be dislodged out of our heart and we would never arrive at the pureness of the image of the firstborn Son. So our God sees to it that the carnal part of us is often 'trampled underfoot'—sometimes by the negative circumstances of life, and sometimes by His own convicting power. (Of course, the Heavenly Fuller's motive cannot be doubted, for the feet employed in this task are nail-scarred.) Let us welcome the process and submit to the spiritual soap, knowing that God has great plans for us.

When Jesus was yet in His earthly state, on the Mount of Transfiguration, He stepped up momentarily into the glory of the celestial. The Scripture relates that, "His raiment became shining, exceeding white as snow; so as no fuller on earth can white them" (Mk. 9:3 KJV). When He comes again, He will cause us to 'step up' into the glory of the celestial permanently. In that spectacular moment, we will also become "shining, exceeding *white*" as no fuller or launderer on earth could have made us: no religionist, no philosopher, no counselor—only Jesus.

Let us review God's motive. Why does He come as Fuller's Soap and as a Refiner's Fire? That He might *"purify* the sons of Levi...that they may offer to the LORD an offering in righteousness." Under the Old Will, the sons of Levi were the inheritors of the priesthood rights: something all believers inherit under the New. (See 1 Pt. 2:5, 9.) Those referred to as chief priests burned *pure* frankincense before the LORD, laid showbread on a "*pure* gold table" and kept the light burning on a "lampstand of *pure* gold." These were all subtle and constant reminders to them of their calling to be pure. Psalm 24:3–4 questioned, "Who shall ascend into the hill of the LORD? Or who may stand in His holy place? He who has clean hands and *a pure heart...*"

Those who minister to God now as "sons of Levi" must, in an even greater degree, do so with pure motives and pure praise. Therefore, just as Old Covenant priests were washed in water as part of their initiation, "let us draw near with a true heart in full assurance of faith, having our hearts sprinkled from an evil conscience and our bodies washed with pure water": the pure water of the Word of God. (Heb. 10:22, See Eph. 5:26.)

This makes us fit for the priesthood calling.

This renders our worship receivable in God's sight.

This qualifies us to become the "**pure offering**" of praise Malachi foretold would come under the New Will (Mal. 1:11).

THE COLOR WHITE: A SYMBOL OF ULTIMATE PURITY

The color white is a biblical symbol of purity and speaks especially of the future state. God speaks of His redeemed as "they which came out of great tribulation, and have washed their robes, and made them *white* in the blood of the Lamb." Our sins though "red like crimson," will be made "*white* as snow" and "*white* as wool." (Is. 1:18, See Ps. 51:7.) We will be given "a *white* stone, and in the stone a new name written." As the armies of heaven accompanying the returning Messiah, we will ride upon "*white* horses, clothed in fine linen, *white* and clean." As the bride of Christ; we will be arrayed in fine linen, clean and *white*: for the fine linen is the righteousness of saints." And we will be rewarded eternally by the Holy One whose hair is "*white* like wool, as *white* as snow," who sits on a "great *white* throne" (Rev. 1:14; 2:17; 7:14; 19:8, 14; 20:11).

In that future state, everything will be made utterly pure. God has even promised to "restore to the peoples a *pure language,* that they all may call on the name of the LORD, to serve Him with one accord" (Zep. 3:9). This will be a universal and holy language, common to all the inhabitants of the coming kingdom—for the curse of Babel will be lifted and God's blessing will be fully manifested. All the various defiled languages of the world, containing evil and blasphemous words, will apparently be done away with forever. This *pure language,* abounding in worship phrases, praise utterances, and inspired heavenly words taught by the Holy Spirit, will ever be the tongue of God's redeemed. It will surely be the language of God, the language He spoke to Adam and Eve in the beginning.

Isaiah pledged that in that final day the mighty God will *"purely"* or thoroughly purge away all the dross of Jerusalem and cause her to be called "the city of righteousness, the faithful city" (Is. 1:26 KJV). Moreover, according to John's revelation, our eternal abode, New Jerusalem, will come down from God out of heaven like a pure, virtuous bride adorned for her husband. This spectacular, celestial city will appear as *"pure* gold, like clear glass." The street of the city will also be *pure* gold. And from beneath the throne of God there will issue a *"pure* river of water of life, clear as crystal" Yes, everything in the coming new world will be utterly *pure* (Rev. 21:2, 18–21, 22:1).

Thank God for the soon-to-be-fulfilled promise:

> *When He shall appear, we shall be like Him; for we*
> *shall see Him as He is.*
>
> (1 John 3:2 KJV)

John also added to this pledge, "everyone who has this hope in him *purifies* himself, just as He is *pure"* (1 Jn. 3:3). How does this work? Most likely by the following process. By maintaining hope in the resurrection to come, an overflow of resurrection life pours into our lives even now—resurrecting us into purity again and again—in the inner man, the hidden man of the heart.

This, too, is undoubtedly the *deep calling to the deep*—the Mighty God daily stirring up in His everlasting offspring the absolute pureness of His nature and His image. Therefore, it is no wonder that *the pure in heart* are also termed *blessed*—for those who yield to such a God-pleasing character quality discover a source of *supreme happiness* and *spiritual bounty* that is unlimited in scope.

To be pitied are those deceived ones who cling to their uncleanness. To be praised are those *highly favored ones* who make purity their choice. Only eternity will reveal the fullness and richness of the *blessings* and *benefits* that will come to them as a result.

Deep calls unto deep,
*To be **pure**, LORD, we pray—*
Not defiled by this world,
And its death-dealing ways.

Pure hearts and pure minds
Pure consciences and souls;
Pure motives in religion—
God, grant us these goals!

So wash us and cleanse us;
Refine us with fire,
Purge us with hyssop—
God, grant this desire.

'Till we join that
Heavenly white-robed throng,
And on streets of pure gold—
We sing a new song!

Endnotes

*1 There are many other Old Will reasons for uncleanness such as those found in Leviticus 11–15.

*2 Benjamin Franklin, *The Way to Wealth*, as published by Simeon Ide, Windsor VT 1826.

*3 Miller, *Harper's Bible Dictionary*, (NavPress, Inc., Colorado Springs, Colorado) under *Fuller*, p. 208.

THE THIRSTY

THE HUNGRY

Let them give thanks to the LORD for His unfailing love and His wonderful deeds for men, for He satisfies **THE THIRSTY** *and fills* **THE HUNGRY** *with good things.*

(Psalm 107:8–9 NIV)

*For He satisfieth **THE LONGING SOUL**, and filleth **THE HUNGRY SOUL** with goodness.*

(Psalm 107:9 KJV)

*As cold waters to **A THIRSTY SOUL**, so is good news from a far country.*

(Proverbs 25:25)

*For as the rain comes down, and the snow from heaven and do not return there, but water the earth, and make it bring forth and bud, that it may give seed to the sower and bread to the **EATER**, so shall My Word be that goes forth from My mouth…*

(Isaiah 55:10–11)

LONGING SOULS

HUNGRY SOULS

THIRSTY SOULS

EATERS

Deep calls unto deep,
Feed me LORD or I'll die.
Quench this aching within—
Father, do not deny.

Give this day—daily bread
(Not a stone in its place.)
Send celestial waters
(Of life-giving grace.)

For by these I live,
And my heart is in need,
Of its heavenly portion
So Good Shepherd, please feed...

Me the Word and the Spirit,
My meal from above,
O, communion of glory,
O, expression of love.

THE THIRSTY, THE HUNGRY

Let them give thanks to the LORD for His unfailing
love and His wonderful deeds for men, for He satisfies
THE THIRSTY *and fills* **THE HUNGRY** *with good*
things.

(Psalm 107:8–9 NIV)

*T*wo of the main drives resident in the human body are hunger
and thirst. In order to survive in this world we must have food to satisfy
our hunger and drink to quench our thirst. Succeeding or failing in this area
literally means the difference between life and death. If we secure the right
kind of food and drink, we live. If we fail, we die—as simple as that.

And so it is spiritually as well.

Two of the main drives resident in the human spirit are hunger and thirst.
In order to survive spiritually—in this present world and forevermore—we must
succeed in finding the right kind of spiritual food and drink. This is not optional.
This is mandatory. In a spiritual sense, succeeding or failing in this area of
human need also means the difference between life and death.

Most of what the world spreads before us is tainted with the deadly poison
of carnality and sensuality. Even all of its religions are contaminated with enough
deception to prevent their adherents from ever finding the truth. So it becomes
necessary, not only to satisfy our hunger and thirst, but to make sure we are
choosing the right kind of meal. Failing to satisfy our hunger and thirst definitely
means death, but trying to satisfy this dual need with the wrong kind of spiritual
food and drink also means death—the eternal death of the soul.

THE FALL OF MAN

God provided food for Adam and Eve to perpetuate their existence.
Their main source of sustenance was identified as the tree of life. Forbidden
fruit grew on the tree of the knowledge of good and evil. In this Genesis
story, the natural and spiritual aspects of food were blended together.

The fall of man took place primarily because Eve decided what God said
NOT to eat was instead "good for food and, that it was pleasant to the eyes, and
a tree desirable to make one wise…" (Gen. 3:6). Adam afterward succumbed to
her influence and erred also. Whatever this involved, the plunge into sin
occurred primarily because Adam and Eve chose the wrong thing to satisfy
their hunger. It is apparent that Eve longed to be "as God knowing good and

evil" (Gen. 3:5). Quite possibly, she did not desire a totally wrong thing (to be like God); rather, she stubbornly attempted to reach this goal the wrong way (as the majority of religions do).

How strangely ironic it was that when God pronounced the curse upon Adam, it declared man's inevitable and continual struggle to obtain proper sustenance! (God said, "Cursed is the ground for your sake; in toil you shall *eat* of it all the days of your life. Both thorns and thistles it shall bring forth for you, and you shall *eat* the herb of the field. In the sweat of your face you shall *eat* bread till you return to the ground, for out of it you were taken.")

Thank God! The blessing that came through the New Covenant has set in motion the conquering of this curse and spread the table before us that we might feast on the good things of God.

THE TABLE IN THE WILDERNESS
A PROPHETIC FORESHADOWING

The children of Israel were in bondage in Egypt for over four hundred years, eating the meager rations intended for slaves. But then Moses prophesied to Pharaoh, "Thus says the LORD God of Israel: Let My people go, that they may hold a feast to Me in the wilderness" (Ex. 5:1). The arid Wilderness of Sin stood between God's people and the Promised Land, but God pledged to provide. Psalm 107:5 paints the picture of the Israelite people: "hungry and thirsty, their soul fainted in them." These troubled pilgrims questioned, "Can God prepare a table in the wilderness?" The Almighty Provider dispelled their doubts. Psalm 78 celebrates what happened, reminding us how Moses struck the rock and the waters gushed out, and how God "opened the doors of heaven…and rained down manna…Man ate angels' food" (Ps. 78:19–25 excerpts).

Remember, it was God who supplied the meal. He held the feast and invited the children of Israel to participate. 1 Corinthians 10:3–4 claims that the Israelites "all ate the same spiritual food, and all drank the same spiritual drink. For they drank of the spiritual Rock that followed them, and that Rock was Christ." Every day God's supply was abundant and sufficient (quite possibly about twelve million gallons of water and two to three thousand tons of manna).[*1]

So the first grand impression on the minds of the pilgrim Israelites was that God could miraculously supply their food and drink, even in a desert land. At one point the elders of Israel even went up on a mountain with Moses where they "saw the God of Israel" and ATE and DRANK in His presence. (See Ex. 24:10–11.)[*2] So, in a very profound way, God "blessed" the bread and water of the children of Israel. As a result, sickness was taken from them. The Most High "satisfied them with the bread of heaven" and when their hearts were right, amazingly, there was not "one feeble person among their tribes." (Ex. 23:25, Ps. 105:37 KJV, 40, See Neh. 9:15.)

Furthermore, every time they partook of their peace offerings at the brazen altar, they understood the symbolism. They were sharing a meal with God. They were fellowshipping with the Creator. No wonder the altar was called "the table of the LORD" (Mal. 1:7, 12). In eating the flesh of the sacrificial animals, their relationship with God was restored and atonement was made for their souls. So feasting, forgiveness, freedom from sin and fellowship with God all went together in the minds of the seed of Abraham. And all of this happened at God's table.

Little did they understand the profound, prophetic picture being painted right before their eyes. Veiled minds could not comprehend that a New Covenant meal was coming that would far surpass this meal of the Old Covenant—as much as heaven surpasses earth, as much as eternity surpasses time.

THE NEW COVENANT TABLE

✺ Moving from the Natural to the Spiritual

Right before He launched His ministry, Jesus faced the same evil seducer that originally enticed Adam and Eve. Once again, food was the object of temptation! (This was no coincidence.) "Turn these stones into bread," hissed the tempter. But the Son of God answered, "It is written, Man shall not live by bread alone, but by every word that proceeds from the mouth of God" (Mt. 4:4). Jesus was simply revealing that the eternal, living Word of God is a far more important meal than the natural food our bodies crave.

Later on, He reemphasized this, saying to His disciples, "I have food to eat of which you do not know... My food is to do the will of Him who sent Me, and to finish His work" (Jn. 4:32–34). These two statements blend together as one, for the Word of God and the will of God are interrelated. Because God's Word is the revelation of His will, both are inseparably part of the same living loaf—something Jesus rejoiced to digest into His inner being. So, the last Adam succeeded where the first Adam failed.

The first Adam refused God's will and God's Word—and ate what was forbidden. The last Adam (Jesus) chose God's will and God's Word—and ate that which was pleasing to the Father. In this, as always, Jesus became our example, and He always challenges us to walk in His footsteps. How appropriate it was that His first recorded sermon included the beatitude promise:

> *Blessed are those who **hunger** and **thirst** for righteousness, for they shall be filled.*
>
> (Matthew 5:6)

The NAS says *"they shall be satisfied"*—for only an infilling of the very righteousness of God can *satisfy* man's deep longing. Religious works and self-attained righteousness are insufficient. We must have God's nature, His essence, poured into our famished souls. Such an infilling brings blessedness indeed— the happiness and all the benefits that result from being accepted in God's presence, reckoned righteous before His throne. (See Ro. 4:7–9.)

This is what Adam and Eve lost.

This is what we, the redeemed, are privileged to regain.

Many of the religious leaders had a hard time accepting Jesus' teaching, for they were just too full. They were full of tradition, full of self-righteousness and full of spiritual pride. Their lack of hunger made them disinterested and unreceptive. How they personified the warning of Proverbs 27:7:

> *A satisfied soul (KJV "The full soul") loathes the honeycomb, but to* **A HUNGRY SOUL** *every bitter thing is sweet.*

Not only did they reject the meal that Jesus spread before them, they were shocked at those who responded to His invitation. Matthew 9:11 records the Pharisees saying to Jesus' disciples, "Why does your Teacher eat with tax collectors and sinners?" Why? Because He knew that they were honest in assessing their own need. They were hungry. They were empty. They were unfulfilled. They were spiritually starving and emaciated. Life had left them destitute. They needed the Savior and were so ready to admit their need and respond to Him. Even His 'bitter' words were sweet to their taste (tough commandments, difficult to swallow).

How true was His prophetic observation concerning those who rejected the sumptuous meal He offered:

> *"Woe to you who are full, for you shall hunger."*
>
> (Luke 6:25)

The foolish, rich man who died without God evidently still had cravings like thirst and hunger though he was being tormented in flames. He even pled that the once-poor Lazarus would come from paradise and touch his tongue with cool waters from that realm. But it was too late! On earth his heart had been *full*—full of egotism, full of material riches and full of contentment over his many accomplishments. In the end, he was left empty, hungry and thirsty— forevermore.

And so it will be with all who are *full* in this life. Their table becomes a snare and that which should have been for their well-being becomes a trap. (See Ps. 69:22, Ro. 11:9.) Quite the contrary, though, if we respond, the Good Shepherd spreads a table before us in the presence of our enemies. (See Ps. 23:5.)

Proverbs 25:25 (KJV) declares, "As cold waters to **A THIRSTY SOUL,** so is good news from a far country." In a New Covenant sense, the "good news" is the Gospel. The "far country" is heaven itself. The Son of God came from heaven to bring that 'cool, refreshing water' to **thirsty souls.** Isaiah 32:2 prophesied this Messiah would be "as rivers of water in a dry place." Through this prophet, the LORD gave a profound New Covenant invitation:

> *Ho! Everyone who thirsts, come to the waters; and you*
> *who have no money, come, buy and eat. Yes, come, buy*
> *wine and milk without money and without price.*
>
> (Isaiah 55:1)

When the Father finally sent the Messiah into this world, how perfectly He fulfilled the praise-filled statement that flowed from the lips of Mary:

> *"He has filled* **THE HUNGRY** *with good things."*
>
> (Luke 1:53)

The LORD of glory did it two thousand years ago—and He is still doing it now. Of course, there is a reason He fills only **the hungry** with good things. Those who are hungry for God normally do not make idols out of the "things" God blesses them with—because they are not hungry for "things," they are hungry for God. So He delights to do them good.

God's Word came in a bodily form for a purpose: to give "bread to the **EATER**" (Is. 55:10). His Word still comes from above to fulfill this purpose. And if mere crumbs falling from the Master's table could heal the Syrophoenician woman's daughter, how much more can we expect to receive—since we are partaking of the full loaf of a covenant relationship with God (Mt. 15:27, Mk. 7:28).

❧ Identifying the Bread of Life

Not only did Jesus point out the error of those who rejected His meal. He described, in unforgettable symbolism, its amazing content. In one of His most profound messages, He stated:

> *"Most assuredly, I say to you, Moses did not give you*
> *the bread from heaven, but My Father gives you* **the true**
> **bread from heaven.**
>
> *For the bread of God is He who comes down from heaven*
> *and gives life to the world."*
>
> (John 6:32–33)

The hearts of the disciples, so hungry for God, must have leapt within them as Jesus' continued:

> "I am **the bread of life**. He who comes to Me shall never hunger, and he who believes in Me shall never thirst."
>
> (John 6:35)

What a mystery! What a contrast! Those who are full in this life spend eternity empty, unfulfilled and dissatisfied. But those who come to God with hungry and thirsty hearts—once they depart from this world—never hunger and never thirst again. Everlastingly they feast on the good things of God.

This is the more glorious New Covenant meal, far greater than the manna that came down from heaven and the water God miraculously provided during the Israelites' wilderness journey. Though *supernaturally* supplied, these provisions only temporarily satisfied their *natural* need. Later on, in the same 'Bread of Life' sermon, Jesus further identified this spiritual staple of the redeemed. He boldly claimed:

> "I am **the living bread** which came down from heaven. If anyone eats of this bread, he will live forever: and the bread that I shall give is My flesh, which I shall give for the life of the world."
>
> (John 6:51)

Because Jesus was "the Word made flesh," eating His flesh speaks of eating the Word and digesting it into our inner being. Of course, his audience did not understand this truth and quickly challenged, "How can this man give us His flesh to eat?" Jesus confidently responded:

> "Most assuredly, I say to you, unless you eat the flesh of the Son of Man and drink His blood, you have no life in you.
>
> Whoever eats My flesh and drinks My blood has eternal life, and I will raise him up at the last day.
>
> For My flesh is food indeed, and My blood is drink indeed.
>
> He who eats My flesh and drinks My blood abides in Me, and I in him."
>
> (John 6:53–56)

Upon hearing this, many of the disciples were offended at the Son of God and refused His doctrine. Not only was it unreceivable; it sounded cannibalistic. Little did they know that by turning away from the Messiah's offer, they were sealing themselves into the dark destiny of utter spiritual starvation. On the contrary, those who believed began feasting at the very table of God, a table that stretches from time into eternity.

❧ Identifying the Water of Life

Jesus also asserted that we have to drink His blood in order to be heirs of eternal life. This, too, was extremely difficult for His Jewish audience to embrace. According to the Mosaic law, they were not even allowed to drink the blood of an animal, much less the blood of a human being. So what did Jesus mean by this radical new doctrine? The biblical symbolism is beautiful.

If the flesh of Jesus was the Word manifested, then it follows that His blood was the Holy Spirit manifested. Scripture reveals that "the life" of an animal is in the blood of the animal. (See Gen. 9:4, Lev. 17:14.) In like manner, the life of God is in the blood of God. And if God ever had blood, He had blood when He incarnated in the form of His Son. Without argument, that precious blood was divine. Acts 20:28 explains that we are the "church of God which He purchased with His own blood."

The life of God is the Spirit of God. The Holy Spirit is even called "the Spirit of life" in Romans 8:2. So to drink Jesus' blood is to drink in His life-giving Spirit. The two are inseparably intermingled. This life-giving Holy Spirit is also termed "the water of life"—living waters that refresh the most sin-sick soul. Jesus informed the woman at the well:

> *"If you knew the gift of God, and who it is who says to you, Give Me a drink, you would have asked Him, and He would have given you **living water**…*
>
> *Whoever drinks of this water will thirst again, but whoever drinks of the water that I shall give him will never thirst.*
>
> *But the water that I shall give him will become in him a fountain of water springing up into everlasting life."*
>
> (John 4:10, 13–14)

Later on, He opened the door to all humanity, saying:

> *"If anyone thirsts, let him come to Me and drink.*
> *He who believes in Me, as the Scripture has said, out of his heart will flow rivers of living water."*
>
> (John 7:37–38)

Both of these scriptures bring out a new and intriguing concept. Once the water of life flows into believers, quenching their spiritual thirst, it reverses its circuit and begins to flow out. Certainly this means that once God satisfies our thirst, we are then called upon to satisfy His thirst (the thirst for fellowship, for worship, for sweet communion)—and the thirst of the unsaved for spiritual truth? The Most High is definitely thirsty—but only those who receive His Spirit can give back to Him the spiritual praise He yearns to hear.

Psalm 107:9 reveals that He satisfies "**THE LONGING SOUL**" and He fills "**THE HUNGRY SOUL** with goodness" (KJV). But it is also true that we satisfy His longing and hungry soul—by filling Him up with our worship.

This is also *the deep calling to the deep.* And only those people termed "**His waterspouts**" and "**a well of living waters**" can fulfill this awesome charge (Ps. 42:7 KJV, Song 4:15).

✿ The Table of the LORD

When Jesus broke the bread and passed the cup at the Last Supper, He instituted a memorial that would remind His New Covenant people of their mystical union with Him. As we partake of the bread and the wine, we are reminded, again and again, of the supreme privilege of experiencing oneness with the spotless, sinless Lamb of God. There is an old saying that "You are what you eat!" There's a lot of truth in that, both naturally and spiritually. If we eat the flesh of the Son of God and drink His blood, in a certain qualified sense, we digest His nature, His attributes and His divine abilities into our inner being. We commune with Him at a totally new kind of 'table' or altar. Hebrews 13:10 says, "We have an altar from which those who serve the tabernacle have no right to eat."*[3]

In other words, unless a person submits to the revelation of the New Covenant, he has no right to eat the New Covenant meal. Furthermore, Paul warned certain worldly and doctrinally erring Christians in the Corinthian church:

> *You cannot partake of the LORD'S table and of the table of demons.*

> (1 Corinthians 10:21)

To participate in this New Covenant feast, it is only right that we share, not only the great victory of the resurrected Savior, but the suffering of the cross. In fact, that's what the very word *communion* implies. All four times it appears in the Kings James Version of the New Testament (1 Cor. 10:16, 2 Cor. 6:14; 13:14) it is translated from the Greek word *koinonia* which means *having in common, a sharing, a partnership or fellowship.*

Those who eat at His table *share* the experience of the cross—the self-denial that is demanded there and the salvation that is available there. But they also inherit the privilege of *sharing* His crown—the glory, the victory, the rest and the restored dominion that is available to all who are enthroned with Christ. This is all simply part of the meal—and it is proper etiquette, even in a spiritual sense, to *"eat what's set before you."*

COME AND DINE

Psalm 22 portrays in graphic detail the horrendous suffering that the crucified One endured. Then toward the end of the psalm, twice, it speaks of *eating* of the benefits of this substitutionary death. Verse 26 (KJV) foretells that "the meek shall *eat* and be satisfied" and their heart shall live forever as a result. Verse 29 then declares that all "**the prosperous of the earth**" or, as rendered in another translation, "all the **rich of the earth** will feast and worship" (NKJV, NIV). In other words, by eating this New Covenant meal, bankrupt, famished souls, who come with meekness and repentance, are prospered beyond measure with the very riches of the kingdom of God.[*4]

In John 21 we read about Peter and the disciples going to fish after the resurrection of the LORD had taken place. They caught nothing. Then Jesus appeared on the beach. After directing a miraculous catch of fish, He invited the disciples to *"Come and dine!"* He proceeded to fix them a meal. It was as if He was saying that the time of misery was over. It was time now to celebrate, to indulge in all the benefits Jesus procured. IT WAS TIME TO FEAST NOT ONLY NATURALLY, BUT SUPERNATURALLY! Of course, not only did He invite the apostles in their day, He invites us to feast with Him as well.

In Revelation 3:20 we find an opposite yet complementary slant on the revelation. The resurrected Christ actually requests that we provide a feast for Him:

> Behold, I stand at the door and knock. If anyone hears
> My voice and opens the door, I will come in to him and
> dine with him, and he with Me.

The 'door' is the human heart and within its confines God delights to 'feast' on sincere worship and loving adoration. So again this 'feasting' is a reciprocal thing. He invites us to His home and we invite Him to ours. We dine with Him in the inner chamber of His heart and He dines with us in ours.

This is also *"the deep calling unto deep"*—something that will reach an awesome climax during the Millennial Reign of Christ. He prophetically announced to His chief disciples:

> I bestow upon you a kingdom, just as My Father
> bestowed one upon Me, that **you may eat and drink at
> My table in My kingdom**, and sit on thrones judging
> the twelve tribes of Israel.

> (Luke 22:29–30)[*5]

This scripture could be a reference to the marriage supper of the Lamb.

The Bible proclaims we are blessed if we are merely invited. (See Rev. 19:9.) Why! Because once we partake of God in His fullness, we will hunger and thirst no more. Though we will apparently enjoy celestial food forevermore, the aching, the longing, the pain of hunger and thirst will be over. Furthermore, the perfect nourishment that Adam lost will finally be restored to God's people and sustain us throughout all the ceaseless ages. The assurance of this truth is discovered in promises found in the last book of the Bible. God said, concerning His people:

> *They shall hunger no more, neither thirst any more; neither shall the sun light on them, nor any heat.*
>
> *For the Lamb which is in the midst of the throne shall feed them, and shall lead them unto living fountains of waters: and God shall wipe away all tears from their eyes.*
>
> (Revelation 7:16–17 KJV)
>
> *Blessed are those who do His commandments, that they may have the right to the tree of life, and may enter in through the gates into the city.*
>
> (Revelation 22:14, See John 6:27.)

Yes, we have a blessed assurance. One day, the hungry will hunger no more. The thirsty will thirst no more. *The deep* in God will merge with *the deep* in us until our contentment and fulfillment know no bounds. It goes without saying—we hunger—we thirst—for that day.

Endnotes

*1 Of course, the manna did not come on the Sabbath, so quite possibly, the water did not flow on that day either. Also, it is quite amazing that in Deuteronomy 32:20 this same generation of Israelites was described as being "children in whom is no faith." If the Almighty supplied such sustenance for those who did not believe, what will He supply for those who do? He later stated that if they had listened to Him, He would have given them, not just water, but "honey from the rock." (See Ps. 81:13–16.)

*2 This could have well been supernatural food, a foreshadowing of the marriage supper to come.

*3 For a more full treatment of the beauty, depth and symbolism of the communion ritual, and what it is to be *Partakers of the LORD's Table*, see the chapter on *One Bread* in Volume Four of **Our Glorious Inheritance**.

*4 To fully explore this wondrous truth, see the chapters entitled, *The Prosperous of the Earth* and *The Rich of the Earth* in Volume Seven of **Our Glorious inheritance**.

*5 Though we may feel unworthy of such a wondrous privilege, God delights for us to partake of this heavenly feast. David's gracious and generous invitation for Mephibosheth to eat at his table wonderfully foreshadowed God's goodness toward us. Even as Mephibosheth was the son of David's enemy (Saul) so we were at one time the sons and daughters of God's enemy (Satan). Even as Mephibosheth was crippled at an early age, so we were crippled spiritually as soon as we came into this world. But through the mercy of our God, we have been lifted from our low estate to eventually eat at the table of the King of all kings. (See 2 Sam. 4:4; 9:6–13; 16:1–4; 19:24–30; 21:7–8.)

WATERSPOUTS

Deep calleth unto deep at the noise of Thy **WATERSPOUTS:** *all Thy waves and Thy billows are gone over me.*

(Psalm 42:7 KJV)

Deep calls unto deep,
Stir the 'eddy' within.
Draw us upward to heaven
From this 'ocean' of sin.

Whirling wind, frothing water:
Lifts the soul, now earthbound—
To its heavenly sphere,
With blest worshipful sound.

'Tis the 'noise' of **God's Waterspouts,**
Responding to His call;
Sweet Spirit, still brooding,
Hovers over us all.

To change us, transform us,
To awake us from 'sleep.'
Even now, our hearts surge —
For **"deep calls unto deep."**

WATERSPOUTS

Deep calleth unto deep at the noise of Thy
WATERSPOUTS: *all Thy waves and Thy billows are*
gone over me.

(Psalm 42:7 KJV)

*I*n the very beginning, we are told that "darkness was upon the face of *the deep*. And the Spirit of God moved [brooding and hovering] over the face of the waters. And God said, *Let there be light*" (Gen. 1:2–3 KJV, NIV, Amp).

"And there was light"—brilliant, clean, infinite and Word-birthed.

What God did then, at the onset of creation, He has done again and again—in bringing forth each one of His everlasting sons. There was a time when our lives were simply "without form and void." We were helpless captives of spiritual ignorance, miserably lost in our sins. We were exiled from the presence of God in a strange world at enmity with Him.

Darkness was upon *"the face of the deep"* in each one of us.

For the *deep* potential of being conformed to the divine nature and the *deep* heritage of walking in intimacy with the Almighty were instead shrouded with "the covering cast over all people, and the veil that is spread over all nations" (Is. 25:7). This covering, this veil, is the inescapable, dark, suffocating prison of flesh-consciousness that resulted from the fall of Adam.

Thank God for that wonderful day when the Spirit of God brooded, then moved over the churning, dark waters of our wayward souls. In a sense, the God of all grace once again said, *"Let there be light."*

"And there was light"—brilliant, clean, infinite and Word-birthed.

"The *deep* uttered His voice and lifted up His hands on high" and we were miraculously transformed (Hab. 3:10 KJV). We became the children of light, no longer limited by mere sense-knowledge.

The moment we were born again, the covering was removed, the veil was pulled back. We saw the glory of the firstborn Son of God and He restored us to our rightful place of inheritance. We received the mind of Christ, illuminating our minds with divine inspiration. ("O LORD—Your thoughts are *very deep*" Ps. 92:5, See 36:6.) As part of **Our Glorious Inheritance**, we became "rooted...in love" that we might comprehend "the width and length and *depth* and height" of who God is and who we are. (See Ps. 95:4, Dan. 2:22, Ro. 11:33.)

Yes, in that *deep* initial experience, God opened up a *depth* in us as everlastingly unfathomable as the Almighty Himself. Psalm 64:6 admits that "both the inward thought and the heart of man are *deep.*" How much more true this is when redeemed hearts are filled with the infinitely deep Spirit of God. Then, from out of this infinite, inward *depth* springs forth an incessant flow of the pure and pleasant water of life.

Psalm 42:6–7 (KJV) could well be a reference to this phenomenon:

> *"O my God...deep calleth unto deep at the noise of*
> *Thy waterspouts."*

Such beauty lives within this passage of Scripture.

The deep in God is the brooding Holy Spirit who still hovers daily over every born again "well of living waters" as if to echo the song of Israel:

> *Spring up, O well! all of you sing to it—*
>
> (Numbers 21:17)

It is God yearning to be completed through a full union with His delightsome bride, calling us to fill up this spiritual stature.

The deep in every child of God is the inward and upward surge of longing that often rises to the surface especially when we fall to our knees or lift our hands to worship. Then, more than any other time, *"deep calls unto deep."* The fountain of holy desire, welling up within, gives birth to Spirit-filled praise and adoration, returning grace to the very God who gave it. These anointed worship utterances—spoken in time, but ascending into eternity—partially make up *"the noise"* that proves the true location of **God's Waterspouts!**

This title-position speaks of an awesome longing.

In the first verse of Psalm 42, the psalmist declared, *"As the deer pants for the water brooks, so pants my soul for You, O God"* (Ps. 42:1).

Of course, this *deep* thirst for true communion and intimacy is not just something that churns in the hearts of sons. God Himself 'pants' or longs even more deeply for such communion and intimacy with us. So this is definitely a reciprocal experience. *"Deep calls unto deep."* The longing flows from eternity to time and from time to eternity: from heaven to earth and from earth to heaven.

A chord of deep-seated desire, with all its minors and sevenths, must have struck in the heart of the Creator the very moment He scooped up a handful of dust and said, "Let Us make man in Our image." Then, the very moment Adam's eyes flickered open for the first time, as God-breath flowed into him, certainly the same chord was struck in his spirit, and began resounding in his inner being.

Of course, this 'song of the soul' became quite obscure after the fall, and how very few could ever claim the privilege of hearing it. (For this is a song deeper than music and a poem deeper than words.) But for those who have been blessed to truly hear and feel its reality, existence becomes so much more than just the boisterous and chaotic, white-tipped waves that crash continuously on the surface of the ocean called 'mere existence.'

We reach far beneath the waves and discover the *deep*, still current of the divine purpose underlying all things. And we feel that same current, with near-irresistible pull, daily drawing us closer to the bosom of the Father.

Surely it was this profound flow of emotion from God's heart (this eternal call) that welled up within Paul's heart toward the Galatian church when he wrote:

> *My little children, of whom I travail in birth again*
> *until Christ be formed in you.*
>
> (Galatians 4:19 KJV)

This very statement reveals God's all-consuming desire for us.

This is *the deep calling to the deep*. This is the image of all perfection urging imperfect ones to come forth in His perfect image. We know that all the circumstances of life really do work together for good—to bring forth this eternal purpose in us. So we can always walk in confidence. (See Ro. 8:28–30.)

Though "waves and billows" of tribulations, temptations and trials crash over our lives, we can still be full of faith. We know that:

> ...*the LORD will command His lovingkindness in the*
> *daytime, and in the night His song shall be with me, and*
> *my prayer unto the God of my life.*
>
> (Psalm 42:8 KJV)

Every Christian should have this blessed assurance. Even the lowest places and the most painful experiences can be ultimately beneficial. Deuteronomy 8:7 (KJV) even declares that there are "fountains and *depths* that spring out of valleys."

In the valley, we learn how to thirst.
In the valley, we learn how to trust.
In the valley, we learn how to believe.
In the valley, we learn how to love.
Most of all in the valley, we learn how to pray.

More often than not, we learn more in the valley than we do on the mountaintop. No wonder the question was presented, and the answer given, in the last verse of this "song of longing":

> *Why are you cast down, O my soul? and why are you*
> *disquieted within me? hope in God; for I shall yet praise*
> *Him, who is the health of my countenance and my God.*
>
> (Psalm 42:11)

Yes, of all people we can possess hope when there is no hope. We can persist, even when hope seems hopeless.

We know that we are "saved by hope" and that our hope is "an anchor of the soul, both sure and steadfast, and which enters the Presence behind the veil" (Ro. 8:24, Heb. 6:19). This spiritual anchor assures us that long after all the disquieting events of life are over, God's everlasting purpose in us will reign supreme. We place our confidence now in the fact that "our light affliction, which is but for a moment is working *for us* a far more exceeding and eternal weight of glory" (2 Cor. 4:17).

This is the conclusion of the whole matter.

And this is the reason that even in the worst of circumstances, any sincere, humble-hearted, believing child of God can still lift his hands and say, *"I shall yet praise Him"* (Ps. 42:11).

DEFINING THE REVELATION

Those God has called to be waterspouts should consider the following two definitions:

(1) A **waterspout** can be anything through which water is carried, or out of which it is spouted (to spout is to issue forth with force).

(2) A **waterspout** can be a whirlwind over some body of water, a funnel-shaped or tubular column of rotating cloud-filled wind, usually extending from the underside of a cumulus or cumulonimbus cloud down to a cloud of spray torn up by the whirling winds from the surface of an ocean or lake.

This second definition is most likely the one intended by Psalm 42:7 and the one on which we will focus our attention. The great difference in air pressure (a low pressure inner core and a high pressure outer shell) is the very thing that causes the waterspout. This peculiar act of nature is, in a sense, the atmosphere calling to the ocean—invisible wind above forcefully drawing the visible water beneath. The ocean disturbance caused by the waterspout is called an *eddy*, a phenomenon in which the sea seems to lift up as though it were pushed from below.

There is a subtle and beautiful message to be discovered in all of this.

The swiftly circulating wind represents the mighty, transforming power of the Holy Spirit in an individual's life (something that, at times, causes turbulent side-effects).

Out of the ocean of humanity God calls certain individuals to arise and become containers of His life. God does His part—"He sent from above, He took me; *He drew me out of many waters*;" and we must do ours—"Out of the *depths* I have cried to you, O LORD" (Ps. 18:16; 130:1). Thus, we become God's waterspouts, made up of water and wind—containing elements of both the human and the divine. We are 'caught up' in a unique and curious union of that which is natural and that which is spiritual.

For those who receive such a heaven-sent visitation, life is never uneventful, for wind is notably unpredictable and uncontrollable. Often we find ourselves overwhelmed by a surge of divine influence that is fully intent on subduing the natural part of us. A supreme example of this is found in Job, who, in the midst of all his tribulation, poured out his soul to God, crying:

> You lift me up to the wind and cause me to ride on it;
> and dissolve [me in the storm].
> For I know that You will bring me to death, and to the
> house appointed for all living.
> (Job 30:22–23 NKJV, LB)

God's purpose in each one of His chosen is to dissolve the fallen-nature and work in us the stormy death of Calvary. This transpires so that the life also of Jesus might manifest in us, bringing us to the 'house' of victory, joy and power appointed for all those who know Him in resurrection life.

This developmental process, at times, can create circumstances just as disturbing and just as difficult to endure as the loud and fierce, whipping winds of a waterspout. Nevertheless, we welcome such divinely-allowed pressures of life—as challenges to our faith—for we know the ultimate outcome.

Often, the "low pressure" of our fortitude on the inside seems no match for the "high-pressure" trials, afflictions, and persecutions on the outside. But then, as if lifted from beneath, our travailing souls rise upward in trust and spiritual desire. The awesome roar of Holy Spirit wind is all around us, constantly discipling, overpowering and challenging the "natural man"; but simultaneously, a wellspring of life opens up within us, exalting us by stirring up the "inner man," the "hidden man of the heart." (See Eph. 3:16, 1 Pt. 3:4 KJV.)

This end result justifies the means, making it well worth enduring.

Admittedly, this *waterspout* experience speaks of more than just a gentle wooing from heaven, for this is a transfiguring process sometimes quite forceful, often intense and always compelling. Through it all, though, we have the blessed assurance that one day the *whirlwind* will subside, for the LORD will have "His way in the whirlwind," and the heartrending calamities of life will be no more (Nah. 1:3).

What will be the outcome for the sons and daughters of the Most High? They will be fully absorbed in the infinite bliss of absolute oneness with God. The *whirlwind* will finally carry us supernaturally, as it did Elijah, into the unutterable splendor of the heavenly realm.

Then the transformation will be completed.

But this portion of our calling will not altogether cease—because, throughout the unending ages, in an even more perfect sense, we will remain *His waterspouts*—everlasting fountains of Spirit-unctioned praise. We will be living containers and infinite channels of the crystal-clear river of life that flows from the throne of God.

This living water will constantly flow from the Father toward us. And this living water will continuously and rapturously flow out of us toward the Father.

Yet there will be one major difference.

The *deep* will no longer yearningly and even sorrowfully call unto the *deep*—for that experience will be gone forever (hidden somewhere in the *deep* regions of the past). Instead, the *deep* in us will be utterly one with the *deep* in God. This is truth unspeakable—for there are no earth-born words that can sufficiently describe such a celestial state of being.

But for those who know, and for those who feel, there is a witness beyond words. Often, when we contemplate the glory of such a wondrous destiny, in a very gentle and loving way, God-breathed wind suddenly stirs around us and a spiritual *eddy* wells up within our hearts.

Then, even as the LORD answered Job out of the midst of the *whirlwind*, so He answers us. We hear the echo of His voice, like the sound of many waters, saying:

Where were you when I laid the foundations of the earth…when the morning stars sang together, and all the sons of God shouted for joy?…have you entered the springs of the sea? Or have you walked in search of the depths?

(Job 38:4, 7, 16)

O how these questions, posed by God Himself, always cause our hearts to churn within—for questions from God are often more comforting than answers from men. In a responsive way, the thoughts of our minds, like trembling hands reaching through the darkness, grope for the fullness of understanding (the golden knob on the golden door).

Where were we then? What was the condition of our existence? What did God mean by such a question?

But even more than reaching toward the *deepness* of the infinite past, we ask ourselves, again and again—where will we yet be, and what will we yet possess, in the *deepness* and vastness of what we call the infinite future.

We know basically where we are headed, but the full truth of what it will all be like is still somewhat cloudy (for "we see through a glass, darkly"— 1 Cor. 13:12). Yes, we "see but a poor reflection as in a mirror" of who we are and what we shall be (1 Cor. 13:12 NIV). Now we know in part. Then shall we know, even as also we are known. What an awesome metamorphosis when we possess complete understanding of all of God's mysteries! We long for that "moment" of full revelation and transformation. Yes, we long—until that inrushing of divine insight comes.

We are reduced to love and trust.

We are given to patient waiting, convinced of the faithfulness of our God. We realize that we will never fully understand until we complete our journey. But until that day, we understand one thing quite well, and we have only one choice way of saying it.

"Deep calls unto deep."

This is the main theme, the primary revelation, and the key explanation of what God is doing in us right now. And this is our heritage, our character and our calling forever, for we are—

HIS WATERSPOUTS

We will spend eternity *yet praising Him* for such a privilege and such a gift.

Deep calleth unto deep
at the noise of
***THY WATERSPOUTS**:*
all Thy waves
and Thy billows
are gone over me.

(Psalm 42:7 KJV)

BIBLIOGRAPHY

BIBLES:
A number of different translations of Scripture have been referenced in this book. Most of the following do not have complete bibliographic information; those that do are particularly noted for their commentaries on the King James Version made by the authors.

Listed according to the names of the versions:
Amplified Bible (Amp); Darby's Version (Dar); King James Version (KJV); Living Bible (LB); Modern King James Version (MKJV); New American Standard (NAS); New English Bible (NEB); New International Version (NIV); Phillips Modern English (PME); Revised Standard Version (RSV); The Septuagint (Sep); Today's English Version (TEV); Young's Literal Translation (YLT)

Listed according to the names of the authors:
Harrison, R. K., *The Psalms for Today: A New Translation from Hebrew into Current English* (Har—from 26 Tr.)
Vaughan, Curtis, *The Bible from 26 Translations*. Grand Rapids Michigan: Baker Book House.
Williams, Charles B. *The New Testament: A Translation in the Language of the People*. (Wms—from 26 Tr.)

Presentations of the King James Version with commentary—listed by author:
Bullinger, F. W., *The Companion Bible*. Grand Rapids, Michigan: Zondervan Bible Publishers, 1974. (CB)
Dake, Finis Jennings. *Dake's Annotated Reference Bible*. Lawrenceville, Georgia: Dake Bible Sales, 1979. (DARB)
Thompson, Frank Charles. *Thompson Chain Reference Bible*. Indianapolis, Indiana: B.B. Kirkbride Bible Company, Inc., 1988. (TCR)

BIBLE DICTIONARIES:
Achtemier, Paul J. *Harper's Bible Dictionary*. San Francisco, California: Harper and Row Publishers, 1985. (HBD)
Smith, William. *A Dictionary of the Bible*. Nashville, Tennessee: Thomas Nelson Publishers. (SMD)
Unger, Merrill F. *Unger's Bible Dictionary*. Chicago, Illinois: Moody Bible Institute, 1967. (UBD)
Vine, W.E. *Vine's Expository Dictionary*. Minneapolis, Minnesota: Bethany House Publishers, 1984. (VED)

COMMENTARIES:
Bethany Parallel Commentary on the New Testament. Minneapolis, Minnesota: Bethany House Publishers, 1983.
Bethany Parallel Commentary on the Old Testament. Minneapolis, Minnesota: Bethany House Publishers, 1985.

CONCORDANCES:

Strong, James. *Strong's Concordance*. Nashville, Tennessee: Thomas Nelson Publishers, 1984. (SC)

Young, Robert. *Young's Concordance*. McLean, Virginia: McDonald Publications, 1984. (YC)

OTHER WORKS:

Bainton, Roland H. *Here I Stand, A Life of Martin Luther*. Nashville, Tennessee: Abington Press, 1978.

Halley, Henry H. *Halley's Bible Handbook*. Grand Rapids, Michigan: Zondervan Publishing House, 1967.

Lockyer, Herbert. *All the Divine Names and Titles in the Bible*. Grand Rapids, Michigan: Zondervan Publishing House, 1979.

Lockyer, Herbert. *All the Parables of the Bible*. Grand Rapids, Michigan: Zondervan Publishing House, 1963.

Illustrated World Encyclopedia. Woodbury, New York: Bobley Publishing Corporation.

ORDERING INFORMATION

"Our Glorious Inheritance"
Volume Three

To order another copy of this book
send $17.95 plus $5.00 shipping and handling to:

Deeper Revelation Books
P.O. Box 4260
Cleveland, TN 37320-4260

Be sure to include your complete shipping information
(P. O. Box or street address, etc.)

Possible discounts may be available for multiple orders.
You can also order other volumes in this series online.
For information visit our website:
www.shreveministries.org
www.deeperrevelationbooks.org
or call: 1-423-478-2843